STOCK PICKER

STOCK PICKER

How to develop the mindset, temperament, and strategy to outperform Wall Street

IAN CASSEL

Harriman House

I dedicate this book to my wife Amanda and children Jack and Madelyn.

Amanda – Stock picking is a life lived at the extremes. The constant ups and downs. The fear and greed. The buying and selling. There is rarely a middle ground. When the violent swings of the market, multiplied by the volatility of microcaps, made me feel like a piñata, you were my center. In a career that can feel transactional and often strips away one's empathy, thank you for being my rock, for calling me out on my bullshit, and for loving me through it all.

Jack and Madelyn – I hope this book helps you understand my journey. Stock picking can be a lonely craft because you are always living in the future, waiting for tomorrow's gains. You two forced me to live in the present. I don't know where this book sits in the timeline of my life, but my greatest success was working from home and being there: Hugging you every morning, the walks to and from the school bus, and helping your mother tuck you in at night. I am proudest of the fact that I never let my obsession with stock picking and other professional pursuits come between us.

Harriman House

HARRIMAN HOUSE
www.harriman-house.com

First published in 2026 by Harriman House, an imprint of Pan Macmillan
EU Representative: Macmillan Publishers Ireland Ltd, 1st Floor, The Liffey Trust Centre, 117-126 Sheriff Street Upper, Dublin 1, D01 YC43
Associated companies throughout the world
www.panmacmillan.com

Paperback ISBN: 978-1-80409-412-9
eBook ISBN: 978-1-80409-413-6
Audio ISBN: 978-1-80409-414-3

British Library Cataloguing in Publication Data
A CIP catalogue record for this book can be obtained from the British Library.

01

Printed and bound by CPI Group (UK) Ltd.

Cover design by Paul McCarthy.

CONTENTS

WHAT IS CHASING YOU?

At the turn of the 20th century, a delicious white flaky fish known as cod was gaining popularity in the United States. The fish was found in the North Atlantic and word quickly spread to the West Coast.

The question was, how could you get the cod fish across the United States and keep it fresh?

At first, they tried to freeze the fish and ship it by railcar, but when the fish was defrosted at the other end it was mushy and lacked flavor.

Then someone had the great idea of turning a railcar into a large aquarium and shipping the cod fish alive across the country. The fish would certainly stay fresh. But unfortunately, it didn't improve the result. Even though it was transported alive, the cod was still mushy and tasteless.

Finally, someone studied the cod fish and discovered its natural predator was the catfish. They put a few catfish in each tank and shipped cod fish across the country. During the journey the catfish would chase the cod fish. When the cod fish arrived on the West Coast it tasted fresh.

For the cod fish to be fresh it had to be in an environment with catfish.

We all want to go through life anxiety free, comfortable, and without obstacles. But God, destiny, whatever you want to call it, puts catfish in our lives for a reason.

Don't go through life just standing there. Fresh means being uncomfortable. Fresh means you are being chased.

Why?

Because you run the fastest when someone is chasing you. You pray the hardest when something is after you. You go further, harder, faster when you are being chased.

I've been a stock picker all my life. I started when I was a teenager, and in college I told my family and friends my goal was to become a full-time private investor. I wrote down on a napkin "$10k and two 10-baggers = Millionaire." Some smiled. Some laughed. Some looked confused. Most told me to go work for my dad in the family business.

The desire to prove them wrong chased me.

When I was 28 and became a full-time private investor, I was frugal. I had the ability to travel light and travel far. I learned to live on a dime so I could turn on one. It is amazing how disciplined you can become when your livelihood and survival depends on it.

The fear of having to work for someone chased me.

In 2009 at the depths of the Global Financial Crisis, a friend invited me to attend a cocktail party in New York City with a few prominent investors and fund managers. I was one of 20 guests. I think the other 19 were the last people who still had jobs on Wall Street.

At the party I remember getting into an argument with a fund manager. I told him I was a full-time private investor and he looked at me with pity. After everyone had a few too many drinks he told me, "So I guess you weren't good enough to keep a job."

I smiled and replied, "You know how I define a fund manager? Someone who isn't skilled enough to support themselves with their own capital."

Sometimes the biggest motivator is someone that disrespects you. For years I woke up thinking about that guy.

Anger chased me.

After I got married, bought a house, and had a daughter, the pressure mounted. When you support your family by managing your own capital it's a different mental game. If you take a big loss managing other people's money it hurts your bonus. If you take a big loss when you're a private investor you hurt your family.

The fear of failure chased me.

A few years later my wife lost her mother to ovarian cancer. One year after that I lost my mom in a car accident. There is something about losing your parents and watching your kids get older that speeds up time.

When your kids are young you start thinking about how they will view you once they are old enough to see who you truly are.

Will they like what they see? I didn't. I would pray every night, "Please God help me change. I still have time to be the father they deserve."

Time starts to chase you.

As you get older you start to think about the skills you have developed and how they could be used for something bigger than yourself. You start to see young people that remind you of you when you were young. You feel the urge to mentor them and pass onto them what you've learned. You quickly realize you aren't going to be remembered for what you did for yourself, but what you do for others. You want to plant trees that others can shelter under.

Now my legacy is chasing me.

When you are focused on building your capital base from thousands to millions in 10 years and then supporting yourself and your family on that capital for another 10 years, you aren't in a reflective mindset.

You are too busy surviving.

Now that I've hit the mid-point of my life, it's time to get it all out on paper.

PREFACE

Every stock picker has an origin story, but few of us recognize its shape until we've survived enough cycles to look backwards with clarity. For most of my early life, I didn't understand what was pushing me forward. I only knew I felt chased by expectations, by fear, by ambition, by time itself. That pressure became the invisible engine of my investing journey. Years later I realized there was a pattern, and it traced perfectly through the structure of this book.

Section 1: The Making of a Stock Picker begins with the raw ingredients that shaped me long before I knew what a balance sheet was. A small town in Pennsylvania. A tight-knit family. A father whose business burned to the ground and who shrugged it off and rebuilt. A decision at 16 to invest my college fund instead of spend it. A tech bubble that turned $20,000 into $120,000, and then into $8,000. A bus ride to New York City with a fake business card to meet the CEO, a bet that became my first 10-bagger and permanently rewired my brain. This section is about the formation, the upbringing, early mentors, wins, wounds, and obsessions that molded me into a microcap investor before I ever named it.

Section 2: The Evolution of a Stock Picker chronicles the next decade, when curiosity turned into craft. These were the years of grinding through message boards, conducting management interviews in borrowed conference rooms, taking red-eye flights to company visits between graduate school classes, and learning from mentors who were equal parts brilliant and flawed. It is where I learned that microcaps – the smallest, most inefficient part of the public markets – are where individual investors can still have an edge. It is also where I learned that edges dull if you don't keep sharpening them. I became a concentrated, conviction-driven investor, slowly building the capital base that would allow me to go full-time in 2009, and then launching MicroCapClub in 2011 to build a global community around the craft I loved.

Section 3: The Reflections of a Stock Picker explores what happens once survival turns into longevity. Success brings scars, drawdowns, bad management teams, emotional baggage, and the mental wear that accumulates over 20-plus years of concentrated investing. It examines fear, ego, patience, discipline, and the invisible psychological forces that compound just as powerfully, perhaps more powerfully, than capital does. This section is about the inner game, the parts of investing that spreadsheets can't model.

Section 4: The Skills of a Stock Picker brings it all together. The practical tools and frameworks I've developed through decades of learning, failing, and refining. How to talk to management. How to conduct due diligence. How to build conviction. How to spot deterioration early. How to survive volatility. How to find great companies before institutions can touch them. These skills are learnable, repeatable, and available to anyone willing to do the work most investors avoid.

This book is my attempt to distill a lifetime of being chased by challenges, by markets, by mortality into something useful for the next generation of stock pickers. This isn't an invest like ME book. This is an invest like YOU book.

SECTION 1

The Making of a Stock Picker

CHAPTER 1

My Journey

I've been a stock picker all my life. I've never had a normal job. I've never worked for anyone or any firm. I have no other skillset. I can barely screw in a lightbulb. Just ask my wife.

I'm addicted to stock picking. The thrill of the chase. I love finding and buying small stocks no one wants and then selling them 10 times higher when everyone wants them.

It all started when I was a teenager.

In 1997, on my 16th birthday, my parents sat me down and gave me a choice.

They told me they had saved approximately $20,000 for my college education. They had also co-signed paperwork so that I could open an account with their financial advisor. I could choose what to do with the money.

I had always been interested in money and the stock market. Technology stocks were starting to make daily headlines. I called the financial advisor and he sent me a few analyst reports to review. I bought $5,000 of a technology stock. It doubled in two months.

I was hooked.

I filled out applications to a few private and public colleges. I realized I could spend all my money on one semester at a private college or attend a less expensive public university, live at home and commute, work part-time, and continue to invest. I chose the latter path. I was in love with investing.

By 2000, I was a sophomore in college and working part-time for a financial advisor. We had over 1,000 clients, so we were a sizable office. My job was that of a glorified secretary who worked on marketing materials and answered the phone. The money I made working was enough to pay for my college tuition. The $20,000 from my parents, I turned into $120,000 riding the technology bubble.

I didn't realize I wasn't skilled – I was lucky. A monkey could have picked winning stocks in that environment.

I enjoyed working for the financial advisor. It kept me close to the markets. The financial advisor liked having me there as well. By my second year on the job, I was having discussions with him about becoming a financial advisor upon graduation. He even offered to give me some of his clients to get started.

When the technology bubble burst, so did my portfolio.

By 2001, my portfolio of smallcap technology companies fell so much they turned into microcaps. My $120,000 was now $8,000. I was financially and emotionally bruised.

Adding insult to injury, my day job consisted of answering calls from emotional clients and calming them down before sending them to my boss. I didn't realize that, in addition to my undergraduate degree in economics, my day job would give me a master's degree in investor psychology. I realized I didn't want to be a financial advisor. It is hard enough navigating your own emotions when investing, let alone the emotions of others.

It's often how we navigate the valleys in our lives that dictates our future direction.

Since my portfolio turned into microcap stocks I decided to focus on this area. I found a special one. I was still in college but made some fake business cards and traveled to New York City to see if I could meet with the CEO. After the meeting I invested my remaining $8,000 into the stock. In 18 months the stock went from $1.70 to $34 per share. I was back in the game. I also became hooked on microcap investing.

Microcaps make up a majority of the public companies that exist globally. They are the smallest public companies in the world. Most of the best investors ever started their careers in microcap stocks. Most of the best-performing stocks ever were microcap stocks. The structural advantage in microcaps has persisted for 100 years. This is the only area of the public markets where the small, astute retail investor has the advantage over institutions. I devoted myself to becoming one of the best investors in this niche of investing. All great companies started as small companies.

I didn't have enough capital at the time, but I was supercharged by the notion of becoming a full-time private investor. I wrote down on a piece of paper, "$10k and two 10-baggers = millionaire."

I would stare at it every day. It seemed preposterous to most people, but it became my vision statement. One 10-bagger down, one more to go.

From 2002 to 2009, I was relentlessly focused on building my capital base as quickly as possible. During my senior year in college, I realized I wasn't employable. I had average grades, didn't do any internships, and hated the thought of working for anyone. I almost joined a prop trading firm where they teach you to trade and give you money to trade, but it just didn't feel right.

Instead, I applied for a graduate assistantship position at Villanova University, and somehow, I got accepted. As a graduate assistant I would work for two professors on their research projects, and in turn I would receive free tuition to the two-year MBA program. They even paid me a small monthly stipend to help with bills. This was the perfect scenario because it was a socially acceptable way to continue to focus on microcap investing while getting a degree.

I learned the art of stock picking from experience and mentors. My first mentor was a full-time gambler and stock picker. I met Skip in 2002 on a stock message board and he taught me everything he knew. He taught me how to communicate with management. He taught me how to find a great story. He was tough and opinionated, but he could move mountains as soon as he opened his mouth. He was the most "convicted investor" I would ever meet.

Skip also taught me the qualitative art of investing. He was a maestro at Dale Carnegie's *How to Win Friends and Influence People*. During graduate school we would go on a few company visits each semester. I had a system where I knew exactly how many classes I could miss.

Villanova is 30 minutes from the Philadelphia International Airport. I would take early morning flights and catch red eyes home, so I only missed one day of studies and work. I loved every second of it.

I graduated with my MBA in 2005. I wanted to become a full-time investor, but I didn't have enough capital. What was I going to do? I loved microcaps, but how could I pay my bills? I decided to do some consulting with microcap companies. I took on a couple clients at a time and helped on a variety of tasks ranging from writing press releases to strategic decisions with the business. I really enjoyed it. It paid my bills while I focused on building my capital.

By 2007, I felt I had enough capital to become a full-time investor, but something kept me from making the leap. My strategy was a bit of an oddity. I was concentrated, investing in three or four stocks at a time. I was also a story stock investor that was only starting to appreciate fundamentals and profitability. Value wasn't part of my vocabulary. You could say I was a concentrated, convicted, momentum investor. I did very well, but it was the opposite of what Warren Buffett preached. *Could I be right if I contradicted Buffett?* In order to be sure my strategy was viable, I wanted to test it through a recession. I didn't realize one was right around the corner.

I quit consulting and became a full-time private investor in 2009.

You achieve financial independence by saving more than you spend and investing those savings into an area where you have an advantage. For me it was microcap stocks, the smallest public companies in the world.

Becoming a full-time private investor is the pinnacle of financial achievement. Why? You don't need the help of others for anything. You don't need a boss. You don't need clients. You don't need customers. You don't need their money. You have your own.

Here is a fact that few in the financial world want you to know. Individual investors have an edge over investment managers, advisors, analysts, or anyone forced to prove how smart they are to others. You don't need to have an opinion on *everything*. You don't have distractions. All you must focus on is making a few good investment decisions per year and living a great life.

When I started dating my wife it took her six months to understand what I did for a living. She saw me working from home, on the phone, and occasionally making trips to "visit companies." It didn't help that I bought a new Porsche 911 the same week we started dating. I'm pretty sure she thought I was a drug dealer. To this day, explaining to people what I do for a living is excruciating. It's easier to tell them I'm unemployed; then they look at my wife in sympathy.

In 2011, I launched MicroCapClub.com, a private online community for experienced microcap investors to share ideas and collaborate on due diligence. Today we have over 1,000 microcap investors from around the world discussing their best ideas. The community has found 300+ microcaps that have doubled or more.

In 2016, I co-authored *Intelligent Fanatics Project*. "Intelligent fanatic" is a term Charlie Munger used to describe an exceptional founder who builds a business from scratch into one that dominates an industry, geography, or niche. He mentioned several of these intelligent fanatics in his speeches. We researched these individuals, their companies, pulled out some valuable lessons, and wrote a book. The smaller the company, the more important management becomes. If you want to find great companies early, you must find great leaders early. The main goal for me was to fine tune my qualitative lens for great leadership and apply that to microcap investing.

In 2019, roughly 10 years after becoming a full-time private investor, I was ready for another challenge. After all those years of saying no to outside capital, I pivoted and started saying, "Yes." I formed my firm, Intelligent Fanatics Capital Management LLC. We now work with over 70 families to provide them with intelligent exposure to the smallest public companies in the world.

In 2026, I acquired a microcap in-person events business called Planet MicroCap. The combination of the MicroCapClub online community and Planet MicroCap in-person events is a powerful flywheel that I look to leverage to positively impact the microcap space globally. The goal is when the good Lord finally takes me from this Earth that I leave the microcap ecosystem in a much better place than how it was when I entered it.

I'm now in my mid-40s. I'm still young in years, but stock pickers age in dog years so I feel like a veteran. When I was building my capital base from $8,000 to $1 million, I was in three to four stocks. Today my fund consists of 12–15 stocks. I'm still a concentrated and convicted stock picker. Being concentrated has allowed me to learn the hard lessons quicker because each decision's outcome is amplified.

One of the hardest parts of aging as a concentrated stock picker is the emotional scars and baggage that build up over time. You get callused by all your experiences and you must put up emotional safeguards, so you don't lose your edge. Many stock pickers can't go the distance. The boldness gets scared out of them. They slowly deteriorate into a riskless diversified portfolio, afraid to pull the trigger.

I love stock picking. I'm still learning and evolving. I've been doing this for 25 years and I am nowhere near the best investor I can be. I have so much more to do. There are more great companies that must be found before the institutions find them. Remember, all great companies started as small companies.

Now that I look back at my journey, I realize how much my environment, parents, and values influenced the type of stock picker I have become. During the journey nothing seems to make sense because you are living through it in the present. It's only when you stop and look back that you understand the things that shaped you.

CHAPTER 2

The Things That Shape You

I was born and raised in Lancaster, Pennsylvania. This is a rural area mostly known for being the home of the largest Amish community in the United States. In fact, more than eight million tourists come to Lancaster every year to visit the Amish. Tourists watch the Amish milk cows. Go on horse and buggy rides. Buy some handmade furniture. Eat some Pennsylvania Dutch food and then leave. Thank goodness.

Most people think the Amish are simpleton agrarian people, stuck in a lifestyle meant for the 1800s. I will tell you from experience, the Amish are some of the most business savvy people you will ever meet. They have no cars, no electricity, no TV, no internet, they wear the same style of clothes, they have no debt – they have no vices. All they have is time to think. Go ahead and underestimate the mind that has this much time to think and that has no distractions. All they think about is family, God, and business.

I was once at a real estate auction where an auctioneer sold a farm. An Amishman pulled up in his horse and buggy with a pickup bed in the back. He unloaded six 5-gallon metal milk jugs full of cash. Paid $2 million, shook the cashier's hand, and rode away likely to make it home in time to work in the fields before sundown.

I still remember the first time a tourist asked me if I was Amish. I was only seven years old. I was riding my bike with a friend, and we were at a stop sign. A car pulled up and the driver yelled out the window. "Are you Amish?!" I was really confused. I remember thinking, "Am I wearing all black clothes? Do I have a bowl haircut? Do I smell like a farm?"

Not everyone in Lancaster, PA is Amish. Lancaster county has a population of 550,000.

40,000 are Amish.

I am not Amish.

Another odd fact about Lancaster, PA.

In 2022 it was ranked #1 in US News and World Report's "Best Places to Retire." A big reason is Lancaster is also ranked #1 for most retirement communities per capita in the United States. More than Sarasota, Naples, Scottsdale.... Yes, Lancaster, PA.

My cynical view of Lancaster is people come here for two reasons – to stare at the Amish and to get old and die.

My father was a small business owner. My grandfather started the business in 1945. My father took it over in 1980. I was expected to take the business over after him. I worked at the family business since I was "knee high to grasshopper," child labor laws be damned. It was a very small business. Two employees and my mother did the bookkeeping. We weren't rich, but we weren't poor. My dad earned enough to buy a new pickup every four years and put food on the table. That is how "success" is defined for 90% of small business owners.

I was truly blessed. I came from a great family with great parents who loved each other. My parents were 100% in love with each other 100% of the time. My Mom passed away 13 years ago, but they are still in love. Their marriage represented the pinnacle of what God wanted marriage and love to represent.

My parents also loved my sister and I and let us both know. Sometimes it feels like your backstory isn't inspirational unless you overcame some massive hardship or absentee parents. You almost feel like you should hide the fact that your upbringing was as American as apple pie. It took me years to realize that mentality is disrespectful to your parents and the work it takes to keep a family together. Now I know it's a huge advantage to know what love feels like from an early age.

My family wasn't Amish, but we were raised in a conservative Brethren Church. My parents were active in the church. We went to church every Sunday and every Wednesday. We even went most Saturdays to help clean, mow, pull weeds, etc. 10%+ of our income went to the church. My dad would say, "The 10% is before tax, not after tax. God gave you everything, so don't try to give him less."

Most of my friends growing up were from the same church. They were also sons of fathers who owned small businesses. My best friend today is still my best friend from when I was five years old.

Our family business was next to our house in an old barn that was partially renovated into a working space. When I was 12 years old the barn was struck by lightning, and I watched it burn to the ground. I remember feeling horrified watching the flames and watching the local firefighters try to save it.

I was standing with my dad staring at the ashes after the last fire engine and firefighter left. I asked him, "What are we going to do?" My dad looked at me and said, "I'm hungry, let's go out to eat."

I remember thinking to myself, how can he be this calm? How do we have money to eat? How are we going to make money? These were the thoughts going through my 12-year-old brain. But that was my dad. He shrugged off the loss and had already moved on. His goal was to rebuild bigger and stronger. He did.

I still remember the day the direction of my life flipped. I was 14 years old. We didn't watch much TV so we listened to a lot of radio, mostly a local Christian radio station. I was listening to the radio while I was helping my dad clean up around the business, and I heard the host say, "You weren't put on this Earth to be average."

I don't know why but that sentence resonated with me. It replayed over and over in my head. That statement planted the seed in me to have *a conversation* with my dad.

My grandfather started our family business in 1945. My father took it over in 1980. I was expected to take it over from my dad. Everyone expected this. No one turns down a third-generation golden goose of a business. But I didn't love it like my dad and grandfather did. I felt like my life had already been planned out for me. It felt claustrophobic.

I still remember when I was 15 years old telling my dad I wasn't interested in taking over the business.

I was so emotional. I had been thinking about the conversation for months. I remember breaking down crying because I was letting my hero down. My father accepted it with such grace. He just gave me a hug and said, "It's okay, I just want you to be happy."

This was one of my first life lessons. When you are stressed out about a hard conversation, the more you worry about it, the longer you wait to address it, the bigger the problem gets in your mind. It becomes bigger than it needs to be.

You should always have hard conversations as soon as you can.

What does all this have to do with stock picking?

Your experiences, your environment, your past, shape your temperament and your stock picking.

When I saw my father working hard at his business – I knew what hard work and focus looked like.

When I saw my father taking calculated risks in business – I knew what appropriate risk taking looked like.

When I saw my parent's tithe to the church on a consistent basis, even in the bad years when the business barely made any money – I knew what commitment looked like.

When I saw my father stay calm after watching his entire business burn to the ground – I knew what self-confidence, bouncing back, and moving on looked like.

When I watched my parents have a 35-year love affair up until my mother died – I knew what conviction looked like.

What does any of this have to do with stock picking?

It has everything to do about stock picking.

Reflect on your own journey. Whether it's childhood, family, business, or your first few investment experiences – they all shape the stock picker you will become.

CHAPTER 3

All Great Companies Started as Small Companies

There are a bunch of small stocks that will 10x over the next five years that are waiting to be found.

Institutions can't buy them.

Only you can.

The opportunity in microcap stocks exists because institutions can't own them until they go up. It is the small, astute investor's duty to find great companies early and collect the reward for doing so. Don't follow the institutions. Invest where they are going to go.

I've been a microcap stock picker all my life. I look for small stocks that can produce big returns. I buy before the institutions can buy them and then sell them to the institutions 10x higher.

A microcap is a public company with a market capitalization less than $500 million. Microcap stocks are the smallest public companies in the world and more than half of all public companies are microcaps: Of 60,000 public companies globally, 30,000 of them are microcaps. In many ways, microcaps are small businesses that just happen to be publicly traded, which means you can buy shares in a brokerage account just like you can buy shares of Google or Tesla.

Every public stock exchange in every country around the world has microcaps. In fact, in Canada, 80% of publicly listed stocks would be considered microcaps.

The crazy thing is that even though microcaps make up a majority of public companies, most people have never heard of these companies.

In fact, 99.9% of financial professionals have never heard of these companies. Institutions can't own microcaps. Microcap companies are too small and too illiquid for institutions to care about them. This is the opportunity for the small, astute investor.

Warren Buffett, Peter Lynch, Joel Greenblatt, and many other famous investors started their careers as microcap investors. Why? It's the only place in the public markets, and perhaps even private markets, where an astute investor managing a small sum has a structural advantage over institutions. Where YOU have the advantage.

Walmart, Netflix, Celgene, Amgen, Intuitive Surgical, Monster Beverage, even Berkshire Hathaway, were once microcap companies. In fact, 87% of all global stocks that went up 1000%+ between May 2012 and May 2022 were microcap stocks.

A quick recap:

- Most of the best investors ever started in microcap stocks.
- Many of the best-performing stocks ever started as microcap companies.
- Most of the best-performing stocks over the last 10 years came out of the microcap ecosystem.

Why isn't anyone talking about this amazing area for investment?

Microcap gets zero positive attention from the mainstream financial media. In fact, the only thing that is written is the negative side. It's more fun to write articles about venture capital and private equity.

Microcap is too small for anyone with real money to care about. If you rolled up all 10,000 microcap companies in North America into one company, it would have a $500 billion market capitalization. This seems large, but there are currently 20 individual companies that are valued at more than $500 billion.

Once again, this is not something to worry about – this is the opportunity.

Microcap as an investment class has sustained its structural advantage for 100 years.

Why?

First, institutions manage too much money to invest in these small, illiquid public companies. Second, the great investors that start as microcap investors quickly evolve up and out of the space in the same way the best minor league baseball players are promoted up to the major leagues. Once you're ready to pitch for the Phillies, you don't pitch for the Lehigh Valley IronPigs anymore.

And the same is true of investors. Almost all the greatest stock pickers started in microcap and as they launched funds and their capital grew from millions to billions they were forced out of microcap. The best investors are constantly leaving, creating a hole. I want to fill that hole.

If you still don't believe me, here are some facts.

The smaller the better

From 1927–2016, the smallest decile of the public market (<$114 million market cap) has outperformed all other market cap classes. A 17.45% annual return, almost five percentage points per annum more than the next highest decile. You can see this in Table 3.1, where as company size decreases, compound annual return increases. This is staggering outperformance by the smallest public companies.

Table 3.1: Performance of size deciles of stocks (1927–2016)

Decile:	1 small	2	3	4	5	6	7	8	9	10 large
2016 avg. market cap (millions)	114	499	941	1,557	2,295	3,384	5,157	9,092	18,412	88,945
Avg. return 1927–2016 (%)	25.86	18.66	16.88	16.12	15.05	15.23	14.33	13.52	12.91	11.11
Std. dev. (%)	49.67	41.44	32.7	31.65	27.65	26.55	26.33	23.76	22.15	19.64
Compounded return (%)	17.45	12.54	12.43	11.95	11.53	12.01	11.16	10.90	10.48	9.21

Source: Mark Vonderwell, "The Excessive History of MicroCaps," MicroCapClub.com.

In addition, Jenga Investment Partners wrote a white paper titled, "Global Outperformers," that researched all global stocks that returned 1000% or more between May 2012–2022. 446 companies out of 55,000 global stocks produced 1000%+ returns; 87% of them were microcaps.

The more illiquid the better

Roger Ibbotson is a Yale finance professor and the chairman and CIO of Zebra Capital. He has written several white papers, including "Liquidity as an Investment Style," where he argues that liquidity should be given equal standing to size, value, growth, and momentum as an investment style.

He examines stock-level liquidity in the top 3,500 market cap universe of US equities from 1971–2017 and subjects it to the four style tests of Sharpe. One of his conclusions is that liquidity dominates size as a return predictor and he provides evidence illustrated in Table 3.2. Illiquid microcaps have produced 16.05% annual returns, beating all other market caps under the same liquidity factors. Illiquidity means volatility. Volatility means opportunity.

Table 3.2: Performance of stocks by liquidity (1971–2017)

Quartiles		Low liquidity	Mid-low	Mid-high	High liquidity
Microcap	Geom. Mean:	16.05%	15.68%	9.57%	0.11%
	Arithm. Mean:	18.38%	19.23%	14.77%	5.23%
	Std. Dev.:	22.67%	28.52%	34.54%	33.07%
	Avg. No. Stocks:	345	181	124	98
Smallcap	Geom. Mean:	15.65%	14.32%	12.26%	6.00%
	Arithm. Mean:	17.29%	16.83%	15.52%	10.11%
	Std. Dev.:	19.35%	23.73%	26.86%	30.09%
	Avg. No. Stocks:	199	201	173	174
Mid-cap	Geom. Mean:	14.03%	13.88%	12.89%	8.40%
	Arithm. Mean:	15.38%	15.54%	14.99%	11.87%
	Std. Dev.:	17.59%	19.47%	21.54%	27.35%
	Avg. No. Stocks:	130	177	203	238
Large-cap	Geom. Mean:	11.44%	12.28%	11.97%	9.07%
	Arithm. Mean:	12.66%	13.39%	13.46%	11.99%
	Std. Dev.:	16.22%	15.40%	17.61%	24.53%
	Avg. No. Stocks:	74	188	248	238

Source: Roger Ibbotson.

The less institutionally owned the better

By default, the smallest and most illiquid microcap companies are not widely held by institutions. The illiquidity in these small public companies provides an embedded barrier of entry for larger pools of capital. This barrier creates an opportunity for skilled investors managing smaller sums to find, evaluate, and deploy capital into undiscovered companies where larger pools of capital can only buy them when their equities are higher and more liquid.

Additionally, when the market shifts from bull to bear, institutional investors look to reduce risk in their portfolios. They pull capital from investment vehicles such as smallcap ETFs and smallcap focused mutual funds and hedge funds. When institutions pull their capital, redemptions hit these investment vehicles, causing constant selling pressure. Put simply, high-quality microcap businesses perform better through bear markets because institutional investors don't own them. They can't sell what they don't own.

The power of discovery

Finding a great idea in microcap before others is important – discovery is important – because one or two investors can move the market. Many think the opportunity in microcap is because there aren't many smart investors looking at these small companies. It is the opposite, I know a ton of smart investors in this space. The opportunity is that the discovery phase of a small great business produces returns you can't get anywhere else. The great thing about small market caps is they can go up two, three, five, or 10 times or more, and still be small companies, and still a new idea to most everyone else.

Caveat emptor – buyer beware

> The definition of an inefficient market: You can make or lose a fortune. Skill matters. For the one willing to cautiously grind over a decade+, this is great news. For the part-time amateur, it's a recipe for an expensive education.
>
> **– Brent Beshore**

Microcap investing is the most inefficient area in public markets. This means extreme outcomes are the norm. Big winners and big losers. This means you will lose money as you learn. Investing's greatest lessons can't be taught in a book or in a classroom. They must be experienced and oftentimes the best teacher is loss. Every successful stock picker has paid the price of admission.

The smaller the better.

The more illiquid the better.

The less institutionally owned the better.

The less talked about the better.

These statements horrify most professional investors and financial advisors. It spits in the face of mainstream financial theory.

But guess what?

You make the most money by driving through the fears of other investors. The greatest advantage a microcap investor has is the rest of the financial world thinks you're an idiot for investing in microcap stocks.

A majority of the financial world believes if you find, buy, and hold a great company early you were a lucky gambler. Instead, they love it when you buy after the 25th analyst covers the stock from a broker who is charging you a commission.

The financial machine loves to discredit courage and produce lemmings and followers. Institutions hate it that you can buy things they can't. They hate it that you can make money in ways they can't.

> You don't have to invest like a big bureaucratic institution. If you choose to invest like one, then you're doomed to perform like one.
>
> **– Peter Lynch**

Microcap stocks aren't owned by institutions or covered by analysts. This means you must do the work to find them and diligence them to form your own conviction. Institutional research and opinions aren't spoon-fed to you like you're a child. This independent mindset is crucial to being a successful stock picker. It isn't a fluke that most of the best investors ever started in microcap.

When you do the work others haven't done to discover a small winning stock, people will say you are wrong. When you hold a winner, people will say you are stupid. When you get rich from a winner, people will say you got lucky. You tell them you love being wrong, stupid, and lucky.

Your first big win is important because it proves to yourself it can be done. The bad thing is often you mistake skill for luck. I got lucky with my first big win.

My first big win

From 1999–2001, I was in college while also working part-time as a branch office administrator for a local financial advisor. During the bull market I loved it because the job kept me close to the markets and my rising portfolio. During the bear market I hated it because of the daily reminder of how much poorer I was getting.

My portfolio of smallcap technology companies that ascended from $20,000 to $120,000 fell off a cliff and turned into microcaps. My $120,000 was now $8,000. My ego was crushed.

During the bull market I thought I would become a financial advisor after I graduated. After the crash I also realized there was no way I was going to become a financial advisor. Dealing with my own emotions was bad enough, let alone the emotions of 1,000 clients layered on top of it.

I would soon be faced with some big decisions. Mainly, what was I going to do after graduation? Everyone around me said I should go back and work for my father. It pained me to even think about becoming the prodigal son. I needed more time.

My Junior and Senior years in undergraduate studies were spent diving into the underbelly of microcap investing. I subscribed to a few newsletters and joined a few stock message boards. Since microcaps were mainly owned by retail investors, most of the discussion and diligence on microcaps was on public stock message boards. I would meet my first mentor on one of these message boards.

It was at this time I stumbled upon XM Satellite Radio (XMSR). XM Satellite was also licking its wounds from the dot-com bubble bursting. In less than a year the stock was down 90% and hovering around $1.80. I loved the story: no commercials, nationwide coverage, consistent station listings, and digital quality. If you are under the age of 40 you probably don't even remember how inconsistent normal terrestrial radio was at the time.

However, XM had several issues. First, they had a mountain of debt from spending a couple billion dollars launching satellites into space. Second, they had very few subscribers or OEM agreements with car manufacturers. Short sellers controlled 42% of the float, betting the company was going bankrupt.

In 2001, XM produced $533,000 in revenues with a $284 million dollar loss. The company needed a $50 million cash injection just to make it through the next 12 months. *What a great investment opportunity?* Sarcasm.

But I loved the story.

I was down to $8,000 in my brokerage account. I was desperate. One of my new rules was to do everything possible to meet the CEO of my next investment. I didn't have much money left. I needed a win.

I noticed that Hugh Panero, CEO of XM Satellite Radio, was presenting at an investor conference in New York City. I registered for the event under a fictitious business name, "Cassel Capital." The conference organizers didn't know my "assets under management" was less than $10,000.

I skipped a day of college and took a bus from Lancaster, PA to New York City. I printed out XM's annual report, which gave me ample reading material for the three-hour bus trip.

When I checked-in to the conference, to my amazement investors were able to schedule one-to-one meetings with the companies presenting. Evidently my fake business card hadn't impressed them, since they restricted me from scheduling one-to-one meetings.

I walked into the main presentation room and sat in the back of the room. I listened to a few CEO presentations, including Hugh's presentation and the Q&A that followed. After Hugh concluded, I followed him out of the presentation room and into his one-to-one room. He was likely surprised and disappointed to see this 20-year-old with no money staring at him.

I was so nervous. My palms were sweating. When I shook Hugh's hand I remember saying, "I… uhh… uhh… was just in the bathroom and washed my hands." I don't think I even said who I was.

I remember thinking, "Whew, that wasn't too embarrassing," as Hugh nodded in affirmation of my good hygiene.

To my amazement he was polite and didn't call security. We sat down and spoke for 10 minutes before his first actual one-to-one arrived.

In retrospect, Hugh's humble demeanor probably had more to do with his company's market valuation dropping from $2 billion to $200 million in less than a year. I'm sure he was getting beat up like a piñata every day by shareholders, creditors, and analysts.

He explained his vision for the company to me. Over 50% of radio listening was in the car. Once consumers experienced crystal clear, commercial free radio in the car they would demand it in the home and elsewhere. Car manufacturers were slow to adopt new technology, but he was confident they would be successful.

When his next meeting arrived, I stood up, shook Hugh's hand with my sweaty palm, and thanked him for his time. I also told him I liked the story and was going to buy some stock. I remember him smiling at me like I was the first person to tell him that in a long time.

I took the bus home that evening. The next day I bought 5,000 shares at $1.78.

Almost immediately the tide turned in the business and the stock. The company refinanced their debt. They signed multiple OEM agreements to install their radios in new vehicles. Shorts were forced to cover.

The stock ran from $1.70 to $34.00 in 18 months. I sold out around $15.00. I was back in the game.

This is when my love affair with microcaps began.

The ability for an idiot like me to sit across the table from a public company CEO was electric. When I spoke to Hugh that day, I felt I had an edge.

It's been a couple decades since my first meeting with a CEO took place, and it's been surreal to look back and realize how important that meeting was. It's also surreal to look back and realize how important that big win was for me and my self-confidence.

Yes, the outcome was 110% luck, but I proved to myself it could be done.

Today, the relationships I develop with management teams is my moat.

CHAPTER 4

Talking to Management

The difference between what you modeled in a spreadsheet and the outcome you get is management. Businesses are people, not Excel spreadsheets. Get to know the people.

Talking to management is the most important thing I do as a stock picker. Some investors disagree and say that reading public filings, press releases, and other surface due diligence gives them all the information they need.

Their argument against talking to management is that management won't give you an honest assessment because they are paid advocates for the company. They say, the facts are in the filings, so no reason to talk to management.

Let these investors think this way, because they are wrong.

Do you really think that talking to the leaders of a business won't give you additional insights?

In almost every circumstance you will gain differential insights by talking to management.

The management team is the brain and the business is the body. The quickest way to destroy a great business is to put an idiot in charge of it.

Mediocre or bad management teams are the same as the zero property of multiplication. Any opportunity, no matter how big or obvious, when multiplied by zero is zero.

Think about the extremely gifted people you've known that never lived up to their potential because of bad decision-making. All their natural gifts and talents flushed down the drain.

Similarly, it doesn't matter how great a company's product or service is if the management doesn't make the right decisions. It doesn't matter that a technology is 10x better and 50% cheaper than the competition. It doesn't matter that a company has $10 billion worth of gold, silver, and copper buried in the ground. If the management team implements the wrong sales strategy, the wrong financing, the wrong plan, shareholders will lose money. If the head is incompetent, the body is useless.

A big fallacy is that people believe talking to management is about acquiring insider information. This is not true. Joseph P. Kennedy, the father of President John F. Kennedy, made a large fortune in the stock market as well as real estate. In 1934, President Roosevelt appointed Joseph Kennedy to be the very first chairman of the Securities and Exchange Commission (SEC).

Thomas Phelps, author of *100 to 1 in the Stock Market*, asked Joseph Kennedy if he regarded insider information as a major problem or hazard for investors. Kennedy responded, "If I had all the money that has been lost on inside information, I'd really be rich." To put it simply, most of the "inside information" management teams tell you isn't true or doesn't come true.

The management teams that talk too much normally execute too little. It is always a red flag when a management team crosses the line and tells you information they shouldn't. When I talk to management, I'm looking for their help to answer questions I have about the business and strategy.

Legendary investor Phil Fisher would make it a point to become an expert in the business he was evaluating prior to talking to management. He is known for saying an investor won't know the right questions to ask until they do all the upfront scuttlebutt research. I believe this is true for small-, mid-, and large caps, but not microcaps.

When investing in small public companies you can't afford to wait until the end of your due diligence to talk to management. Why?

Oftentimes one management conversation unearths differential insights that make the company completely uninvestable, or three times more interesting than you originally thought. I normally talk to management earlier in the due diligence process after I have a broad understanding of the business.

I talk to management to better understand management's plan, strategy, and time frames. This is crucial so you know how to benchmark management's progress and to make sure the risk–reward matches your time frame.

The edge in building relationships with management is it helps you spot the signs of progress and deterioration quicker. It's the same with anyone you have a close relationship with. My wife doesn't have to tell me that she is angry with me. I know when she is angry with me. When you truly know someone, you can tell when something is wrong.

The relationships I develop with management allow me to hold longer and sell quicker. I've been a successful stock picker for 20+ years not only from holding big winners, but also because of the losses I didn't take. I was able to sell before others when my spidey sense started tingling that something changed – and this spidey sense was attuned to what management was doing.

All of this leads to an important question.

How do you access management teams?

If you are a small retail investor, do not expect to get an audience with management. You must first earn this right. In most cases you will find resistance in trying to talk to the CEO. Put yourself in the CEO's shoes – would you want to take time away from running a business to talk to you? Are you worthy of that time? In addition, management teams are solicited daily by all sorts of service providers including investor relations firms, investment banks, consultants, and attorneys trying to sell them services. This means that management teams naturally have their guard up. Professional persistence is key to breaking through their barrier. You must prove you are worthy of their time.

Here are some approaches.

Annual General Meetings (AGMs)

Most public companies have an AGM, which is the yearly gathering of a company's interested shareholders. At an AGM the management team and board of directors present the company's financial performance and shareholders vote on the issues at hand. All holders of stock are entitled to attend the meeting; this is a meeting set up for shareholders. This is a great way for shareholders to meet management while not asking for additional time out of the CEO's schedule. I love attending AGMs since so few other investors do so. If you want to make an immediate impression on a CEO, attend an AGM. A CEO is more likely to reply to your next email or phone call if they met you in person at the AGM.

Earnings calls

Most public companies have quarterly earnings calls. The CEO and CFO give an overview of the preceding quarter's accomplishments, some commentary on the future, and then open it up to questions. The Q&A portion of an earnings call is another great opportunity for an investor to ask questions and make a positive impression on management. You aren't asking management to take time out of their busy schedule to have a one-to-one conversation with you. You are simply participating on the earnings call. Similar to attending an AGM, a CEO is more likely to reply to your next email or phone call if they thought you asked thoughtful questions on the earnings call.

Conferences

Smallcap and microcap companies present at a variety of conferences throughout the year. Some conferences can only be attended by institutions, but there are several that retail investors can attend. The companies that present at these conferences are trying to raise awareness about the company. Some are looking to raise capital. These events are a good place to meet management teams and find ideas. We now host two microcap conferences annually under the Planet MicroCap brand to help quality investors meet quality management teams. These events are free for retail and institutional investors.

Cold email and phone calls

Most public companies list an investor relations contact on their website and on press releases. Sometimes this person is the CEO. Sometimes it's someone else within the company. Sometimes it's an external investor relations firm the company pays to handle its investor relations. In whatever case, when you contact them keep it short and be genuine.

What would I say in my first email or phone call?

Be direct. Be genuine. Be a shareholder. Management treats you differently when they know you own shares. A tactic that worked well for me was communicating I'm a shareholder and I'm thinking about making it a much larger position. This would immediately give them a reason to reply to me. Sometimes I would tell them exactly how many shares I owned so they would take me seriously. I keep all written communication short and on point. In business, real doers don't waste time. A communication from me might look like this:

> My name is Ian Cassel. I'm a new shareholder in the company. I've been following [Company Name] for years and I'm impressed with the recent progress. I own [number of shares] and I'm thinking about making it a much larger position. Would you have 20 minutes to answer a couple questions? I'm not here to waste your time.

Nine times out of 10, I would get a reply from the CEO or the investor relations contact. From there I had the hook in the fish's mouth, and all you must do is reel them in. None of this is done in a coercive way. I was genuine in my ownership and my interest.

How do you interview management?

Full-time Canadian investor Chip Maloney wrote a wonderful article for the MicroCapClub community covering this topic. I'll blend his thoughts with mine since we both have experience talking to hundreds of management teams.

Combat fear with preparation

If a CEO is giving you 30–60 minutes of his or her time, show some respect by preparing. Do all the work you can to learn about the business and its strategy so you can ask the right questions. Go through all the past annual filings since the CEO was at the company. Make note of any material change in business strategy and the reason for it. Rank order a list of questions that are most important.

Build rapport with management

During your research, before you talk to management, try to find something personal in common with them. It may be something as simple as a link to the city they are headquartered in – maybe you traveled there previously. Have a look at their LinkedIn summary. Maybe you know someone who worked with them in the past. Maybe you share the same alma mater. Mention it to them at the beginning of your initial conversation. A connection, however small, can help you to build rapport early on and get them to open up to you. It could be something as simple as joking around with them, which might help them to lighten up and drop their guard.

It's also impressive if you can weave into the conversation a few details where it's obvious you have done your research. Perhaps you spoke to a couple customers that alerted you to a product change or increase in SKU count. Perhaps you spoke to a competitor that mentioned they are pulling out of the market. Perhaps you spoke to an ex-employee who said he wished he still worked at the company. Whatever it is, I've found CEOs are happy to give time to people that have done the work. Once you build rapport with a CEO, they are much more likely to give you better quality information.

Ask open-ended questions

Open-ended questions are questions that can't be answered with a yes or no answer. An open-ended question often involves the words what, how, or why, and to a lesser extent who, when, and where. These types of questions that encourage a subject to describe or explain have a better chance of giving you a complete response.

A close-ended question yields a yes or no answer. Close-ended questions are fine if you are trying to verify core information, but they do not yield detailed answers. An example of a close-ended question would be, "Do you still think you can improve your gross margin to 50%?" On the other hand, an open-ended question would be, "What specific steps do you plan to take to improve your gross margin to 50%?" It is a subtle difference, but the open-ended question will probably yield much deeper information compared to the close-ended question.

Questions should be lean

Keep each question short and focused on a single subject. Some management teams have had media training and have learned how to tactfully avoid answering your questions and divert the discussion to their own agenda. Questions that are unfocused and cover a broad subject matter allow them too much range to do this. The more focused your questions are, the more meaningful the answers you will get back.

Questions should be neutral

Neutral questions are free of values or opinions of the investor. Avoid using charged words and try to keep your opinion out of your questions as that can distract management. When values or opinions are added by the interviewer, either positive or negative, it may bias the executive into answering your question how you want it answered. In the very worst cases, the subject closes up because they feel they have been criticized, and it may be difficult to get them to open up again.

For example, a microcap company I have a holding in granted a large amount of stock options to management. I could have asked the CEO, "A lot of shareholders are angry about this option grant, how do you defend it?" Instead, I asked, "What criteria did your board use in rewarding management in the recent stock option plan?" Instead of using charged words in my question, and him getting defensive, I got a very thoughtful answer that made sense once it was looked at from his standpoint.

Listen to answers and build new questions from there

Don't be in too much of a rush to get to the next question on your list. By listening and asking them to elaborate, you will help management to articulate the subject matter. Also, by doing this, you are showing that you are listening, and it builds trust and credibility, which will allow management to open up deeper.

When I first started interviewing public company management, I would stick very close to my question list, because I didn't want to sound like an idiot ad-libbing off script. However, as my interview technique has improved over the years, I have noticed that a lot of the best information comes from going off script and asking for elaboration of an answer. As you gain experience interviewing management, don't abandon the possibility of deeper information by jumping too quickly to your next question. Instead, pick up on a comment and follow-up.

Use acknowledging words that show you are listening

When management are answering your questions, say things like, "I understand," and "go on." This builds trust and rapport, and encourages them to open up further.

Use an uncomfortable silent pause to your benefit

When I first started interviewing management, they would be finishing up their answer to one of my questions, and I would be starting to look for the next one on my list. I sometimes would pause for a brief period until I could find my next question. A funny thing happened. Some of them continued to talk when there were a few seconds of silence. Humans hate lulls in conversation, and it makes a lot of people uncomfortable. So, they feel the need to fill the void with something better. Sometimes those extra little nuggets of information contain gems. You must use this technique sparingly, but I have found it can be very effective for getting management to open up.

And here are some things to avoid when talking to management.

Things to avoid when talking to management

Don't ask questions with multiple parts to them

Ask one question at a time. When long, multi-part, convoluted questions are asked, they may end up leaving management confused about what information you are looking for. Or it may give the executive the option to answer either one question or the other. If they are good at diverting questions, they may answer none of your questions and will go off on their own carefully rehearsed message track and by the time they are done with their answer you will have forgotten your original questions.

I see this all the time during conference calls when analysts ask long questions with multiple parts to them. I don't know if it's because they fear that they will only get to ask one question on the call, but by the time the executive is done answering they have often picked which part of the question they want to answer and left it at that.

Don't ask leading questions

When you convey your expectations to management by way of a leading question, it limits the possible answers, and their answer may not reflect the truth. I have seen this happen on conference calls, when investors are trying to tease guidance out of a CEO who is reluctant to provide it. The question will often go something like, "I am using a 50% gross margin in my model for next quarter. Is that a reasonable expectation?" Management will often reluctantly confirm that it is reasonable, because they have been influenced by the leading question. If they were willing to answer the direct question, "What will gross margins look like next quarter?" I am sure it would be a different number than the investor suggested most of the time. The investor is worse off than before they asked the leading question because they then plug this faulty information into their earnings model.

Another example of a leading question asked on conference calls is when an analyst's or investor's question starts off with, "You probably can't answer this, but..." and then they go on to ask their question. You've just given management an out to not answer your question, if they are at all hesitant. Nine times out of 10, management will say something like, "We can't answer that because we haven't given out that information to the market for competitive reasons," or something along those lines. Whereas if they had just asked the question without adding "You probably can't answer this, but..." management might answer the question 50% of the time.

Don't interrupt them

You are trying to get information out of management, so let them talk after you ask them a question. We like the sound of our own voices, and we want to demonstrate that we are knowledgeable about the subject being discussed, so we interrupt. Let management finish talking. You'll get more complete answers to your questions.

The next time you listen to a conference call, or even a reporter interviewing someone, listen to the types of questions they ask. You will notice a pattern that good-quality questions result in good-quality answers.

You build self-confidence by putting in the reps. Don't be too hard on yourself when you are learning. When I was getting started as a microcap investor, the thought of talking to management was very intimidating.

I fell in love with the microcap space because even a small investor like me could gain access to management. I fine-tuned my skills over years and now decades. Most investors don't even try.

To beat the market, you must do things most investors aren't willing to do.

I was lucky that I had a mentor who showed me how to communicate with management. He was an established and wealthy investor, and he could buy hundreds of thousands or millions of dollars' worth of their stock, so of course management was going to respect him.

We would do many management interviews together. In the beginning he would take the lead, and every so often I would interject with my shaky nervous voice to ask a few questions. After several calls, he encouraged me to lead the calls, and I gained more confidence. Just like most things in life, practice makes perfect.

Mentors are important. I would like to tell you more about mine.

CHAPTER 5

Mentors

Mentorship is best described by this verse in the Bible:

> As iron sharpens iron, so one person sharpens another.
>
> **– Proverbs 27:17**

Mentors help people by giving advice and sharing what they've learned from their own experiences. They can guide you when you face problems or tough choices. A mentor can make you feel more confident and supported. They can also open doors to new opportunities through their networks. Having mentors can make it easier to reach your goals and it fosters accountability.

Here is an unpopular opinion that will get me banned from presenting at all value investing events:

Warren Buffett is not your mentor.

A mentor is someone you can share a personal relationship with. *How do you find one?* Look out 10 years and visualize who you want to be. Then go find that person today and learn from them.

When you find this person, don't reach out asking for help.

Most successful habits in life and investing are counter to our human nature. The key to success isn't getting everything you can out of everyone you meet. It's about adding value to everyone you meet. The way you get someone to want to work with you is showing value to them – proving to them you will be additive to their already rich and complex life.

In 2002, when I was learning how to invest in microcaps, also known as losing money, I stumbled upon the person that would become my first mentor. I met Skip on a stock message board. He communicated through written word like no one I had ever met. He wrote in a clear, informative, and authoritative tone.

Have you ever been part of a group or team where no one was officially the team leader but there was a person in the group that after they spoke you knew they were in charge? They exuded the confidence you wish you had. Deep down you wanted them in charge. You wanted to follow them.

This person was Skip on the stock message boards in the early 2000s. He had a massive following. I wanted to get closer to him. I sent Skip a private message. I heard nothing back. I sent another message. Nothing. Sent again. Nothing.

Finally, I decided to give him a reason to respond. I knew the stocks he liked, so I did a deep dive into one of his favorite stocks. My goal was to find some piece of information that even he didn't know existed. It took me 30 days, but I finally found what I needed and posted the information on the company thread on the message board. I knew he would see it and be impressed. But I heard nothing. I just kept digging and kept posting interesting insights into his own positions.

Finally, at 1am on some random day, I received a reply. "Hey kid, let's talk, here is my number." We spoke over the phone and immediately started working together on due diligence.

Skip had a deep radio announcer type voice. He spoke like he wrote on the message boards – with authority. In his previous career he trained stockbrokers. He managed the brokerage arm of a large national firm before starting his own firm and building it up to 150 stockbrokers.

His firm was focused on small cap stocks. He ended up selling the firm in the mid 1990s. Well, he would say he "got [insert expletive]" because his partner stole the business from him. Skip had decades' worth of experience in three things: training brokers, selling people stocks, and getting people to like him quickly.

He was cut from the cloth of the 1970s and 1980s stock markets.

When Type A personalities ruled and were respected. When the Michael Steinhardts of this world with their "I'm your competition" and "I'm right and you're wrong" mentality were the norm. No touchy feely "we can all win together" like it is today. It was a different time of different men. A time that produced opinionated, callused men.

I grew to love that about him. The certainty. The conviction. The willingness to piss people off at any moment if he disagreed. The type of man that will stop a conversation mid-sentence or get up from a dinner table and end a 30-year relationship if certain lines are crossed. The type of man that has a lot of colleagues but few friends. These personalities are lightning rods, and you only have to wait to hear the crack.

But their personality is also what you respect about them. You know exactly where they stand and where they stand with you. I didn't agree with him all the time or how he lived his life. Neither did his three ex-wives. But I loved him, nonetheless.

I met him when I was 22 years old during my first year of graduate school. I was obsessed with microcap investing, but I had an assistantship where I worked for two professors and the school paid my tuition. I had to keep my grades above a B– average to keep the assistantship, so my goal was to get Bs. The effort to get As wasn't worth the time away from focusing on microcap investing.

A few months into our friendship, I flew to meet Skip in person. He picked me up from the airport in a silver Porsche 911. I grabbed my bag off the baggage claim, walked outside, and I heard his booming voice yelling my name. When I got in the car, he looks at me and says, "You ready to gamble?" I had no idea what he was talking about, so I just replied, "Sure, absolutely."

I would quickly learn Skip was also a full-time gambler. He literally went to the casinos every day.

When we arrived at the casino, he stepped out, threw his keys to the valet, and briskly walked into the casino. I chased after him. He walked straight to a craps table. "Mr. Davidson, good to see you again," the stickman said from behind the table. Soon a couple more dealers stepped behind the table. "You want your usual?" Skip nodded, and threw his player's card at them and said, "You know you should have at least named the men's room after me for all the money I've pissed away at this casino." They all erupted in laughter.

The boxman brought over a receipt for him to sign and they laid out $10,000 in chips. I would later learn he had a marker [line of credit for patron gamblers] for $100,000 at that casino. I stood beside him feeling out of place and intimidated staring at the stack of chips. My eyes were as big as saucers. This was real money.

I had never played craps before, but the way he navigated the board, moving bets, shouting orders at the dealers, and throwing dice was like watching a maestro. Out of the gate he hit a hot streak, and his pile of chips grew bigger. He pressed his bets.

After 10 minutes he looked at me and said:

> I'm going to teach you some things about investing at this craps table. The first lesson is when you have a hot hand, you press your bets. It's the same for stocks. I know you think you're young, but you will only own a dozen big winners in your lifetime. Those are your chances to get rich. But you aren't going to get rich if you don't press them and hold them.

I nodded my head in agreement, too nervous to comprehend anything he said.

"We started with $10,000. How much money did we have out on the felt when we started?" I said, "I don't know, just a couple hundred dollars." He said, "Yes, that is close. We were betting small when we got started. In craps you normally have two or three rolls and then you lose. The key is to lose small. We want to let the table determine our bet size. If we are rolling dice and hitting numbers, we'll let our betting positions naturally get bigger while holding some of the winnings back. We've had a hot hand since we got here. How much is out on the felt?" I looked at the felt, "I would say $4,000." He replied, "Yes, and we have about $20,000 off the table."

He continued.

> Did you notice the table was empty when we got here. It was just us and the dealers. When we started winning and hitting numbers,

> excitement started to build. The dealers are rooting for us because when I win, they win. My tips get bigger the more we win. Did you notice it didn't take long for other players to join the table and now the table is full. There is also a crowd around us. Winning attracts people. They want to win too. It's the same thing with stocks. Investors love to buy stocks that are going up. Whether it's stocks, craps, business, or life, people are attracted to winners.

The dice eventually went cold. The next player had two throws and done. Skip looked at me and said, "Let's get out of here. This table is dead." He threw a $500 chip at the dealers and yelled, "I'm getting out of here before I pay for another one of Jimmy's [the casino owner] paintings in his office." The dealer laughed, took the chip, knocked it twice on the tip bin, "You're a wise man!" to which Skip replied, "Tell that to my three ex-wives!" as we walked away.

We went outside and while we waited for the valet to bring around the car, he said, "The last lesson for the day and perhaps the most important part of gambling and stock picking is knowing when to walk away. You don't want to get into the habit of trying to turn a bad table. You can't tell the market it's wrong. Even if you're right – being broke and right is the same as being wrong. When you are losing and feel the itch to double down to make it back quicker… walk away."

Skip was just a force of nature. He was addicting to be around, and he also had many addictions. I would fly out to his house at least a dozen times over the next two years while I was in graduate school.

What would we do?

He would give me a stock, let me study it for a couple hours, and then I had to pitch him and convince him it was a great situation. At first, I stumbled and stammered. As you can imagine it was uncomfortable.

I still remember when he stopped me mid-sentence: "Remember this – People don't listen to unconfident people. People don't write checks to unconfident people. People don't follow unconfident people."

He trained me to pitch an idea quickly and know a company so well I could answer any follow-up questions. He put me through the full training gauntlet. I think he missed training brokers, so I became the person he trained.

Skip had no patience for "uhmmmms" or "I thinks" or half convictions. There was no gray. It was only black or white. A stock was either a buy or a sell. Never a hold. A hold just meant you couldn't make up your mind, so it was a sell.

I would be wavering on a position, and he would scream, "Hold ratings on stocks should be illegal. A stock is either a buy or a sell, not a hold. Which is it?! Make a decision!"

The other thing he taught me was "skin in the game." He had no interest in hearing about stocks I thought were interesting. He only cared about stocks I owned. He only cared about what I was doing, not what I was saying.

I remember it like it was yesterday. I pitched him a stock and he asked me, "Do you own it?" and I said, "No." He put a finger in my chest and looked me dead in the eyes and said, "This world is full of analysts and not enough investors. Put your money where your mouth is or shut your mouth."

He was the first conviction investor I met. He owned four stocks and spoke to management frequently. Like any mentor–mentee relationship, his best four ideas became my best four ideas and so we started traveling to meet management teams together.

He was insanely good at getting people to like him. He would say, "There is no money to be made being an asshole. People tell you more when they like you." He was extremely likable. He just wasn't lovable for most.

He would normally take the lead in conversations and meetings. At dinner he would have a few cocktails with the CEOs while I took notes. I remember one night I flew into Pittsburgh and his flight was canceled. I took the lead with the CEO and also had a few cocktails. I didn't know how a person could do both those things at the same time and remember anything at all. I learned it just took practice.

Skip influenced my approach. He was exactly what I needed at the right time. Even though he was independently wealthy and a better investor, he treated me as an equal.

When I was building my capital base through college, then graduate school, and struggling to figure out how to support myself, he was always there to listen. For some time I thought it was odd he never offered to financially support me, but I don't think he wanted an "employee."

He was unusually warm, but cold at the same time. When he knew I was struggling, there was no shoulder to cry on. He would say, "As stock pickers we eat what we kill. If you want to eat, then go kill."

He would share his stock ideas through email to a list of a hundred or so people. These people were investors he met over the last decade. I would meet half of them in person over those first few years of traveling with him. They probably ended up making a little more money than they lost, but even after the big losers they still respected him. They knew he had 10x more skin in the game in each idea than they did.

Skip lived by a certain code. His father was a Lieutenant General and Superintendent of United States Military Academy at West Point. Those principles stayed with him. He may have been the first one into his stock ideas, but he was also always the last one out. He would tell a few of his closest colleagues, "I'll hold the door open while you leave and I'll shut it behind us." That was his code and it was hard not to respect it. It led him to make more on some stocks but lose a lot more on many others. I adhered to this same code when I was building my network.

Toward the end of his life, we grew apart because I kept evolving and he stayed how he was. Any normal person would have cut ties with him completely, but I loved him too much.

Mentors don't have to be perfect; they just need to be great in an area where you want growth.

Over the years you realize people come into your life for a reason. They are meant to show us what we can become or shouldn't let our lives become. Seeing the bad is just as educational as seeing the good.

It was 15 years after I had first met him. The years and decades of hard living finally caught up to him. Years of gambling would strip him of almost all his wealth. His health began to fail. His son called me and told me his dad's health was deteriorating quickly. I was married, but I jumped on a plane. I showed up on his front doorstep unannounced.

He opened the door using a walker. He could barely walk, but he still had that personality. That baritone voice you could hear across the room. He still had that spark. The type of person that if you met him for the first time, within five minutes you would have thought, "I wish I could have met him 30 years ago to see what he was like."

After we embraced, I held up an envelope with $10,000 in cash and said, "Let's go gambling." His eyes lit up. It's like I rewound time 15 years back to when we first met. Back when I knew nothing, and I thought he knew everything. It was the best money I ever lost.

The first line of his obituary reads: "Alan 'Skip' Davidson lived for the long shot. After passing away on July 31, he is now running the poker game with the angels, aces wild."

I love you Skip. RIP.

I would have a few more mentors during the journey. Each one played a critical role in my personal and professional growth.

Mentorship Rule #1: Never take advice from people that aren't happy people.

Mentorship Rule #2: Don't take advice from someone who has never done what you are about to do.

You gain wisdom by learning from others and making mistakes. The next step is to grow yourself.

CHAPTER 6

Grow Yourself

In 1831, John Mackay was born in Dublin, Ireland. At the age of nine, the Mackay family immigrated to the US, living in the notorious Five Points in lower Manhattan, which was known as the worst slum in the United States.

John's parents scraped together enough money to send him to school. He was only able to attend for two years, but he learned to read and write. This was the only formal education he would ever receive in his life.

At age 11, John's father died suddenly, so he quit school to work to support the family. He would work selling newspapers for the next four years and then became an apprentice at a ship builder for another four years.

From 1846 to 1848 the Mexican–American War was fought. Nine days before the treaty was signed between the two countries whereby the US was given California and New Mexico, gold was found in a riverbed in California that would spark the greatest gold rush in history.

On January 24, 1848, John W. Marshall, a carpenter and sawmill operator who worked at Sutter's Mill, made a gold discovery. He told John Sutter, the sawmill owner and no one else. Sutter tried to keep it quiet but the news broke by March.

It would be a few months until news of the gold discovery hit New York, and a few months more before the excitement really hit. The trigger point were articles written about mining laborers making $50–70 per day, which was 50 times what a normal unskilled laborer made in the United States.

Tens of thousands of people started flooding into California and the gold rush was the main catalyst that kickstarted people moving from east to west during that time period. But during this time Mackay stayed at the shipyard earning $1-2 per day.

When you think about the California Gold Rush and how it ignited an excitement that pulled so many people west, it's easy to think these people were dumb, undisciplined gamblers. I would encourage you to put yourself in the position of an unskilled laborer making $1-2 per day in the 1850s.

You had no advancement opportunities. Your best-case scenario as an unskilled laborer was in 10 years you would be doing the exact same thing making the same amount of money. That was your upside.

What would you do? Stay at home making $1–2 per day for the rest of your life, or go west and see if you can make 50 times more. You too would be on the next horse or boat out of town headed west.

By late 1851, two full years into the gold rush, Mackay quit his apprenticeship, boarded a ship, and headed for the west coast. He was late to the party. By this time there would have been thousands of people already coming back east from the Sierra foothills empty handed. The easy pickings were picked and by late 1851 the cost of living had exploded in and around the gold rush.

In three years, the population of San Francisco exploded from 800 to 35,000 as it became the fastest growing city in America. San Francisco became the melting pot of culture – you could hear English, Spanish, French, German, Chinese, Malay, and Hawaiian all spoken on the same city block. San Francisco was a place of new beginnings, because the city itself had no past.

At the same time, anyone that came west with a moral compass left it on the boat. Mining was extremely hard, with the odds of success not much better than gambling. Many people went broke.

Disease was rampant in mining towns. Violence and murder were common. Drinking, gambling, and gold were the top three endeavors. California quickly became the devil's playground.

When Mackay landed in San Francisco in late 1851 he went straight to Downieville, California. This was 100 miles north of Sacramento. He lived there for seven years mining gold in the gulches. He never made a big strike during these years, but he earned enough to support himself and send what he could back to his mother and sister.

Mackay loved the mining life – the outdoors, the physical work, the camaraderie, the chaotic menacing life of the mining camps. In his first few years Mackay built a hard-working reputation. No one worked harder than John Mackay. He was well liked among his peers. What made him different was at night when everyone drank and gambled, he stayed home and read about mining, geology, and also studied great men. He visualized himself in situations competing and winning.

In Downieville, at the start of the gold rush if you worked with a good team, you made $20 per day. But the pay was steadily coming down as the easy gold was taken out of the earth. By 1855 miners made $5 per day, and by 1858, you were lucky to make $3 per day.

By 1858, Mackay was 27 years old and had been mining for seven years with nothing much to show for it. He was working hand to mouth just like the first day he arrived. The Downieville gold district was dying, and it was time to make a move. Mackay and a friend packed up and literally walked 110 miles to Virginia City in Nevada, a location that would later become the Comstock Lode.

It's hard to imagine that within 20 years John Mackay would own the entire district and become one of the richest men in the world.

I often think about the perseverance it takes to become who you want to be, and how it doesn't happen by accident. It is the result of deliberate thought, effort, and discipline. Mackay studied while everyone else drank and gambled. His effort in self-improvement wasn't a guarantee he would become successful. But he would have surely guaranteed himself to be poor if he hadn't put in the hours that others wasted.

This is a valuable lesson for life, business, and investing.

Growing yourself ahead of your portfolio

Shyam Sekhar, founder and CIO of ithoughtPMS, said:

"When you make a lot of money ahead of when you should have, it is your duty to grow yourself first and then handle that money. You need to grow yourself ahead of your portfolio."

I love the concept of growing yourself ahead of your portfolio. I experienced early success in investing. Instant success can be a great impostor because you think it's skill instead of luck. Your head starts to swell. We all want fame and fortune, but the problem with instant success is you rarely have the power to keep what you haven't earned.

I penned this chart 15 years ago to illustrate the maturation of a stock picker:

Chart 6.1: The psychology of stock picking

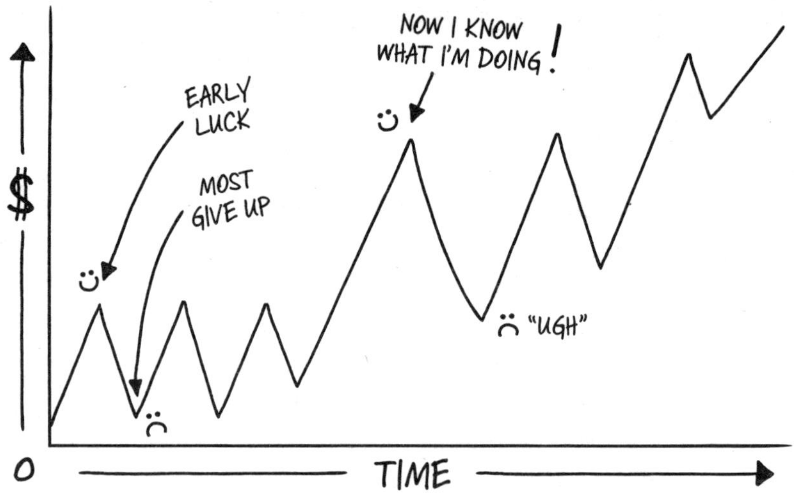

Source: Ian Cassel.

The key to learning is continuous improvement and humility. The market loves to destroy egos because only through humility can it prepare your mind to accept truth. Just like military training, the market needs to tear you down and destroy all your selfish beliefs and tendencies before it can build you back up. It is no accident that the greatest lessons occur when we are the most confident.

My biggest losses have all occurred after my biggest wins. During periods of over-confidence is when we decide to get lax with our checklist, analysis, maintenance due diligence, or expand too quickly outside our circle of competence. This is when the market comes in and destroys our ego again. It is not surprising that many successful investors are not arrogant or brash, but self-reserved and humble.

"Wisdom flows into the humble man like water flows into a depression."

In Pennsylvania, we get all four seasons. I normally start mowing my lawn in April and I'll stop mowing in early November. The grass doesn't grow in the winter. There are also a few weeks in the middle of summer when the grass stops growing and even turns brown.

Grass grows in a temperature band between 40–90°F. Grass stops growing when it's very cold and very hot. The grass doesn't die. It just turns brown and stops growing.

People are the same.

When you're too cold, you lose self-confidence and start reaching everywhere for guidance. When you're too hot, you're overconfident and you think you have all the answers.

When you are too hot or too cold you stop growing. It's important you stay in the middle so you can grow.

The hardest part of achieving a great long-term investment track record is over half the time your returns will look average. You can go years where it feels like you are working hard for mediocre returns. Then suddenly it changes. The previous year's efforts, perhaps helped by a better macro environment, create circumstances where you don't have to work as hard for your returns. The world finally works for you and pulls forward five to 10 years' worth of returns and riches into a single year.

Then it's up to you whether this is your new base from which to grow, or will you stop growing yourself by letting your ego take control? Will you revert slowly and then quickly back to immature tendencies? If so, your wealth will revert slowly and then quickly.

The growth and maturity to manage $10,000 is different than $1 million. The maturity to manage $10 million is different than $1 million. You must always be growing yourself ahead of your portfolio.

Two-time Major winner Zach Johnson learned to play golf when he was 10 years old. He was the #2 player on his high school golf team. After high school he enrolled at Drake University in Des Moines, Iowa. He was the #2 player on the Drake golf team. Zach Johnson didn't win a single junior golf tournament or college golf tournament.

When he was asked about how he became a top professional golfer he said, "I just kept getting better." He would turn professional in 1998 and played on several development tour circuits before obtaining his PGA Tour card in 2003. Johnson would go on to win 16 professional golf tournaments, including two Majors, and has earned over $60 million during his career. Not bad for a guy that wasn't even the best player on his high school or college team.

The #1 player on Zach's high school team said: "Zach wasn't the best in high school, not the best in college, but every single year you saw continual improvement. In a sport where a lot of guys peak early, level off and plateau, he just got better."

Deliberate practice

The key to continuous improvement is deliberate practice. Deliberate practice is a method of training that is specifically designed to improve performance in a particular skill. It involves setting specific goals, breaking down the skill into smaller components, and focusing on the areas where improvement is needed. It is typically done with the guidance of a teacher, mentor, or coach, and it involves repeating the skill over and over, with constant feedback and adjustments. Deliberate practice is often seen as the key to achieving mastery in a particular field.

Professional athletes, artists, and musicians are most common in using deliberate practice. For example, professional golfers spend hours every day practicing specific shots and working on their swing. They often do video analysis and work with coaches to identify areas of improvement. They then go out and practice full rounds and put all the skills together.

Deliberate practice becomes more difficult in areas where the feedback loops are longer. You hit a bad golf shot, you see it and correct it. You play a bad note, you hear it and correct it. You make a bad investment, you might know tomorrow, next month, or next year. In stock picking it takes longer to know when you are wrong, and then even longer to implement changes, and wait for the results. At the same time, the world, and the markets are changing all around us.

Many average stock pickers like to deceive themselves. They use the long feedback loops as an excuse to be lazy. You can't sit around waiting to learn from your last decision. Every minute should be concentrated on continuous improvement. Every minute you waste is a chance for someone else to find the next great idea or uncover something new about your own investments. Every minute you waste is time you could have spent further developing your skills through journaling and studying. You can speed up the maturation process and be light years ahead of others if you devote yourself to mastering the art of stock picking.

Stock picking isn't a game of perfection. It's a game of continuous improvement. An exceptional professional baseball player earns $15–20 million more per year for getting a hit 5% more often than an average professional baseball player. A small increase in batting average and slugging percentage can greatly increase your earnings.

The nine steps of continuous improvement in stock picking

Continuous improvement in stock picking can be broken down into nine steps.

Step 1: Study accounting and industries

Before you start researching a company you must understand the basics of accounting. Accounting is the language of business, and you can't expect to understand what the business is saying unless you know the language.

Unlike 50 years ago, today you have many engaging options to learn accounting. Purchase an introduction to accounting book, or take an online or in-person accounting course. Once you know the basics, start looking at large competitors in the same sector or industry and study their financials. You will find similarities and differences and start to know how they make money. When you study the pioneers of an industry you will learn how they paved the way for the rest of the world. You can then study the next-generation leaders to see how they disrupted the pioneers.

Step 2: Study the greats of investing

Pablo Picasso, Vincent van Gogh, Leonardo da Vinci, Claude Monet, Salvador Dali, Rembrandt, Andy Warhol, etc., were all so uniquely talented and different. The greats of investing are the same way. Buffett does it his way while Schloss did it another way. Icahn does it his way while Lynch does it another way. Tepper does it his way while Andreessen does it another. Some are long term. Some are short term. Some are value. Some are growth. Some are activist. Some bet on change. Some bet on things that won't change. Many of the best investors ever had completely different, almost opposing, strategies.

When you study great investors, you will connect with one or two investors more than the others because they align with your own strategy. This is good, but don't use it as an excuse to not study the others. I often learn the most by studying successful investors that invest differently than me. They normally approach investing with a different lens and value things that I don't, so you can uncover your own blind spots by studying them.

As an example, perhaps you study venture capitalist investors on how they identify promising founders. You then start applying those techniques in the public markets. Your advantage is often in the areas you are different from other investors. Study the greats and then go paint your own painting.

Step 3: Study great stocks, great businesses, great leaders (intelligent fanatics)

A way to speed up the maturation process is being a student of history and studying past winners. This is what I did through the Intelligent Fanatics Project, which I'll discuss in a later chapter. When you study hundreds of winners you start to develop pattern recognition, so you will know what to look for when seeking future winners.

You have all you need to create a Multi-Bagger University Course right at your fingertips. All multi-bagger stocks have a public track record of earnings releases, filings, transcripts, and interviews. Pick 10 stocks and go study everything about them. At the same time you'll be learning about the history of different industries.

Step 4: Investment journal

The best way to learn investing is by investing and you supercharge learning by keeping an investment journal. Create a file system for every business and industry you analyze, and keep it updated. For every investment you make, write out your investment thesis, and then write out what would kill your investment thesis. Keep your thesis updated, in writing, after every earnings report. Keep a shorter form thesis (one page) for every company on your watchlist. Write a note under your original thesis for every earnings release with the numbers, commentary, and what would make the watchlist company actionable (stock price, catalyst, etc.). Rank order your current positions and watchlist companies based on expected two- to three-year IRRs (internal rates of return) and upside to downside ratios.

Step 5: Develop the skills of stock picking

I believe there are five core skills in stock picking: identifying, analyzing, buying, selling, and holding. You don't have to be great at all of them, but you do need to be good at all of them. Good means you have a thoughtful repeatable process that you can refine and improve. You can't refine something you aren't applying consistently. Over time you will find the one or two skills that become your strengths. We will get into these skills in more detail in later chapters. As you develop the skills you will make mistakes. Don't blame others. Fully own your past mistakes so you learn from them.

Step 6: Feedback from mentors and peers

Feedback can be difficult because successful investing means seeing the future in a different way than the majority. Most successful investments are disliked by most investors, so you aren't looking for "acceptance" or "buy in" to the idea when you are looking for feedback. The feedback you are searching is finding holes in your thesis, or differential insights into areas where you lack expertise.

Step 7: Repeat steps 3–6 a few hundred times

In 1973, Herbert Simon and William Chase wrote a paper for the *American Scientist* on developing the skills of chess. It was the preeminent work that Malcolm Gladwell made famous with his 10,000-hour rule. He concluded in his book, *Outliers*, that anyone could master anything if they devoted enough time to deliberate practice. 10,000 hours was found to be the magic number, equivalent to practicing four to five hours per day, five days per week, for 10 years.

Chip Maloney wrote about Dan McLaughlin, a 30-year-old commercial photographer, who conducted a 10,000-rule experiment. He spent 6,000 hours practicing golf, a sport he never played before. He was able to reduce his golf handicap from 50 to 2.6 before he injured his back and stopped the experiment. I'm not sure if the right number is 5,000, 10,000, or 50,000 hours. You must put in the time and reps. It's the only way to develop the skills of investing and become the investor you were meant to be.

Step 8: Evolve

As you mature as a stock picker it's imperative you remain humble and curious towards new techniques that can be applied to your strategy. If you aren't looking back at your past losers and past winners in horror, you aren't growing. Don't ever label yourself as a specific type of investor. Once you put yourself in a box, it's too hard to get out of the box. You are going to evolve in small and big ways. Embrace the change.

Step 9: Mastery

You can't "master" stock picking until you build up a 20+ year track record of beating the market. To accomplish such a feat, you must grow yourself along with your capital. You must be a student of the craft and evolve your strategy. You must become good at all the skills of stock picking. You have likely fully developed your principles and committed to them.

Give yourself the time to go through the process to be who you want to be. Impatience is the killer of process. Continuous improvement is filled with hundreds or even thousands of disciplined, boring days. The stock market is like life. Wrong decisions are often punished quicker than right decisions are reinforced. Successful investing is delayed gratification. It is called delayed because it always takes longer than we think it should.

I've always been a concentrated stock picker, but when I was first getting started I was extremely concentrated. The highs were high and the lows were low. It helped me learn the hard lessons faster.

CHAPTER 7

Life Is Too Short to Diversify

I've always been a concentrated investor. From 2001 to 2010 when I was building my capital base to $2 million, I was in three to four stocks. In 2005, I launched my blog with the tagline, "Life is Too Short to Diversify." I focused on knowing a handful of businesses better than anyone else. This was my edge.

Today, I manage my capital alongside 70 other families that want intelligent exposure to microcaps. We own 10 to 15 stocks.

The beauty of holding only a handful of stocks is that it has allowed me to learn the hard lessons faster because the result of every decision is amplified financially and emotionally. It's like Charlie Munger said: "Extreme outcomes, good or bad, often educate best."

My journey to concentrated investing

My ideas around concentration and focus started when I was in college. One day a professor handed me the book *Think and Grow Rich* by Napoleon Hill. I devoured it in two days. I read it again and again. The book was originally published in 1937 during the Great Depression. Since then it has sold over 100 million copies, making it one of the top selling books of all time.

The book originated when Napoleon Hill was doing research on successful leaders for an article he was writing. He interviewed Andrew Carnegie, one of the richest and most powerful men in the world at the time. Carnegie was so impressed with Hill that he gave him the task of interviewing other successful men and women.

Hill's compilation of research and interviews took 25 years. During those years he studied and interviewed over 500 of the most successful people in the world, mostly made available because of Andrew Carnegie's influence.

Hill interviewed Henry Ford, Alexander Graham Bell, Elmer Gates, Thomas Edison, Luther Burbank, William Taft, John D. Rockefeller, and many others. After Hill studied and interviewed all of these successful men and women, he noted there was a formula to success. Thirteen steps to riches. He published the formula in *Think and Grow Rich*.

The first step is to create a vision for yourself and a burning desire to achieve it. Hill wrote:

"There is one quality which one must possess to win, and that is definiteness of purpose, the knowledge of what one wants, and a burning desire to possess it."

After my big win with XM Satellite Radio my burning desire turned to becoming a full-time private microcap investor. How was I going to achieve it? I wrote down my vision statement:

"$10k and two 10-baggers = Millionaire."

The term "multibagger" was first coined by legendary investor Peter Lynch, drawing parallels from baseball. For instance, a 10-bagger implies a stock that returns 10 times the original investment.

XM was technically an eight-bagger, but close enough. I loved the simplicity of the statement "$10k and two 10-baggers = Millionaire." I wrote it down in my journal when I was 22 years old. I stared at it every day. Most people think it's a preposterous statement. For me it was a rallying cry. It was my BHAG (big hairy audacious goal). It was perfect.

The best part of being human is when we overestimate our potential.

Thank goodness we do. We would never push ourselves or reach for anything if we didn't.

I recently shared my old vision statement on social media. It went viral, but 90% of replies were negative. People get so angry at the thought of making big returns and then they act surprised when it doesn't happen to them.

When someone says something is impossible, what they mean is it's impossible for them, not you.

Did I achieve two 10-baggers in a row? Absolutely not. But the pursuit focused me.

The goal was to compound capital as quickly as I could. If compound interest is the eighth wonder of the world, then the compounding effect of great decision-making is the ninth. String a few great decisions together and it will change your life. That is what I ended up doing.

When I was getting started, I read every investment book I could get my hands on. I quickly realized most of the great stock pickers had concentrated, high-turnover strategies during their peak-return years. Not surprisingly most got their start in microcap stocks.

The concentrated investments of the great investors

Warren Buffett's right-hand man, Charlie Munger, is quoted as saying, "The first $100,000 is a bitch." Warren Buffett made his first $100,000 in the early 1950s when he was still an individual investor. $100,000 in 1950 is equivalent to about $1.2 million today. So perhaps Munger's 2026 version would be, "The first $1.2 million is a bitch."

In 1948, through his company Graham-Newman Corporation, Ben Graham bought 50% of GEICO for $712,000. By 1972, this investment was worth $400 million, a 562-bagger. The gain in GEICO would contribute more profit to Graham's partnership than all the gains from all the other investments he made combined. The irony is that Graham rarely invested more than 5% of the firm's capital in one company, but with GEICO he invested 20% of the firm's capital. Graham's most successful investment ever came when he broke his rules and made an educated concentrated bet.

Warren Buffett, at age 20, was introduced to GEICO in 1950 when he was Graham's student at Columbia Business School. Buffett would soon travel to GEICO headquarters to conduct due diligence on the company. He talked for hours with Lorimer Davidson, who would later become CEO of GEICO, and gained valuable insight into the business. Less than two days after the meeting with Davidson, Buffett put 75% of his net worth into GEICO. Roughly two years later he sold for a 50% gain.

Buffett later joined GEICO's board of directors even though he didn't own the stock. This changed in the 1970s when he started buying shares again, adding through two decades, and finally in 1995 buying the remaining 49% of GEICO he didn't own for $2.3 billion. I love how old stock ideas can come back around and become new ideas decades later.

Throughout his early 20s, Buffett continued allocating capital to only his highest conviction investments. In some cases, this meant placing big bets on one, two, or three companies. When reading Warren Buffett's early partnership letters, he often used phrases like, "I bought as much as I could." You don't hear him using phrases like, "I was worried about owning too much."

From 1949 to 1954, Buffett averaged ~50% annual returns, growing his capital 10 times and breaking the $100,000-mark, equivalent to $1.2 million today.

Some of you might be thinking it's easy to cherry pick the greatest investor ever as a justification to focus and concentrate. He had above average intellect and discipline. For most others it can end in disaster. But it isn't just Buffett. Most successful people in business and investing that preach diversification built their early wealth by concentrating on their best ideas.

We look at business titans today and how diversified they are in business ownership, investments, income streams and say, "That is how I should start." You are analyzing how to start by how these people finished. In fact, 90% of their wealth was likely accumulated or dictated by ferociously concentrating on one or a few things.

The good news for us mere mortals is Warren Buffett didn't have it all figured out when he was getting started, and his investment philosophy evolved over time.

When I was managing $100,000, my approach wasn't nearly as disciplined as it is now. Unlike Buffett I was human and I sustained severe losses during my early capital-building years. Most people will also experience their fair share of losses along the way. That's why it's best to start early, so you can fail early. When you fail you know what will work the next time. Most give up. Few push forward.

Warren Buffett's success can be summed up in one word: focus. In his early years he wanted to grow his capital as quickly as possible. He didn't do that by investing in 50 good companies. He did it by finding one, two, three great opportunities and buying as much as he could. He didn't have position sizing rules. The higher the risk-adjusted return, the more he owned. Even Graham broke his own rules and bellied up to the bar when he saw a great opportunity in GEICO.

When I was building my capital base from $10,000 to $100,000 to $1,000,000, I was at most in four positions. I found the best investments I could find and bought as much as I could. If you want to build capital quickly, only invest in your best ideas.

Another important lesson from Buffett's early years is he conducted due diligence, visited companies, and spoke to management. Most wouldn't be surprised by the first one, but many would be surprised that he went as far as visiting companies and speaking to management.

In many cases price was his due diligence, but he still took the initiative to meet management. When you're concentrated it gives you the time to know your investments better than most. In addition, the amount of work you do on an investment correlates with the amount of volatility you're willing to endure. The more you know what you own, the more volatility goes from being a risk to an opportunity.

Finding sustainable multi-baggers

If you want to grow your capital quickly you must find companies that can be multi-baggers. Most investors assume this means taking on more risk. This isn't the case at all; you must be extremely disciplined.

Find undiscovered businesses that can grow revenues and earnings without diluting.

Concentration doesn't mean you are reckless; it means you have high standards.

My favorite Charlie Munger quote: "The goal of investment is to find situations where it is safe not to diversify." This doesn't mean you will find them every month, quarter, or even year. He meant that you get 10 or 20 no-brainer buys in your entire investment career. When you do, you back up the truck.

For whatever reason, when people hear "multi-bagger" or "10-bagger," they think of a story stock with no fundamentals ascending quickly. Yes, it can be those types of companies. In fact, I was a story stock investor for the first several years of my career. But as I matured, I grew tired of buying stocks I knew I would have to sell within a few months.

The goal is to find and invest in sustainable multi-baggers – those companies where the fundamentals drive the stock price. The only thing these sustainable multi-baggers do quickly is rapidly grow earnings.

Professor Hendrik Bessembinder studied 26,000 stocks from 1926 to 2015. Only 42.1% of common stocks beat one-month Treasury bills over that horizon, and more than half delivered a negative lifetime return. 86 stocks out of 26,000 accounted for over half of the wealth creation.

Most people will read these statistics and conclude that stock picking is too hard. I invert it and say this is proof the stock market is made for stock pickers. I don't want to own all those losers. I want to pick winners.

$10k and two 10-baggers = Millionaire.

XM Satellite Radio represented my first 10-bagger. One 10-bagger down, one more to go. Instant success is awful. My head started to swell. I started thinking, "Warren Buffett who? They better make a spot for me in the Forbes 400 list. Move over Grandpa."

The greatest trick the market plays on beginners is making you think luck is skill. It waits for you to double or triple down on your next bet and then it teaches you your first lesson.

My maturation as a stock picker was just beginning.

The one thing I did right in these early years was starting to build out my network. As you mature as a stock picker, your biggest asset becomes the network you build through reciprocation and trust with investors, industry experts, and management teams. Getting to the truth quicker than someone else is the ultimate edge.

CHAPTER 8

Building Your Network

In 1982, Warren Buffett was 52 years old with a net worth of $900 million. He crushed the market for 26 years. If he had quit or died suddenly, I'm sure plenty of books would still be written about him.

But Buffett didn't die so he didn't quit. He kept compounding. Buffett found what Juan Ponce de Leon couldn't – his fountain of youth was a daily intake of Cokes and See's Candies. Buffett now has a public track record dating back 70 years since he first established his partnership.

It's Buffett's longevity and those few extra decades of compounding that puts the exclamation point at the end of GOAT! (GOAT = Greatest Of All Time). He is the greatest investor ever because he started young, outperformed, and has lived a long time.

If you were to ask Buffett, "What is your edge?" he would probably say it's his ability to do rational things during irrational times. I would argue his edge quickly evolved from rationality and intellect to one of reputation.

Reputation

Buffett has been compounding his reputation for 70 years with investors, operators, financiers, world leaders, everyone. The result is people desire his opinion and approval. Business owners are willing to sell to him for less. Financiers are willing to give him a better deal to have him involved. When the markets are in free fall, investors look to him to put in the floor and tell us it's going to be okay. Reputation means influence.

Reputations take time to develop and can only be earned. They normally start from humble beginnings. Most of the people you admire today weren't known by anyone the first 10 years of their career. They kept their heads down. They weren't seen. They worked in unglamorous positions, but they started building a reputation that they could be relied upon.

If you're an investor looking to build your reputation, find a great company early before institutions. Do the work. Be public about it. Be the axe in that stock (axe = no one knows the company better than you). Most importantly, be right.

Then do it again and again. If you can do this, it won't matter whether you went to Harvard or flunked out of the fourth grade. Investors, employers, and money will find you.

Twenty years ago, I would pound the table on stocks when I liked them. I wanted people to know I was the axe in the stock. I would post on public message boards and on my blog about my convictions. Not all the ideas worked, but some did. Fund managers and larger private investors would reach out and want to talk about my ideas. The seeds of many great relationships started 20 years ago.

My best advice to young people is work hard. Be positive. Be intense. A positive attitude and extreme intensity produces a gravitational force that pulls great people into your orbit. Winners want to be around winners. They want to be around that positive energy.

As you mature as a stock picker, relationships become your greatest assets – those relationships with investors, CEOs, and industry experts you've built over years and decades through reciprocity. These relationships are the gold plating on your reputation.

A great reputation manifests itself for stock pickers in three ways:

1. **Opportunities find you**. Investors and operators bring you opportunities. You're the first call.
2. **Companies listen to you**. They respect you.
3. **Expert truth seeker**. You can get to the truth quicker than other investors because you know the individuals that have the answers.

The motivations for building your network shouldn't be transactional. The motivation is to make everyone better. What you learn over time is 95% of the people you meet are transactional, and very few deserve to be a part of your inner circle. This doesn't mean you shouldn't let new people into your life. In fact, it's important to lead with grace and keep your eyes and ears open.

Give people a chance to take too much from you, so you can see who they really are. Building your network spans decades and you'll be constantly adding and pruning people from your network. This network will become your greatest asset.

How do you get started building your network?

First, build yourself

Here are the aspects to building yourself.

Be a good person

Whether you're 15 or 75 years old, there are two people in all of us. The person you are and the person you ought to be. It's your job to make sure they meet. Every day, get a little closer to the person you were meant to be. The biggest part of building a great network is being a person that is worthy of that network. Be a person that attracts people.

Be a positive person

If you want to increase the velocity of your relationships, every time you think something good, say it. Every time you think something good about someone else, tell them. Don't underestimate a single word of encouragement. People are attracted to positive people. Do you ever hear successful people complaining? No, because they are too busy doing. A big part of a positive mindset is acknowledging that opportunity rarely knocks at convenient times. You will have doors slammed in your face and that's okay. Develop an inner belief that if one door closes it's because another will open to something better.

Work hard and do it with intensity and consistency

Attitude and work ethic attracts people and opportunities. Think of some of the people you've met that left an impression on you. It was probably their energy and intensity. Intensity is contagious and once you are around it you want to be around it more.

Set goals and have the discipline to achieve them

Goals are accomplished through hard work and great discipline. Discipline is choosing what matters most in the long term over what you want now in the short term. Discipline is also pushing forward with a positive mindset no matter how you feel that day. Give yourself the time to go through the process. The process is filled with hundreds or even thousands of disciplined boring days with little to no recognition and then one day someone notices, and then thousands of people notice.

Build self-confidence by keeping the promises you make to yourself

It might be something small like waking up early to workout, or eating healthy, or not missing your kid's basketball game, or not having a drink, or telling your spouse I love you – but do it every day, every time, no excuses. Your life gradually builds momentum. You will start accomplishing things you didn't think you could ever accomplish.

Better yourself

The only thing I have in common with Warren Buffett is we both took the Dale Carnegie public speaking courses to better ourselves. Buffett said, "That $100 course gave me the most important degree I have. It certainly had the biggest impact in terms of subsequent success." My experience was the same. Don't be afraid to better yourself. Developing a strong presence and charisma, and improving your verbal and nonverbal skills, is a big multiplier in attracting people. The art of storytelling is probably the most underappreciated leadership skill a person can develop. Stories move products. Stories move people. Stories move stocks. Become a great storyteller.

Be a good listener

You can win over almost anyone by just listening to them during a conversation. It's hard to dislike someone that listens too much. It's easy to dislike someone that talks too much.

If you do all the above, you will become a magnet. The next step is to build your network.

Build your network

Put yourself in situations that showcase your potential. You supercharge the power of serendipity by putting yourself in situations to meet new people and sharing your ideas. It can be uncomfortable, but growth is rarely comfortable. Here are some ways to be proactive.

Show value to people you admire

Reach out to people you would like to emulate or who could mentor you. Don't ask anything of them. I'm not talking about famous people or public facing people. It could be someone you admire in your small town. Learn all you can about them and find a way to show value to them. Try to become an asset to them even if it's in small ways. Over time they will want to bring you in closer, and over years, perhaps even into their inner circle. During the process you will learn how they think and what made them successful. You will gain invaluable knowledge, friendships, and trust.

Create your brand

Start a blog, Substack, or newsletter. Start sharing your longer-form thoughts on a consistent basis. You can use it for general thoughts on investing and also to share your thesis on your current holdings. I think it's important to share something twice per month. Over time this will become your public journal where people can connect with you and see how your views have evolved. I started posting my thoughts on my own personal blog, and then on MicroCapClub's blog. I've met so many wonderful people by doing this. You have no excuse. Get started.

Connor Haley, founder of Alta Fox Capital, summed it up perfectly: "One of the reasons I tell young investors to start a blog is it timestamps your investing views, process, and ideas. That is more valuable to someone in a hiring seat than any potential case study, which is by definition a single point in time."

Share your thoughts on X or social media

I started on Twitter (now X) in 2009, and now I have a big following. My following is the result of authentic commentary, consistency, and time. I've always aligned with X because I've always enjoyed summarizing complex investing or life topics in simple statements. X has also been a catalyst for my writing. When you can get real-time feedback, it shows you what the public is interested in. If a tweet gets a lot of engagement, you know it will be a great blog post or article topic. To do anything consistently over the long term you must be fueled by something bigger than you. For example, my main agenda on X has been to pull quality investors into the microcap arena. If you want to attract quality into your life, whether it's relationships, investors, customers, achievers, opportunities, then project quality with your actions and words.

Find a great company early and attach your name to it

There is no better resume builder for an investor than finding a great company early. My mentor would say, "Find it early and be right." You want to be "the axe" in the name, where people know you were first, and you know every nuance about the company.

This happened to me a few times in my 20s. I got in early, blogged about it early, and as the company performed, institutions stumbled upon my articles. Then they reached out to me through my blog or through MicroCapClub and wanted to talk to me. This is how you build your network.

Share your struggles

In 2006, professional golfer John Daly was interviewed after playing with Tiger Woods. Daly was well past his prime. He was overweight. He drank too much. He gambled away his fortune. John Daly's life had been a roller coaster ever since he burst onto the golf scene in 1991 by winning the PGA Championship. He was widely considered the most talented golfer in the game, but his addictions and bad habits impacted his golf. He fell out of the world rankings several times over his career. Then out of nowhere he would get clean, devote himself to practicing, and win a golf tournament. Then his demons would pull him back down again. This happened a few times over his career.

Tiger Woods accumulated 82 PGA Tour wins. John Daly had five wins. The fascinating thing was Daly's fan base was just as big as that of Tiger Woods. Daly was asked how this was possible: "When people see Tiger, they see perfection. When they see me, they see imperfection. When people see me, they see themselves. When they see me win, they believe they can win too." You impress people with your successes, but you connect with people through sharing your struggles. If you want to build real connection, it's more valuable to be authentic than perfect.

Make a presentation. Teach a course

The best way to learn something is to teach it. This is also one of the best ways to meet new people. I remember the first presentation I gave on my progression as an investor. I had been a full-time private investor for four years. I was building a reputation and network by doing all the things I've mentioned in this chapter. Finally, an opportunity struck and Saurabh Madaan at Google asked me to come to Google HQ and present on microcap investing. You can still find that presentation on YouTube, "All Great Companies Started As Small Companies." I practiced that presentation 50 times. I prepared so much I think I could have delivered it effortlessly while being hung upside down and under water. My presentation was broadcast across several of Google's campuses. I could tell it impacted people. There is no better feeling than overpreparing and crushing it.

Join a private forum, message board, Reddit

I grew my reputation on public stock message boards like Raging Bull, Yahoo Finance, InvestorsHub, and Silicon Investor. Since most microcaps are owned by retail investors, I went where retail investors congregated. Sometimes posting on these message boards felt like Thunderdome in Mad Max. It could get ugly, but you built up a thick skin and the strong and the right survived. These venues have slowly died off and others like Discord and Reddit emerged. I founded MicroCapClub in 2011 because I wanted to share ideas with a smaller private community. I wanted quality of discussion over quantity of discussion. But those larger venues are still great places to share ideas and network with likeminded investors.

Ask questions on earnings calls and AGMs

Not all microcap companies have earnings calls, but if they do then use it as an opportunity to be seen and heard by management and other investors. I can't tell you how many times I've asked a question on an earnings call, and then people hear me on the call and reach out wanting to ask me questions. The same with an AGM. I've met some really good fund managers simply by being the only other investor at a company's annual shareholder meeting. Simply showing up can become a big advantage with management teams and investors.

Reach out to large holders of companies

If you own a position in a company that you know better than anyone else, and then you see an institution file as a 5% owner, reach out to them. They would likely love to hear from you if you feel you have substantial knowledge on the company. The closer you get to big money, the better.

Maintaining and pruning your network

In Dale Carnegie's classic, *How to Win Friends and Influence People*, he emphasizes the importance of regular, thoughtful communication, such as sending a note of congratulations or remembering a birthday, as a way to build and sustain relationships.

In an article written by investor Chip Maloney, he mentions Keith Ferrazzi, author of *Never Eat Alone*. Ferrazzi calls keeping in contact with your network "pinging." For those you have a closer relationship with, you might reach out weekly or monthly. For others, it could be every two or three months. This could involve sending a private message, a brief email, or making a short call to discuss a specific stock or investment idea. It might also mean sharing content regularly on your blog, contributing to forums you frequent, or tweeting valuable insights to your followers. Since strong relationships grow over time, maintaining regular contact and following up is essential. Each interaction you have with your network gradually strengthens the connection, deepening the relationship.

I'm not successful doing this every week, but this is my weekly relationship habit:

- Connect with one new person that inspires me and have an uninterrupted conversation.

- Connect with one person that impresses me – a younger aspiring person who likely looks up to me.
- Connect with one person you haven't connected with in a while but know you should.

There isn't enough time in the day to maintain contact with everyone you meet. The hard truth is many people aren't going to be additive to your investing or your life. After one or two interactions you will know if maintaining the relationship is worth your time.

Don't be afraid to prune back the tree so it can grow stronger. You are a limited resource so you must make peace with the fact that you can't please everyone. You must prioritize and say no to things, but you will find a firm "No" is always respected more than a weak "Maybe."

You will also have relationships that become fruitful but then sour. Walk away from relationships and partnerships that cause you to compromise your core values. You won't reach your full potential unless you are authentic to your core.

Supercharge your network

The most important part of building great relationships is helping people, without any expectation of receiving anything in return. It's the opposite of transactional relationships. In transactional relationships each side is expecting something from the other. These are shallow relationships.

If you want to supercharge key relationships within your network, do this:

How can I help you?

When I was first getting to know the now-famous Morgan Housel, we were communicating back and forth about something, and at the end of the exchange, he simply asked, "How can I help you?" It was genuine. I was taken aback by the selflessness of it. No wonder he probably has one of the greatest networks of anyone I know.

Be a match maker

Successful people want to be connected with other successful people. Bringing people together and helping others form connections is powerful. As you build relationships with more and more people, you will start to see commonalities of goals, personalities, strategies, beliefs, etc. It will become natural to be a connector. When you've introduced two people that become lifelong friends they remember it. I think a part of us wants to "keep our relationships to ourselves," and this is a mistake. Selfishness is the kryptonite to building relationships. Be a match maker.

Small group company visits

I've established some long-lasting friendships by including a few other investors on my due diligence process, and my company visits. It's not only helpful in evaluating a business, and conducting on site due diligence, but it's so much more fun to include others. In addition, if you are a smaller retail investor, management might not be open to a site visit. But if you tell management that it isn't just you, but a few other investors, they might be open to giving you the time.

Host an event

I now host two larger events under the Planet MicroCap brand. These events are a great way to network with microcap investors from around the world. Microcap investors love talking stocks and telling stories. I've also been able to leverage my network in getting some prominent speakers like Morgan Housel, William Thorndike, Jim O'Shaughnessy, Shane Parrish, Brent Beshore, Josh Tarasoff, Jeff Gramm, and many others to participate and present.

Mentorship

As you get older you want to stay relevant and in tune with the younger generation. The best way to do this is through keeping your eyes and ears open for young people that remind you of you. I had a couple mentors early in my journey. I mentioned Skip in an earlier chapter. I worked hard to earn his trust, and I never took his trust for granted. Eventually he opened his network to me. It supercharged my network, but my engagement with his established relationships re-energized these relationships for him as well.

Helping others takes little effort but can greatly benefit your network. By offering small, five-minute favors each week, you strengthen relationships without significant sacrifice. The strongest networks are built on generosity, not transactional exchanges. Those who focus on helping others succeed ultimately create the most valuable connections. The key to building and nurturing your network is to add more value to your network than you get back.

As you build your network your reputation grows, and your influence grows. Then it's up to you to protect the reputation you've built. Work every day to make sure your name, your word, your handshake, and your counsel are worth more than the day before. Reputation means influence.

In the next section, I'm going to tell my story and discuss my evolution as a stock picker from individual investor, to full-time microcap investor, to fund manager.

SECTION 2

The Evolution of a Stock Picker

CHAPTER 9

Story Stocks

In his essay "Best Story Wins," Morgan Housel wrote:

> The Civil War is probably the most well-documented period in American history. There are thousands of books analyzing every conceivable angle, chronicling every possible detail. But in 1990 Ken Burns' Civil War documentary became an instant phenomenon, with 39 million viewers and winning 40 major film awards. As many Americans watched Ken Burns' Civil War in 1990 as watched the Super Bowl that year. And all he did – not to minimize it, because it's such a feat – is take 130-year-old existing information and wove it into a (very) good story.

Stories are powerful. Every great leader is a great storyteller. Abraham Lincoln grew up the son of a poor farmer. His father would burn his books. He had to self-educate himself. He taught himself how to read and attracted friends through storytelling. He would later use this skill to convince colleagues and ultimately to change the course of a nation. Warren Buffett uses stories to educate investors. Jesus used parables to connect with his followers.

The art of storytelling is the most underappreciated leadership skill a person can develop. CEOs use stories to sell their mission and vision to customers, employees, and investors. Especially today, employees want to work for companies that are making an impact beyond profits. Customers like to support companies that are doing more than just selling them something.

I love to find companies with a great story. I love to invest in CEOs who are great storytellers that can execute. Great stories move companies. Great stories move products. Great stories move stocks.

Stock pickers usually get started in either story stocks or cheap stocks. This is ironic because they are opposite sides of the spectrum. If you got started as a stock picker before you took an accounting course, you likely started out like me in story stocks. If you got started as a stock picker after you took an accounting course, you likely started out buying cheap stocks or value stocks.

Why?

If you are a new stock picker and you've taken an accounting course then this is the only tool in your toolbox. The bluntest way to use this is to look for cheap stocks. But on the other hand, stories are the lowest common denominator. Whether you are young or old. Whether you are rich or poor. No matter your gender, race, religion, great stories attract everyone.

It took me several years to learn that the best stocks have two things: a great story and great fundamentals. But from 2001 to 2005, I was a pure story stock investor. I wasn't focused on fundamentals.

A story stock is a company with zero revenues and earnings. All they have is a story. The value of the stock is based on future expectations and potential, as opposed to actual earnings, revenues, or assets.

All story stocks sound amazing and have great potential.

- A potential cure for cancer.
- A potential big gold discovery.
- A potential strategic partner that could 10x the business.
- A potential large contract.
- A potential strategic investor.
- A potential transformative acquisition.
- A potential buyout from a large company.

A story can exist in any number of varieties, and they're normally described as, "The next Amazon or [insert 100-bagger]."

Story stocks are most common in technology, life science, and resource industries, where new life-changing products and new untapped resources can be profound. These industries are also the most capital intensive. Most of these companies must raise $50 million to $1 billion on R&D, clinical trials, permits, or exploration before they produce one dollar of revenue.

When a sub $100 million market cap company must raise $50 million or more of capital, what happens most of the time?

Dilution, pain, and loss.

The story stock arena is filled with storytelling CEOs with big ambitions but limited skills and resources to accomplish their plans.

Microcap service providers and investment banks love story stocks.

Why?

Story stocks must constantly raise money and investment banks earn fees for raising capital. The attorneys rack up hundreds of billable hours preparing documents and filing them. Consultants and investor relations firms are hired to help craft and sell the story to anyone willing to listen.

Rinse and repeat every year. The same companies, sometimes with a different name. A revolving door of investors stream in and out as story stocks make short-term highs and long-term lows. The only people getting rich are the service providers.

Nonetheless, story stocks is where I first learned stock picking. When you can survive in the most savage part of the arena, you know you can survive anywhere.

I kept records of this time, and to be honest I had to cringe a bit rereading some of these experiences.

From 2001 to 2005, I invested in 75 different story stocks. My holding period was measured in weeks and months, not years. You never want to overstay your welcome in story stocks. My portfolio hit a low of $8,000 in 2001, and a high of $350,000 in 2005.

During college and graduate school (2002–2005), I made nine site visits. Let me give you one horror story.

I vividly remember visiting a company called Sky Way Communications. I owned it briefly in 2004 and made a 50% return.

The company supposedly bought 40 broadcasting towers from AT&T and were refitting them with Sky Way technology to provide internet service to commercial jetliners.

They leased an abandoned private airport for their headquarters. The command center looked like it was out of the *Apollo 13* movie. In the front of the room was a huge 50-foot screen showing all the aircraft within the network. It looked amazing.

It was a fraud. They declared bankruptcy in 2005. The SEC charged them in 2009 for defrauding investors and orchestrating a pump and dump scheme.

Ironically, a year after bankruptcy the McDonnell Douglas DC-9 aircraft they used for demonstrations would end up getting seized by Mexican customs officials en route to Caracas, Venezuela. The aircraft was painted to look like a government transport vehicle with a crest that resembled the US Department of Homeland Security. When the jet was searched it had 100 suitcases onboard, each filled with 110 pounds of cocaine, worth around $100 million. A fitting end.

Sky Way represented the worst of story stocks. There were plenty of others that were great stories whose leaders were genuine, but their ability to execute was limited by their skills and capital.

Story alone is never good enough. 99% of story stocks with no fundamentals don't have happy endings. The key is combining great stories with great fundamentals. Great stories influence the multiple of a stock and help it get "overvalued."

The best story stocks have CEOs who are great storytellers that can execute on at least 30% of what they say. Some would argue this is what Steve Jobs and Elon Musk represent. They don't have to be right all the time, just enough times for investors to take their vision seriously.

> Every market valuation is a number from today multiplied by a story about tomorrow, and the stories change much faster than the numbers.
>
> **– Morgan Housel**

Here are a few lessons learned from my story stock years that helped shape my strategy today.

Lessons on story stocks

Visit every company in person

Inspect the quality level of the company's technology, service, and assets. You do this to spot inconsistencies that can save you from significant loss.

Stay close to management

The more you talk to management, the more you will be able to spot the signs of the story changing. I didn't have any big losers in companies where I had consistent communication with management.

Invest in simple stories

Do not underestimate a great story. The story that connects with the most people wins. The market pays a premium for simple stories because more investors can understand them. Stay away from onion stocks where you must peel back eight layers to understand them, only to cry in the end. Try to buy stocks that you can explain in a minute or less. No one will buy your shares 5–10x higher if the upside isn't easy to see. The market discounts complexity and pays up for simplicity.

A microcap investor's biggest risk is dilution

Nothing disrupts stock momentum like a dilutive capital raise. Either stay away from companies that need to raise capital or get out before they must raise capital. Most of my winners didn't dilute while I owned them. I exited before they diluted. When a company does an equity raise it can take months, quarters, even years to churn through the new shares. You want to own companies where investors are forced to buy the stock on the market, not in an equity raise.

Story and discovery go hand and hand. Let's look at discovery next.

CHAPTER 10

Discovery

The Lassonde Curve

In 1978, Pierre Lassonde and Seymour Schulich partnered to run a gold resource company called Franco-Nevada. In 1983, they took the company public as a penny stock on the Toronto Stock Exchange.

In 1985, they approached their investors with a new royalty business model. Investors didn't exactly love the idea. They were only able to raise $930,000 in a secondary offering. Schulich and Lassonde sifted through 43 properties until they found one they liked.

In 1986, they paid $2 million, half the cash on the balance sheet, to acquire a 4% royalty in a small heap leach producer.

Unbeknownst to them, this small producer would turn into Barrick's Goldstrike mine and produce three million ounces per year. This $2 million investment in 1986 would eventually pay out over $900 million in cash flow to Franco-Nevada.

By 1997, Franco-Nevada reported revenues of $99.5 million and net income of $61 million from their royalty portfolio. They paid a substantial dividend to shareholders. By that time Schulich and Lassonde had purchased over 50 royalties across the world.

In 2002, Newmont Mining acquired Franco-Nevada and merged with Normandy Mining of Australia to form the largest gold mining company in the world.

You think the story ends here, but it doesn't.

Five years later Lassonde wanted to get his royalty assets back. He led an investment group to buy Newmont's royalty assets. In 2008, Franco-Nevada raised $1.2 billion in the largest mining IPO ever offered on the Toronto Stock Exchange. Lassonde became the Chairman of the company.

In 1983, Franco-Nevada was a $5 million market cap. By 2025 its market cap sat at $36 billion and it had royalty interests in 113 producing properties, and another 300 properties in various stages of development.

It would have been impossible, due to the Newmont buy-out, for anyone to participate in the full 40-year run, but significant value has been created. From 1983 to 2001, shareholders realized a 38% CAGR. Then from 2008 to 2025 a 19% CAGR.

Extraordinary.

In 1990, Pierre Lassonde formulated what is now called the Lassonde Curve. Lassonde realized that share prices of most junior mining companies followed a similar pattern. Figure 10.1 provides an illustration of the curve.

Figure 10.1: Lassonde Curve

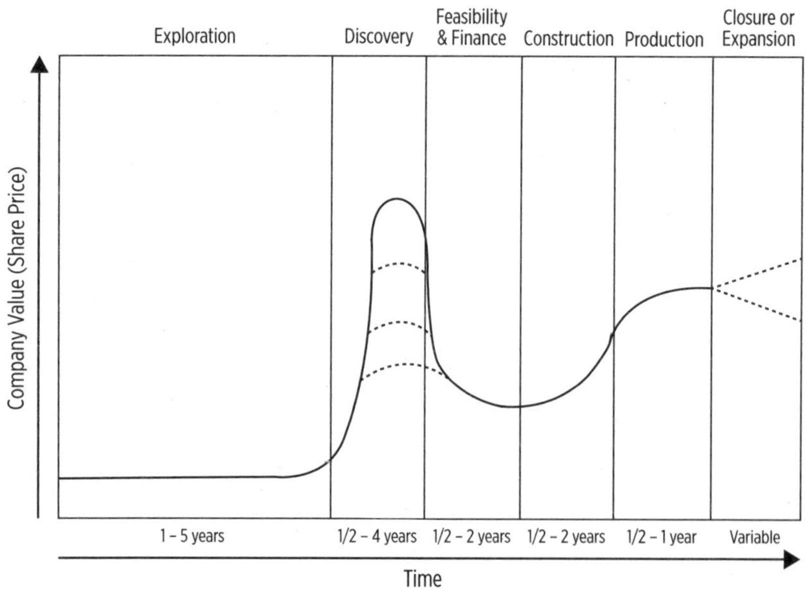

Source: Pierre Lassonde.

In the Lassonde Curve, most of the price appreciation occurs through speculators bidding up the stock price leading up to the discovery of the resource deposit, and then the price languishes as speculators leave.

After discovery, investors realize it's now up to management to figure out how to finance, permit, and construct a mine to get the resource out of the ground. A task that even experienced mining veterans would have a hard time completing.

There is an old saying among mining investors: "You never want to ruin a great discovery by mining it."

The Lassonde Curve is relevant for all story stocks, not just mining stocks. It is really a map of perception versus proof: Early-stage story stocks with no revenue/earnings can levitate on narrative and optionality, then sag when dilution, delays, and "now prove it" reality sets in. The next re-rate only comes when milestones turn the story into measurable fundamentals and economics, but only if the path to it is de-risked without dilution and debt that destroys the upside.

My mining stock adventures

In 2005, I graduated from Villanova with my MBA, though my real focus was microcap investing. I didn't yet have enough capital to live off my portfolio, so I needed income that kept me close to small public companies. Having dealt with investor relations firms before, I understood their role in shaping company stories for investors. Larger companies built in-house teams, but microcaps relied on outsourced help.

Before graduation, I connected with a New Jersey firm serving microcap clients. They offered me an independent contractor role. If I brought in clients, we'd split the revenue. I landed two clients quickly, but soon realized I was doing most of the work, so I launched my own firm.

From 2005–2009, I worked with two or three clients at a time, charging less and doing more than anyone else. CEOs valued my advice because I genuinely cared about their success. While my fees were modest, often less than a secretary's salary, management teams viewed me as an essential partner. That income covered my living expenses, giving me the freedom to focus on building my portfolio and moving toward my goal of becoming a full-time private investor.

During this time, I had started to develop a macro view that the price of gold would move higher. Gold was $500 per ounce, and I thought it could go to $1,000 per ounce. I took my story stock picking skillset to the greatest story stock show on earth – junior mining and exploration companies.

In early 2006, I traveled to Toronto for the Prospectors & Developers Association of Canada (PDAC) convention. There were 15,000 attendees and it was considered the main event for the entire industry. During that year I also traveled to other events in Colorado, Florida, and New Orleans. I was able to network my way into the inner circles of the industry. I sat at the same dinner tables as Peter Schiff, Marc Faber, and many other famous goldbugs and permabears.

My issue was I couldn't find many junior mining companies that had management teams focused on limited share dilution or skin in the game. At least not skin in the game that wasn't handed to them in free shares.

Most junior mining companies were focused on stock promotion so they could raise more money to drill more holes in the ground. The hope was to hit a discovery and attract a large mining company to acquire them.

It took me several months to find two companies that fit what I was looking for.

The first was Gold Resource Corporation (GORO).

I found GORO while attending The Edgewater Research Conference, hosted by David Lavigne in Denver, CO. GORO was presenting for the first time. In 2006, the company completed a self-underwritten IPO at $1.00 per share on the OTC Markets.

GORO was controlled by two brothers that owned 23% of the company. What attracted me was the two brothers had advanced several other mines into production, so they had the experience to execute and hit both waves of the Lassonde Curve. They were the largest shareholders and were deeply focused on their self-interests which were aligned with all shareholders.

GORO owned a property in Mexico, and they felt it had all the elements of being a future low-cost gold producer. They were targeting a $200 cash cost per ounce.

What made the story even more unique was they articulated a capital allocation strategy from the very beginning. One-third of mining cash flow would be paid out to shareholders as a monthly dividend.

The two brothers were mavericks. The plan was to limit dilution and turn this property into a low-cost gold producer within five years and pay a meaningful dividend. It was a preposterous goal. They were attempting to pull off in five years what normally takes 10–15 years. No one in the industry believed them.

I built a relationship with management and bought some stock between $1.00 and $1.50 per share. I also consulted with them on capital markets strategy. Management continued to pound the drum of low-cost production and capital allocation.

Something strange happened. Quarter after quarter and year after year they executed. They pulled it off. They turned a greenfield property into a gold mine in five years. They started paying a monthly dividend, and the annual dividend approached $0.75 per share at its peak.

From 2006 to 2011, GORO went from $1.00 per share to $30.00 per share, and it was the best-performing gold stock in the entire stock market over this period. What GORO accomplished in five years, going from moose pasture to mine, and a $1.00 stock to almost paying $1.00 in annual dividends, was extraordinary.

I sold too early in 2010 around $8–10 per share. Watching GORO race to $30 per share one year after I sold haunted me. It would later turn into a nightmare because I invested the proceeds into a company that would become my biggest loser ever. I'll tell that story in a later chapter.

When I was initially investing in GORO, I was networking my way through the junior mining investment world. Like GORO, I was trying to find another management team that were real operators. Individuals that were business builders not stock promoters.

By late 2006, I ran into Peter Spina, who was around the same age as me, and he had one of the highest trafficked websites in the gold industry, GoldSeek.com. He introduced me to John Swallow.

An investor from an early age, Swallow grew up around the timber and mining industries in Coeur d'Alene, Idaho. Around 2005 he was a "mostly retired" ex-real estate appraiser turned mining entrepreneur. Spina described him as having uncommon business sense in mining. I came to know him as a guy that puts his own money in first.

In the late 90s dot-com days, Swallow saved an old mining shell from becoming a dot-com. By 2003, while holding his day job as a real estate appraiser, Swallow found himself on the board of Sterling Mining. Through a series of events, he almost singlehandedly orchestrated the purchase of the Sunshine Mine out of bankruptcy. The Sunshine Mine was one of the largest historic silver mines in the world, producing over 360 million ounces of silver. At the time he commented that this had the chance to become a home run or an albatross, flip a coin.

In 2003, silver was $4 per ounce. By 2004, silver had moved up 50%+ to $6.50 per ounce. This move excited the crowd and Sterling Mining's stock was seen as a levered bet on the rise in silver.

Rise it did. The stock went from $0.10 to $10.00 per share. The board wanted to push the Sunshine Mine into production themselves. Swallow felt his fellow board members didn't have the experience or skillset, so he left the board and exited around $3.00 per share.

With Sterling, Swallow made his first few million and had built a reputation for doing smart deals and advocating for shareholder rights. He jokingly said it took him 36 years to make his first million and 36 days to make his second.

After Sterling Mining, Swallow watched for a couple years and eventually another opportunity arose in a company called Timberline Resources. His plan was to create a profitable mining services company that used cash flow to explore and find new discoveries. This way he could use operating cash flow instead of dilution to fund exploration. Simple enough.

By 2005, Swallow had purchased 35% of the company through a series of private transactions at $0.10 per share and became Executive Chairman of Timberline Resources. In early 2006, Timberline purchased a drilling company for cash and stock. The drilling company produced $5 million in revenues and was profitable.

What is a drilling company? Exploration and mining companies contract with drilling companies to delineate a deposit for production or exploration purposes. Every junior mining company and major mining company contracts with drilling companies.

In 2006, I flew to Coeur D' Alene, Idaho to meet Swallow. Soon after, I bought a position around $0.65 per share. I also consulted the company on capital markets strategy. As gold, silver, and other commodities increased, so did the demand for drilling services. Over the next two years, Swallow grew the asset base and expanded the drilling fleet from four rigs to 12 rigs. The stock went to $5.50 per share and got listed on the NYSE American.

In 2008, Swallow formed a relationship with the largest underground mining contracting company in the Western United States on a buy-out proposal. The founder and CEO of the mining contracting company was also on Timberline's board. The combined company would have become the one of the largest mining services companies in the United States. Jefferies investment bank was hired to fund the merger and working capital of the combined entity.

The deal fell apart when the global financial crisis caused capital markets to come to a screeching halt. I got lucky and sold most of my position before the crisis took hold. The stock went from $5.50 back to $0.20 per share. Through a series of events, Swallow turned the company around and left the board in 2009.

When Swallow left, Timberline's soul left. As he said, "I had the right assets but too many of the wrong people."

But it was still extraordinary. John Swallow took over a shell of a company with next to nothing and in only two years almost turned it into the largest mining services company in the United States. He didn't quite pull it off, but the third time would be the charm.

In 2011, Swallow and two others bought the drilling subsidiary from Timberline Resources at the low in the commodities cycle. Swallow personally guaranteed the $13 million bank loan. In 2015, when the debt was paid off, he sold his 33% interest back to his two partners for $5 million. Timberline Resources continued to struggle and was taken over by McEwen Mining in 2024.

In late 2013, Swallow became the largest shareholder in another mining penny stock named New Jersey Mining Co. (NJMC) after the founder wanted to retire. I invested alongside him in one of the early financing rounds. He learned from his previous endeavors and put the right team in place and focused on culture as much as the business. Swallow used some of the proceeds from the sale of the drilling company to fund NJMC so it could acquire assets at the low in the commodities cycle and minimize dilution.

New Jersey Mining changed its name to Idaho Strategic Resources (IDR) and the stock is up 2000% since Swallow took control of the company. As of the writing of this book, IDR is my longest-held investment and I consider Swallow a good friend.

From 2006–2010, I was 60% in junior exploration and mining stocks.

During these discovery years I realized four important things that helped shape my strategy today.

Four lessons that shaped my strategy

The smaller the better

The Lassonde Curve is not only applicable to junior resource stocks but all microcap stocks. A tiny $10 million market cap can move up 400% to $50 million market cap simply by more investors discovering it.

It's easier for a $10 million market cap to move to a $100 million market cap than it is for a $100 million market cap to move to a $1 billion market cap. The former is a discovery move. The latter is a fundamental move.

The first wave of discovery can be explosive as retail investors find a new small stock with potential. The smaller you find them, the more of the discovery move you can capture.

With all story stocks, momentum takes them to a place their fundamentals can't keep them. You must have a great story and fundamentals to reach escape velocity and not come back down to earth.

Timberline Resources went from $10 million market cap to $200 million market cap. GORO went from $20 million market cap to $1.5 billion market cap. Each needed fundamentals to get over a $100 million market cap. Both came right back down eventually. Investing is hard.

Don't label yourself as you grow

It takes 10–20 years to learn how to paint with all the colors of stock picking. As you learn and grow, you will study different areas like I did with story stocks and resource stocks. When you are learning a new industry or sector you will become obsessed with the area, and you express that in your portfolio.

When I was learning about precious metals, I was mostly invested in precious metals stocks, but I never labeled myself a resource investor. If I had, perhaps it would have kept me from growing and I would be stuck painting with that one color. Instead, I continued to evolve and grow.

Today I use multiple colors to express myself in my portfolio. Precious metals and resources are just one color out of many on my palette.

Do your own work

It would have been easy to simply fall in line and buy the junior mining stocks that were being promoted. I didn't want to play their game. I wasn't a follower.

The companies I invested in outperformed almost all the pump and dumps from that era. In 2006, PDAC looked like a Taylor Swift concert, and by 2012 it was a ghost town. Most of the promoters and swindlers were broke or driven out of town.

As of the writing of this book, precious metals are booming, and the same characters are back in business.

Invest in owner operators with skin in the game.

Chris Mayer, in his wonderful book, *100-Baggers*, said "People with their own wealth at risk make better decisions as a group than those who are hired guns."

Never invest in a business whose management doesn't have to live with the consequences of their decisions. GORO and IDR represented the first time I held stocks for more than one year. It was nice paying long-term versus short-term capital gains tax. When you invest in owner operators you can trust them more, which means you can hold them longer.

Great stories and getting in early, before they are discovered by others, is extremely important. Next up in my evolution was my framework around scarcity and tailwinds. I wanted to capture lightning in a bottle.

CHAPTER 11

Lightning in a Bottle

In 1746, Pieter van Musschenbroek invented the Leyden jar. It was a glass jar coated inside and out with metal foil that could hold and discharge electricity. Musschenbroek discovered it could produce and store a high-voltage electric charge. It was the first iteration of the modern-day capacitor. News of the Leyden jar spread rapidly among scientists.

Benjamin Franklin learned about it and obtained one of the jars to experiment with in Philadelphia. Franklin theorized that the Leyden jar's inner and outer foils held positive and negative charges that attracted each other.

When connected by a conductor, they discharged in a jolt of electricity. This was a seminal insight into the nature of oppositely charged particles.

In his famous kite experiment of 1752, Franklin flew a kite during a thunderstorm and used the Leyden jar to capture and store the electric charge from lightning, showing its connection to electricity. This proved his theory that lightning was an electrical phenomenon in the atmosphere.

The ability to capture lightning in a bottle led to multiple discoveries and inventions around electricity. The image of capturing lightning, one of Earth's most powerful phenomena, in a jar and holding it in your hands is inspiring.

Great small stocks are lightning in a bottle. They are the most powerful force in the public markets. All this power held within a tiny public company ready to be unleashed.

The lightning is a small, fast growing, profitable business with tailwinds.

The bottle represents the constraints of a scarce business and illiquid stock with no need to raise outside equity capital. In these situations, institutions are forced to buy in the open market, propelling the stock higher.

Lightning in a bottle = scarcity + tailwinds

> Scarcity is the most important law in economics. It's just part of life. There's scarcity in material goods, in resources. Everywhere you look is scarcity. In real savings, in terms of money, other than perhaps credit that is being created. But there's not just scarcity only in visible, tangible resources. There's also scarcity of character in men that you and I would consider to be attractive. Scarcity in all its permutations, is an important ingredient in any action that deploys capital for the future. What makes that painting valuable is not the canvas or the paint but the fact that there's only one.
>
> **– Anthony Deden**

In 1776, Adam Smith wrote *The Wealth of Nations*, and it talked about individuals' need to fulfill self-interest, the invisible hand, division of labor, and rejection of government interference with the market. Adam Smith would also write:

> The word VALUE, it is to be observed, has two different meanings, and sometimes expresses the utility of some particular object, and sometimes the power of purchasing other goods which the possession of that object conveys. The one may be called 'value

> in use,' the other, 'value in exchange.' The things which have the greatest value in use have frequently little or no value in exchange; and on the contrary, those which have the greatest value in exchange have frequently little or no value in use. Nothing is more useful than water: but it will purchase scarce any thing; scarce any thing can be had in exchange for it. A diamond, on the contrary, has scarce any value in use; but a very great quantity of other goods may frequently be had in exchange for it.

Smith referred to this as the "diamonds and water" paradox. Water is essential to life, and yet it is basically free. Diamonds are far less critical, they serve very little purpose, especially in the 18th century, and yet they were quite expensive. One is abundant. The other is scarce.

> The best things in life are free. The second-best things are very, very expensive.
>
> **– Coco Chanel**

Pablo Picasso painted 1,900 original works. Most of these paintings are now held by private collectors or museums that are never selling. Picasso's paintings are always in high demand by the world's elite. They are status symbols.

Only a small fraction of Picasso's original works are available for sale each year. When one or two come up for sale they sell for a premium price. You have thousands of buyers with unlimited resources chasing one or two pieces of artwork. Scarcity.

Just like a Picasso, investors are willing to pay a premium for high-quality businesses that are scarce. Great businesses always trade at a premium because there are so few of them. The businesses are scarce. Their high-quality founders and leaders are scarce.

Scarcity can also be applied to the number of shares a company has outstanding. Illiquidity is the scarcity of shares. It is very powerful when it's combined with a great business.

Why?

As a company gets discovered by institutions there is more demand for the stock than supply, so investors are forced to pay higher prices to own the stock. Microcap CEOs that execute know that an illiquid stock is an advantage, not a disadvantage.

Finding scarce desirable leaders and businesses before others is difficult, but not impossible. It takes an intensely curious and vigilant human being to turn over thousands of rocks to find the one.

> If you want to find the finest tomatoes it is unlikely you will find them at the grocery store. If you want to find the best fish, meat, cheese, it is unlikely you will find it at some supermarket. But if you are truly seeking these things, you will find them.
>
> **– Anthony Deden**

The power of scarcity is amplified even further if a business is a "one of one" in the public markets. A special business that produces a unique product, service, or provides a unique type of exposure that is in high demand.

I love to find these one-of-a-kind Picassos in the public markets when they are small and undiscovered. I'm not interested in investing in undervalued companies that will always be undervalued. My goal is to invest in undervalued companies that will get overvalued. Fairly valued isn't good enough.

This means you must invest before the crowd starts buying or the tailwinds start blowing.

Another way to think about tailwinds is what venture capitalist Josh Wolfe of Luxe Capital calls undeniable directional arrows of progress. Simply put, investing in an area where technology is headed in a direction that is hard to stop.

When you start thinking about tailwinds you start noticing them everywhere. The tailwinds might be geopolitical, consumer related, industry specific, technological, or some combination. Tailwinds produce institutional demand for the stocks that are benefiting from them.

Don't make investing harder than it needs to be. Don't be a contrarian for contrarians' sake. More capital has been torched by stock pickers trying to look smart by being contrarian than has been lost in any bear market.

When you find a tailwind that is hard to stop, and you combine this with a great management team and strategy, then you find an investment that is hard to stop. Invest where there is a tailwind. You will get to your destination quicker with less effort.

Tailwinds can be fads, themes, or trends.

Fads can last for three months to two years. Themes can last for five years. Trends can last for decades.

In most instances you don't know how long the tailwind will last. You only know the duration with hindsight.

Sometimes a tailwind can literally be a hurricane.

In 2005, Hurricane Katrina devastated Florida and Louisiana. New Orleans was under water. $125 billion in damage. The government sent resources, aid, and paid whatever was necessary to get the damage cleaned up as quickly as possible. Disaster remediation companies were the first responders and made a lot of money.

Shortly after Hurricane Katrina, a microcap company called Charys Holdings decided to roll up the United States disaster remediation industry. They bought the third largest firm in the country and had signed letters of intent to purchase the fifth and seventh largest players.

Charys proforma financials inclusive of acquisitions showed $280 million in revenues and $84 million in net income. A bulk of which was responding to Hurricane Katrina. The stock traded around $2 per share at a $60 million market cap.

Charys looked cheap and looked like a great hedge against another active hurricane season. I bought a position. Two months later, institutions poured into the stock once the national weather service forecasted an active hurricane season. The stock ripped from $2 to $11 per share in four months.

What most investors failed to realize, including me, was that the business model required two category three hurricanes to directly hit populated areas to sustain the previous year's revenue and earnings run rate.

Over the following months this reality became known. I held the stock as it dropped back from $11 to $2 per share and I sold out at breakeven. A six-figure gain evaporated.

Of course, hurricane predictors were wrong. The next hurricane season produced no substantial hurricanes. The business was now over levered with acquisition debt and became insolvent. Within two years the company declared bankruptcy. From $2 per share to $11 per share to bankrupt in under 24 months.

This hurricane stock ended in disaster, but it did prove that when you combine scarcity and tailwinds you get overvaluation.

Other examples of the power of scarcity and tailwinds involve a tidal wave of consumer demand hitting a single product category like Tickle-me Elmo dolls, or the Beanie Baby bubble. You see the extreme effects of scarcity when insatiable demand is focused on one product, company, or stock.

In 2010, I started buying a Latino social network called Quepasa (QPSA) when it was trading for $3 per share. A Mexican industrialist owned a large piece of the company and backstopped the social media site with advertising campaigns from his own businesses.

Yes, I know. You are wondering, "Ian why on earth were you buying this?"

Let's go back in time. This was two years prior to the Facebook (now Meta) IPO. Quepasa was the only social network that was publicly traded. It was a one of one public company. Scarcity.

My thesis was simple. The media buzz for Facebook's IPO would lift Quepasa shares. When I started buying QPSA, it was $3.00 per share with an average volume of 10,000 shares per day. Nine months later the stock hit $15.00 per share and traded a million shares per day.

Institutions and retail investors were looking for exposure to the social network trend. For a 12-month period, Quepasa was the only stock they could buy. The stock had only one way to go. Up.

Eventually, more social networking stocks hit the market and scarcity turned into abundance. Quepasa's chart ended up looking like the discovery portion of the Lassonde Curve. I exited on the rise.

What happened to Quepasa? It acquired a few other companies, rebranded itself as MeetMe, and in 2020 was acquired for $500 million by eHarmony owner NuCom.

Today, I'm not interested in hurricanes, Latino social networks, fads, or bubbles, but the power of scarcity and tailwinds can also be applied to unique desirable businesses. The first time I saw the two forces play out in a more sustainable way was my investment in ZAGG.

In 2007, Steve Jobs announced the first iPhone. It was a technological marvel. The screen was huge, but it was glass. It could scratch. It could break. How would you protect it?

ZAGG made plastic screen protectors for cellphones. You could buy them online where you could choose your make, model of cell phone and they would mail you the product right to your home. They were also distributing the product through mall kiosks across the United States.

I traveled to Utah to meet the CEO Robert Pederson in 2008. We hit it off, and I would later consult with them on capital markets strategy. He was a great storyteller and likable. His family's background was starting and managing the Del Sol brand. This was an apparel brand that changed color when you went out in the sun. You can find Del Sol even today in Caribbean resort locations or on cruise ships.

Robert oversaw the inline store roll out for Del Sol. The game plan with ZAGG was to mimic what he successfully rolled out for Del Sol. Online first, mall kiosks second, and retail stores third.

2008 was a crazy time. The global financial crisis was impacting consumer confidence and the stock market.

In July 2008, Hank Paulson was pleading his case to bail out Fannie Mae and Freddie Mac, the two agencies that held or guaranteed half of United States mortgages.

In September 2008, Lehman Brothers declared bankruptcy, and this triggered the global financial crisis.

In mid-2008, ZAGG was $0.65 per share, a $15 million market cap. I started accumulating shares. The iPhone 3G launched in June, and consumers were now aware of their need to protect the glass screen. ZAGG was positioned at the perfect spot at the perfect time.

Over the next several quarters, ZAGG came to be viewed as a peripheral way to invest in the Apple iPhone boom. This was a massive consumer tailwind. There were other ways for institutions to play this trend, such as buying iPhone suppliers like chipmakers, or sensor makers, but no smallcap way to participate.

ZAGG was it. ZAGG became a scarce stock that was in demand that institutions didn't own. ZAGG was more than a story stock. It had the fundamentals to back up the story.

FY 2007 sales were $5 million.

FY 2008 sales would hit $19 million.

ZAGG was a $0.65 per share stock. It earned $0.01 EPS in Q2 2008, growing to $0.05 EPS in Q3 2008. The stock had only moved to $0.85 per share by the fall of 2008. Everyone was too distracted with the global financial crisis.

When ZAGG reported $0.05 EPS in Q3 2008 the institutions finally took notice. The company was growing sales 200%, and earnings 400%, and they were self-funding their growth.

From May 2008 to April 2009, during the worst economic backdrop since the Great Depression, ZAGG went up 280% while the S&P went down 41%. ZAGG went up 1000% from my original purchase price in 12-months.

ZAGG only had 20 million shares outstanding. They didn't raise any equity capital during the rise. Institutions were forced to pay up in the open market.

By 2011, ZAGG hit $200 million in annual revenues. $5 million to $200 million in sales in five years. The stock became institutionalized.

ZAGG was lightning in a bottle.

Most people say you learn more from your losers than your winners. Not for me. My ZAGG experience was the most formative experience in my investing career because of what it represented and when it occurred.

Here are some key lessons.

Lessons on scarcity, tailwinds, and lightning in a bottle

Find scarcity

Great companies always trade at a premium because there is a scarcity of them. Great companies are scarce. Great leaders are scarce. Great stocks have a scarcity of shares which drives a premium valuation. Find one of ones.

Find the tailwinds

Understand how consumers' and investors' behavior will change before they even know it themselves. Don't follow the institutions. Invest where they are going to go.

Lightning in a bottle can happen in any market environment

Bull market, bear market, sideways market, it doesn't matter. Like a moth to a flame, institutional capital is always attracted to undiscovered, fast growing, unique, profitable companies that can self-fund their growth. Let's not forget how small public companies are discovered.

Small public companies are first discovered by smart retail, then by small institutions, then by large institutions, and then finally by dumb retail.

Institutions can't sell what they don't own

During bear markets, institutions reduce microcap and smallcap exposure. This institutional outflow in a "risk off" environment puts constant selling pressure on institutionalized microcap stocks. ZAGG wasn't owned by any institutions. Great businesses with no institutional ownership do better in bear markets because institutions don't own them. They can only buy them.

My win in ZAGG gave me the self-confidence to make the leap to being a full-time private investor. I quit consulting. I had been obsessing over this moment for seven years.

"$10k and two 10-baggers = Millionaire."

Finally, it was time.

CHAPTER 12

Becoming a Full-Time Private Investor

From mid-2009 to 2019 I was a full-time private investor picking stocks and supporting my family from the gains in my portfolio.

Full-Time Private Investing: Full-time private investors are individual investors that actively manage their own portfolio to support themselves and their families. They normally do so with a lower amount than a retiree which means they must produce above benchmark returns when compared to a retiree. The goal is to beat the benchmark after taxes and living expenses.

The financial media loves to glorify asset gatherers and managers – those who have built extreme wealth collecting fees by managing outside capital. There is nothing wrong with this. In fact, today I manage a small fund.

But I would argue that becoming a full-time private investor is the pinnacle of financial achievement. My most significant financial accomplishment was turning a small amount of money into a larger amount of money and then supporting myself and my family on that capital for a decade.

Why is it the pinnacle? Complete financial independence.

Full-time private investors aren't dependent on anyone. You don't need a boss. You don't need clients. You don't need limited partners. You don't need subscribers. You don't need customers. You don't need their money. You have your own.

99.9% of fund managers could never support themselves utilizing their own investing strategy with their own capital. They can only do so after 10 years of taking two and 20 from their investors. This is why full-time private investing is the pinnacle of financial success.

Most private investors have been brainwashed into believing that institutions are smarter than them.

Here is a fact that few in the financial world want you to know.

Full-time, even part-time, private investors have an edge over fund managers, advisors, analysts, or anyone else forced to prove how smart they are to others.

The private investor is not distracted by having an investment committee, investors, and raising capital.

The private investor is not distracted by having to answer questions or voice opinions about a thousand things that don't matter.

The private investor is not distracted by YTD returns and other time frames that don't matter.

All private investors must do is focus on making a few good investment decisions per year and living a great life.

A few years into becoming a full-time private investor I had an aching question: Was there a full-time private investor out there that grew a personal portfolio of microcaps from nothing to $50 million?

My portfolio was a few million dollars, but I wanted to find a person who already did what I was attempting to do, not what I had already done. I was still close to my first mentor Skip, but we were diverging in philosophies.

Of equal importance was finding a person that was a great husband, father, human being, that didn't also have all their emotions and empathy ripped out of them after the volatile decades of abuse the market put on them. I knew this type of person had to exist, but they likely couldn't be found because they wouldn't want to be found.

In 2011, I launched MicroCapClub.com, a private community for experienced stock pickers focused on microcap stocks. I started publishing articles on the blog about my journey and stock picking.

Finally, in 2014, the person I was looking for found me.

Doug reached out through the "contact us" section of the website after reading a few of my articles. He sent me a very nice message. I still have it. He loved my writing because it was raw, genuine, and closely represented his own thoughts on stock picking in small stocks. We wrote to each other a few times before speaking on the phone.

From the early 1990s to 2014, he grew his portfolio from $100,000 to $60 million, exclusively in microcap stocks.

Surprisingly, he still had a day job. He worked this job not because he had to but because he enjoyed it. His non-financial job offered him autonomy, and this gave him time to focus on stock picking and travel to meet companies.

Doug viewed his day job as a productive distraction. I knew exactly what he meant. MicroCapClub became my productive distraction.

Oftentimes a concentrated investor's biggest risk isn't being wrong, but overthinking your positions. A full-time private investor that runs a concentrated portfolio has all day and night to think about a handful of positions.

It's easy to fall into analysis fatigue. You micromanage and overanalyze every new piece of information. You forget that there are a few big things that drive the business and your thesis, and thousands of inconsequential things that don't matter.

A productive distraction is an asset to a full-time private investor as it keeps you close to your craft while distracting you just enough to stop you from overthinking your core positions.

Doug's job also allowed him to fit into society. It shielded him from questions from family and friends as to what he did for a living. He was worth $60 million but few would know it by how he lived his life. He still had the same job. He still lived in the same house. He still had the same friends. He still went to the same church. He still had the same wife. He drove a car his friends could afford.

Mark Brooks, Director of Wealth Management at Convergence Financial said, "There are two types of wealthy people: Those who desperately want you to know they are wealthy and those who desperately don't."

One of Doug's biggest worries was friends and colleagues finding out how much he had accumulated and viewing him differently.

He recently took his wife on a six-month trip around the world. Beyond the millions he's given anonymously to charity, it's probably the only thing he's ever done that would make outsiders think he had wealth beyond the norm.

You don't hear much about successful full-time private investors because publicity doesn't benefit them. In fact, publicity hurts them. Full-time private investors like the fact that even family and friends don't quite know what they do for a living. They like the fact that they've built up an extensive knowledge level in a niche of the market where it doesn't benefit them to arm-wave their successes.

The advantage of the private investor is you can go places bigger money can't and build up extensive knowledge in an area where few others bother. You can live a comfortable life fishing the same small pond because you know where the fish are.

The ability to fit into society, live below your means, give generously, and do so under the radar is a big advantage.

To be successful as a full-time private investor your strategy, spending, emotions, and lifestyle must all be in harmony. The first step to becoming financially independent is realizing money is about freedom, not consumption.

Most make the mistake of thinking they need enough money to be able to do nothing. This is incorrect. You just need enough to say NO to things.

As you grow your capital, you will reach a pivot point when you feel you finally have a choice to do what you want in life. Some of you will choose to keep your day jobs because you love them. But some of you will choose to finally break free from a job and routine that have been holding you back.

For a select few, the freedom you gain when you become a full-time private investor is worth 100x the income and security you lose when you leave your job.

The motivation is never having to work for people you dislike ever again. The next motivation is never working for an organization you don't believe in ever again. The last motivation is you can finally live your life on your terms.

You are now wondering, "Should I quit my job?"

Not if you enjoy it. Doug grew his portfolio to $60 million all while holding down a normal job he thoroughly enjoyed. Especially early on, the job alleviated the pressure of paying bills, vacations, mortgages, cars, saving for children's college education, and a bunch of other things.

The pressure and stress of having to pay for these things out of your portfolio are real. None of this is necessary if you can simply find a job that gives you purpose and autonomy.

When you become a full-time private investor, you are exchanging security for insecurity. For most this doesn't make sense. For a few it makes total sense.

For those of you I haven't scared away, let me answer the question I get asked more than any other:

How much capital do I need to become a full-time private investor?

CHAPTER 13

How Much Capital Do You Need to Become a Full-Time Private Investor?

A personal question deserves a personal answer. The answer depends on your environment, stage of life, expectations, and breaking point. In addition, it depends on the characteristics of your investment strategy.

I'll give you a look into how these areas helped shape my decision.

Your environment matters

I was born and raised in Lancaster, PA. It was home. From 2003–2008 I moved away for graduate school and then launched my consulting business. In 2008, I moved back to Lancaster when I knew I was nearing the time to become a full-time private investor.

Why?

The cost of living is low in Lancaster. The rural lifestyle was also free from distractions of urban life. Lancaster has three international airports within a 75-minute drive, and New York City was only a three-hour train ride. I was close enough to what I needed when I needed it, and I was far enough away from what I didn't need.

I also found that having family and friends close by made the pursuit easier. Most of my childhood friends were married and had children by the time I returned, but it was nice to have that safety net of relationships to keep me balanced.

When I became a full-time private investor, I rented a red barn that had been renovated into an apartment. My neighbors were Amish and my view from the office was a cow pasture. This was home.

Your lifestyle matters

My total fixed costs were $2,000 per month. I laugh now because my health insurance back then was only $104 per month.

I lived a frugal life. When you become a full-time private investor there is no such thing as savings. Just different degrees of spending.

When building your capital base or living off your capital base, keep your fixed costs low and variable costs variable. Learn to live off a dime so you can turn on one. I could flex my spending up or down depending on the market environment.

My worst nightmare was having to get a job.

I was disciplined with my personal finances. I held zero debt and still don't to this day. I believed in no margin debt, credit card debt, or mortgage debt. Whether it's stocks or stuff, when you go into debt to buy something, you don't own the stuff, the bank owns you.

I was conservative with my personal finances so I could be aggressive with my portfolio. I didn't know exactly when the next big win would happen. I was conservative with my lifestyle so I would have the duration to get to the next big win on the other side.

Your stage of life matters

I was single when I became a full-time private investor. This made the decision much simpler than had I been married.

When you are single and you blow up your personal account you only hurt yourself. When you have a family, you hurt your family. The pressure and fear of failure can cripple a strategy that must be nimble and carefree.

Two years after I became a full-time private investor, I did get married. I tried to set up superficial safeguards.

My wife and I had separate bank accounts for the first five years of our marriage. This allowed me to separate fixed costs from variable costs. I covered all our fixed costs.

My wife then used her salary towards all variable expenses. We could flex up or down our variable spending depending on the environment.

The only big expense I had to incur the first few years was buying our home. I would still rent today if I wasn't married. We own our home free of mortgage debt and I still view it as a liability and not an asset. But not every decision is financially motivated. I understand the attachment and connection of owning the home where you raise your children.

Banks don't like lending to full-time private investors. We don't check the normal box on the mortgage application. They couldn't get comfortable with my income swinging from hundreds of thousands of losses to million-dollar gains.

It didn't matter that I could show them a portfolio worth 10x the value of the house. The only way we were able to get a mortgage was for my wife to be the primary applicant. She had a consistent income stream. Of course, she thought this was funny, but I felt embarrassed. I paid the mortgage off within 24 months and will never go through the aggravation again.

During the 10-years I was a full-time private investor I went from being single to married. We bought a house. We had two children. Then we bought a bigger house. My wife went from working a full-time job with benefits to a part-time job with no benefits.

As time and life happened the expenses and pressure mounted.

When your portfolio is doing well, you don't notice the expenses and obligations.

When your portfolio is at lows, selling stocks to pay bills can become excruciating. The emotional and psychological impact is 100x heavier than the financial impact.

I've always been dispassionate toward physical things. One year I bought a new Porsche. The next year I sold it so I wouldn't have to sell stocks at lows. My ego has never been attached to my possessions. I would have sold our house if my wife would have let me.

Your ability to throw away the ego and pull down your expenses is what keeps you in the game.

Your future expectations matter

A few years ago, I saw a young individual investor announce they were becoming a full-time private investor. They produced a 40% CAGR over the previous three years and believed this was a reasonable expected return over the next several years. This individual had a $300,000 portfolio.

You can always tell the markets are reaching a peak when there are a flurry of people becoming full-time private investors or traders. They make the decision at the top. The smart ones do it at the bottom.

Humphrey B. Neill said it best: "Don't confuse brains for a bull market."

If you are thinking about becoming a full-time private investor you should think about target returns, but you should think more about survival and breaking points.

Survival matters

Most people make the leap to being a full-time investor at the end of a bull market when their confidence is at its highest point. Then a bear market hits, and it crushes their self-confidence.

By the end of 2007 I was already thinking about making the leap, but I was hesitant because I knew we were in a bull market. It was too easy. In hindsight I was extremely lucky that the Global Financial Crisis came so quickly. I don't know if I would have waited for one if it didn't show up at my doorstep the next year.

The bear market of 2008 was ruthless. I was in three stocks. GORO was $6.00 in May 2008 and hit a low of $2.25 by November 2008, then bounced back to $11.00 by the end of 2009. Timberline Resource had a gut-wrenching drawdown, but I got out before it really got nasty. ZAGG went up 280% while the S&P 500 got crushed.

In mid-2009 when I felt I had made it through the worst of the bear market, I became a full-time private investor.

I survived and earned the right to the badge.

> No one's success is proven until they've survived a calamity. Serendipity often masquerades as skill, and the only way to distinguish the two is to see who's still standing after a storm.
>
> **– Morgan Housel**

Your breaking point matters

The Global Financial Crisis lasted 18 months. Home prices on average fell 30%, from their mid-2006 peak to mid-2009, while the S&P 500 index fell 57% from its October 2007 peak to its trough in March 2009.

The Global Financial Crisis was a once in a lifetime event in the markets, so I created some safeguards around this type of event happening again.

First, I wanted to have 18 months of cash set aside for living expenses, so I wouldn't have to sell down the portfolio at the wrong time. I placed $100,000 in a savings account.

Second, how much money did I need to become a full-time private investor? I reframed it. How much pain was I willing to endure?

I needed an amount of capital that could sustain a 50% drawdown and not break me. Not only from a financial standpoint, but feeling the pressures to change my strategy and reach for returns at the wrong time. This amount for me was $2 million.

Third, in bull markets you don't think about cash as a position because everything you invest in goes up. Cash feels like an anchor. In bear markets everything flips, and cash becomes your best position.

Bear markets are 10x worse when you don't have cash to take advantage of them. I don't believe in holding 30% cash. When you hold too much cash, you are making a macro bet.

> Far more money has been lost by investors preparing for corrections, or trying to anticipate corrections, than has been lost in corrections themselves.
>
> **– Peter Lynch**

But you shouldn't hold 0% cash either. For me I found holding 3–5% cash as a position kept me mentally sharp. Even today, this amount of cash gives me the ability to average down in current positions or add new positions. Then I'm forced to sell down my least convicted position if I want to buy more. It keeps me and the portfolio honest.

Your strategy matters

Higher-turnover strategies lend themselves better to full-time private investing because smaller, more frequent gains can mimic getting a paycheck. The leap to full-time investor feels more natural. When your gains come every other year in large chunks it feels less natural.

When I was in college I traveled to Florida and spent a day at a proprietary trading firm. The way proprietary trading works is you bring $10,000+ of your own capital, and the firm gives you 3–5x more by leveraging the firm's capital. The firm teaches you how to trade and you split the gains with the firm.

The goal of every new trader was to consistently make $100 per day ($25,000 per year), and work your way up. The goal was to produce an income for yourself and profits for the firm.

Each trader I met had a different focus. One trader was news driven. He sat at a Bloomberg terminal watching headlines. His keyboard had preprogrammed function keys to react quickly. He could place a trade in less than a second.

The most profitable traders I met focused on trading the same one or two stocks, every day, every week, every month. They knew the stocks so well they almost had a pulse on them. They made money off tiny 10 bps (0.1%) moves in the stock. A couple traders I met made $2,000 to $3,000 per day.

The one thing all the traders I met had in common is they spent everything they made and that's what the firm wanted. The firm wanted the traders coming back for more to feed their greed and habits. I ultimately passed on being a proprietary trader.

My strategy was the opposite of day trading. My strategy was consistently inconsistent.

I wasn't interested in making $500 per day. I was focused on making $1 million every few years, and oftentimes it would happen all in one year after a couple down years.

I was confident in my positions and where they would be in three years, but I had no idea where they would trade next month or next quarter.

I wanted to pick great stocks, which means I needed to give them a duration that allowed them to go up. I would love for stocks to always go up like they do in bull markets – a nice stairway to heaven. But that isn't reality. Reality looks like a stock that goes nowhere for two years and then goes up 300% in six months.

Great stocks don't just go up. They also have sharp declines. They have long periods of stagnation as fundamentals backfill, old shareholders get bored, and new shareholders enter. To be a great stock picker you need a smart head, strong stomach, and thick skin.

You will also face times when you make a lot of money too quickly. When you get the timing perfect, and a stock goes up 500% in 12 months. Since you did the work into the business, you know in your gut the stock has gone up too far too fast.

When a stock reaches a valuation where it pulls forward the next five years' worth of returns in a year you must take some off the table.

Why?

The stock is priced for perfection. 99% of the time that company will stub its toe in an upcoming earnings release and fall 50–70% from its highs.

Then the stock will spend the next one to two years churning while fundamentals backfill into the stock price. Maybe then a bear market hits, and it takes one to two additional years to churn as the multiple come down.

When the stock went up too far too fast, you knew in your gut the stock was priced for perfection, but you didn't sell. You hesitated. Now you're stuck selling it 70% lower to pay bills in a bear market.

Lesson learned. Don't do it again.

Some will say it's wrong to sell if you believe in the long term. My experience is it is dumb not to sell if the market is willing to pay you a ridiculous price, especially if you must live off your gains.

The main goal for full-time private investors is survival.

It's like the day traders that trade the same stock every day. They have a pulse on the stock. I felt I had a pretty good pulse on my positions. When you know what you own better than most you know when to buy, when to sell, and when to hold.

This is your edge, but only if you take advantage of it. Play to your strategy, not what other people are doing or saying. If you aren't a buy-and-hold-forever investor, stop trying to be so.

When you are a concentrated long-only investor it's often feast or famine. In the good years, buy a car, buy a house, buy the things you know you will need for the next five years. After that buy some real estate. Buy assets to protect yourself from yourself.

I'm not without faults and vices. There is something about making a lot of money quickly that makes you want to make regrettable purchases. They aren't regrettable because of the purchase price, but because the purchase doesn't represent who you are and how you want to be perceived.

In late 2009, a few months into being a full-time investor, I booked some gains in ZAGG and GORO. I don't know if it was greed. I don't know if it was the stress release of surviving the crisis. I don't know if it was just vindication, and just wanting to give the middle finger to everyone that ever doubted me or my abilities.

I visited the closest Porsche dealership and ordered a new Porsche 911 4S. Black on Black. I think I was the one person buying a new car in 2009. I remember the salesman just looked at me, "How do you intend to pay for this?" I replied, "Cash. Do you want a check for it all now or when I pick it up in three months?"

He smiled ear to ear. Then I drove to the city of Lancaster, to the only Rolex dealer in the county. I ordered a solid white gold Rolex Day-Date watch. The jeweler looked at me, "Young man, how do you intend…" Same question. Same answer.

I remember driving back to my apartment in the old red barn and already feeling guilty for the $175,000 I just spent in a day. I decided right then – If I'm going to spend six figures on stupid stuff, I better give six figures to the Church.

I dropped off a $100,000 check at the church the next day. Atonement.

Sometimes God gives you more to see if you can handle more. God wants to know if he blesses you, will you still thank him or will you forget him? Will you continue to pray to him like you did when you had nothing?

I didn't. I wasn't mature enough to handle the success.

The day I picked up my new Porsche marked a multi-year top in my portfolio. Ironically, I met my wife around this same time.

For years I would tell her, "You met me at my peak." I like to blame her for the destruction in the portfolio that followed, but I was to blame.

Three years into becoming a full-time private investor I was already asking myself, "Can I still do this?"

CHAPTER 14

Can I Still Do This?

Archie Karas was born on the island of Cephalonia, Greece. His father was a poor construction worker. Archie remembers shooting marbles when he was a kid and betting on each game. He made decent money doing it. He worked construction as a teenager. He then worked on a ship for two years as a waiter. Finally, opportunity knocked. The ship set sail for the United States.

At the age of 17 he ended up in Los Angeles. He didn't speak English, so he got a job in the kitchen of a restaurant. In the restaurant was a bowling alley and pool hall. He started playing pool on breaks and soon became an expert pool player. Archie started making more money playing pool than working. He would play $1,000 games, then $5,000 games, then $40,000 games. He amassed $1.2 million from playing pool.

Soon no one wanted to play him anymore, so he started playing poker. He fell in love with poker and poker fell in love with him. He would amass around $2 million in winnings. His nickname was "The Greek." He grew a reputation for having no limit. He played for big stakes and had no fear.

Finally, his luck turned and lost everything. He was down to his last $50 and decided to go to Las Vegas to start over. Archie found someone to lend him $10,000 at 50% interest. At the first table, he tripled the capital in three hours. He paid the person back and kept playing.

This was the start of a legendary three-year winning streak that would later be called "The Run." He turned $50 into $40,000,000.

"The Run" received a lot of public attention, and scrutiny from casinos. They put the screws to him. The casinos started accusing him of framing, and he was arrested five times for casino scams. He spent 73 days in jail. His name was put in the infamous "Black Book" – essentially banned for life from Las Vegas.

Today he's broke and still lives in Vegas. Archie maintains his innocence.

I've found that my style of stock picking can mimic Archie. I can make a lot of money really fast, but I can also give it back really fast if I'm not careful.

Over the years, I've realized a portfolio has a certain rhythm to it and the longer you invest the more you can tell whether the portfolio is in tune or out of tune. The "in tune" moments feel amazing.

When things are in tune, the whole portfolio is in sync, not necessarily from a performance perspective, but every instrument or stock is doing what it's supposed to be doing in perfect harmony. If you added a position or took one away it would hurt the portfolio and the rhythm.

Then in a moment everything feels out of tune. The out of tune moments make you feel like you've lost control. Losing streaks compel you to do the wrong thing at the wrong time.

It might be a surprise negative announcement from your largest position, or just market forces pulling the portfolio lower for no reason. Or maybe it's from being wrong on your last few investments. You start to lose confidence. You become unsettled. Then you start reaching for returns in areas you shouldn't, or you get more concentrated into your losers.

Every successful investor has gone through situations that have rattled them to their core – that made them question their strategy, their abilities, everything. It can happen in an instant, or after a series of mistakes. It forces you to answer a question you never wanted to face.

Can I still do this? Are my best returns behind me?

Don't worry, you aren't alone. It happens to me. It happens to you. It happens to everyone.

The story of Mark Sellers

In 2007, fund manager Mark Sellers gave a speech to a group of Harvard MBA students titled: "So You Want To Be The Next Warren Buffett? How is Your Writing?"

In his speech, he led with, "I'm not here to teach you how to be a great investor. On the contrary, I'm here to tell you why very few of you can ever hope to achieve this status."

Sellers then gave a list of seven traits which he believed were imperative to becoming a great investor. But before he gave the list, he had another gut shot for the aspiring investor:

> The way I see it, there are at least seven traits great investors share that are true sources of advantage because they can't be learned once a person reaches adulthood. In fact, some of them can't be learned at all; you're either born with them or you aren't.

Here is an abbreviated list of the seven traits:

1. Ability to buy stocks while others are panicking and sell stocks while others are euphoric.
2. Obsessed about playing the game and wanting to win.
3. The willingness to learn from past mistakes.
4. An inherent sense of risk, based on common sense.
5. Confidence in convictions and ability to stick with them, even when facing criticism.
6. Keeping both sides of the brain working; details and big picture.
7. The ability to live through volatility without changing the investment thought process.

16 months after giving this speech, Sellers closed his fund.

"I truly love the art of investing, but managing people's money has taken a large toll on my demeanor and psyche," Sellers said in a letter obtained by *The New York Post*. "I feel downright miserable."

"I have found myself neglecting my personal life in order to put 100%

of my energy into managing the fund. I can't continue to do that; it isn't healthy."

Sellers and his wife moved to Grand Rapids, Michigan, opened several bars and restaurants, and lived a much happier life.

"The restaurant-bar business is a lot more fun. It's not the day-to-day volatility and stress of managing other peoples' money. This seems like a walk in the park to me after doing that."

We all have our breaking points.

My losing streak

From 2010 to 2013, I hit a multi-year losing streak and I was seriously questioning myself and my abilities.

By 2013 I had been a full-time private investor for almost four years, and before that it might as well have been full-time. Sitting at a computer staring at stocks was all I've done since I was a teenager.

I had carved out a nice little niche in microcap stocks. But I hit a losing streak, and it was starting to affect me in my personal life and marriage.

I was becoming the person I didn't want to be. A miserable person.

A big part of successful investing is not letting the direction of your portfolio dictate your mood, attitude, effort, and how you treat people. You can't let your portfolio guide your life or you will live a very shallow life.

The slide in my portfolio started in 2010. I bet big on a stock, and I was wrong. Gut-wrenchingly wrong – it ended up being a fraud. The company produced gaming cards for lotteries. The stock had phenomenal margins, a great balance sheet, it was growing 30% organically, and trading at a seven price to earnings (PE) ratio. The company was headquartered in Europe but traded in the US. I met management and the new CEO.

I bet big, putting 50% of my capital in the company. I was up 100% from my cost basis in a few months. Then one day I woke to an 8K filing that said the auditor had resigned. They couldn't verify the cash the company reported on the balance sheet. I just froze. The stock froze too. It was halted.

When the stock reopened it was down 80% and I sold my entire position. A $1.3 million gain on the position turned into a $800,000 loss in two days.

A $2 million swing in a day.

Many other investors were holding on hoping, and I knew that was a mistake. I had witnessed similar announcements before and when you can't trust the financials, you get out as fast as you can.

The stock ultimately went to zero. What made matters worse was I sold shares of ZAGG at $5 per share and half my GORO at $8.00 per share to buy this loser. ZAGG went to $16 and GORO to $30 within 12 months.

It was like a double gut punch to my ego and my portfolio. Few things are as agonizing as watching stocks you used to own outperform the things you own.

The loss happened at a bad time. I was newly married. We had plans to buy a house. Anxiousness and doubt started to creep into my head. It was the first time I realized my actions weren't just impacting me anymore. I had a wife. We wanted to have a family. I immediately sold the Porsche. My portfolio would tread water for two more years.

As a full-time private investor, when you take a big loss and then don't have a big win for two years it takes its toll on you mentally. The bills don't stop.

I started to ask myself; can I still do this?

When a full-time private investor hits a losing streak, it can go from bad to I must get a job real fast. The tendency is to get more concentrated. Since you aren't in a good mental position, you normally make matters worse by becoming more concentrated into losing positions.

By 2013 it had been a few years since I had a big winner, and the longer it went, the shorter my time frames became. When you need a win, it's hard to win.

The more concentrated your portfolio becomes the more likely you will go through long stretches where it feels like nothing is working.

A stock gets discovered and goes up 200% in a year, and then it falls 50%, and you must wait for the fundamentals to backfill.

If this happens to your largest position it means your whole portfolio is held back while you wait. This backfilling can take quarters, years, or maybe it never happens because the business stops performing. You must avoid the latter at all costs.

The key is to always stay anchored to the business and only own businesses that are executing.

The barbell risks

There are two big temperament risks to avoid. They are barbell risks.

On one side of the barbell is the risk of overthinking your positions. You overanalyze every little thing because you have the time to overanalyze every little thing instead of focusing on the few things that matter.

Every macro to micro news event that is indirectly associated with the business you take under consideration. You start nagging management with every little question. The position occupies far too much of your mindshare. You're holding on too tight.

Whether it's relationships or stock positions, when you hold anything too tight you are going to lose it. If the business is performing, you must give the business and stock room to breathe.

The key to holding multi-baggers is giving them a little room to disappoint you and a lot of room to exceed your expectations.

On the other side of the barbell is complacency. You take your eye off the ball. You become less vigilant with your maintenance due diligence. You get lazy. You rationalize your laziness by saying it's patience. It is important for any long-only stock picker to be vigilant and rational.

For me, I try to ask myself every month, based on the current evidence, if I didn't own this position, would I buy it today?

Don't bullshit yourself. It's important to be honest. If the answer is "No," sell and move on. Create positive momentum and energy.

Adapting for new growth

In 2013, I snapped out of my mental rut. I wrote down a list of things that I needed to do to keep me in the game.

I sold the biggest loser in my portfolio. Your biggest loser is always the position you think about most. It has the most mindshare. I had to free up my mind and some capital to focus on new things.

For over a decade I had always been a very concentrated investor – holding three to four positions. This is a great way to start investing, but it's an easy way to end your career in investing. Sellers himself was primarily in three companies when he shut down his fund.

Investing is the ultimate mind game. You need to have a win, even a small win, in the portfolio every so often to keep you positive and sharp. If you are in a rut as a concentrated investor, increase your chances of winning and add a couple positions. I added three more positions.

It's similar to what Stanley Druckenmiller said:

> One of my most important jobs as a money manager was to understand whether I was hot or cold. Life goes in streaks and like a hitter in baseball, sometimes a money manager is seeing the ball and sometimes they're not. If you're managing money you must know whether you're cold or hot, and in my opinion when you're cold you should be trying for bunts. You shouldn't be swinging for the fences. You got to get back in a rhythm. So that's pretty much how I operated it.

The third area that I changed was I stopped thinking like a scientist and started thinking like an artist. In the first few years of my investing journey, I was mainly a story stock investor. I paid very little attention to fundamentals. I then pivoted to mining for a few years and then to GARP (growth at a reasonable price) situations.

By 2013, my portfolio became bland and one dimensional. All different shades of the same color. I realized I needed to keep evolving and painting with multiple colors. There was no evidence in my portfolio of my earlier years, where quite frankly I did very well. So, I repainted my portfolio and used all the colors I had at my disposal.

Great investors evolve or go extinct. I didn't want to spend the next 10 years bragging about the returns I had 15 years ago. It takes 10–20 years to learn all the colors you can paint with as a stock picker. Once you learn them. Go paint your own painting.

One of the new purchases I made was a company called BioSyent that traded on the Canadian Venture Exchange. It was my first foray into Canadian microcaps. At the time there was valuation arbitrage between United States and Canadian non-resource companies.

Canadian investors were so focused on resource stocks that non-resource stocks in Canada had no following. You could find fast growing, profitable companies trading at single digit PEs.

MicroCapClub member, Mike Schellinger, had profiled BioSyent in 2012 at $0.55. There were a couple other Canadian investors that were MicroCapClub members that bought BioSyent around $0.10 – $0.20 per share in 2011. It's funny to think this company was at a $1.5 million market cap.

By early 2013, the stock was trading $1.00 per share, a $13 million market cap. The company was growing organically at 50% and growing the bottom line 100% and was trading at a nine PE. I had already started accumulating when I visited the CEO, Rene Goehrum, in Toronto in mid-2013 along with Paul Andreola of SmallCap Discoveries.

We were impressed. I averaged up to $1.50 per share.

By mid-2014 BioSyent hit $12 per share. The PE multiple expanded from nine to 70. The stock went way too far too fast and was trading for perfection. I sold 90% of the position at $8-9 per share.

It was the win I needed. I made $1.3 million. I got my confidence back.

If you've been a stock picker for 10+ years, a small part of you always wonders if your last big win was your last. You can't ever believe that. Your next big win is right around the corner. Self-confidence is a requirement to be a stock picker.

Only after you've been a full-time investor for 10 years do you realize the ultimate accomplishment is survival.

CHAPTER 15

Survival

What is the #1 characteristic of an exceptional business?

Revenue growth?

Earnings growth?

Return on invested capital?

Return on capital employed?

I would argue the most important characteristic is survival. A business that can endure and survive over a long period of time.

Ian Davis, former managing director of McKinsey & Company, said, "In a very real sense, survival is the ultimate performance measure of a business."

It is true. Story, discovery, finding lightning in a bottle, they mean nothing without survival. Survival is the ultimate quality score.

It is a Japanese custom that the oldest son inherits all the patriarch's wealth, including titles to all businesses. If a business owner doesn't have a son, it was also Japanese custom up until the 20th century to adopt into the family a person they trust, often a son-in-law, to pass on the business.

This is why most of the oldest companies in the world are Japanese companies. It is not unusual to see Japanese businesses that are "still in the family" operate for 100, 200, 500, even 1,000 years. Even the video game company Nintendo is 136 years old.

Kongo Gumi is a Japanese company and it is the oldest company still in operation in the world. The company was founded in 578 AD. The company builds and renovates Buddhist temples. It was still family run until 2006. A family business for 1,400 years.

Kongo Gumi makes it look easy, but surviving is incredibly difficult.

Fortune magazine has compiled its Fortune 500 list every year since 1955. The Fortune 500 list ranks the 500 largest corporations by total revenue in the United States. The list includes public and private companies.

When you look at the Fortune 500 companies from 1955, only 49 companies remain on the list.

In addition, the average lifespan of a Fortune 500 company in 1955 was 60 years. Today the average age of a Fortune 500 company is less than 18 years.

The lifespans of companies are shrinking.

In 1955, the Fortune 500 list was filled with companies like American Motors, Brown Shoe, Studebaker, Collins Radio, Detroit Steel, and others. These companies were the largest companies in the world. They are now gone. Wiped out.

Why is it so hard for a business to survive?

We can look to Winston Churchill to tell us the answer.

The changes during Churchill's lifetime

Winston Churchill is known for being the Prime Minister of the United Kingdom and leading the country through the Second World War. Churchill was a politician, statesman, army officer, and rather prolific writer.

In fact, Churchill wrote 42 books and earned the 1953 Nobel Prize for Literature. John Rockefeller, the world's richest person ever, offered Churchill $250,000 to write his biography, equivalent to $5 million today, but Churchill declined.

Winston Churchill lived to be 90 years old.

90 years is a long time, but what is fascinating about Winston Churchill is the period in which he lived.

He was born in 1874.

In 1874, the year he was born, there was no electricity. No radio. No television. No telephones. There were no lightbulbs. Homes were still being lit by candle and gas. 1874 was only nine years after the American Civil War ended. There were only 37 "states" in the United States.

Winston Churchill died in 1965. Just think how different the world was in 1965.

By 1965, men had orbited the Earth, walked in space, sent a probe to the surface of Venus. An automobile had already driven more than 600 miles per hour. Nuclear power was in use. The Beatles became a member of the British Order of Merit, an honor Churchill himself won 20 years earlier for completely different reasons.

It is rather remarkable to think about the amount of change that Churchill witnessed throughout his lifetime.

Change was constantly on Churchill's mind. Toward the end of his life he said,

> I wonder often whether any other generation has seen such astounding revolutions of data and values as those through which we have lived. Scarcely anything material or established which I was brought up to believe was permanent and vital, has lasted. Everything I was sure or taught to be sure was impossible, has happened.

Now I want you to think about that rate of change through the lens of a business.

How difficult it must be to operate a business for 100 years through that type of changing environment.

Think about the companies that have endured over a long period of time. Many of the products or services that originally launched their businesses quickly became obsolete.

In 1939, Bill Hewlett and David Packard partnered up to launch Hewlett Packard. The product that launched the company was the Model 200A audio oscillator. They literally baked the paint on the first units in a kitchen oven. David Packard's wife said food never tasted the same afterward. They priced the product at $54 when competing products were $200–$600. Sales took off.

I don't think anyone is buying the Model 200A. In fact, it became obsolete by 1950. The company evolved, innovated, and adapted around their customers' needs to become one the world's largest electronic instrument manufacturers.

Old companies are adaptive, not slow

When most people think of "old" they think slow. They think of an older person. When most people think of an old company, they think slow thinking, inflexible, set in their ways, a relic of the past. This is the wrong framing.

The Henokiens is an association of family-owned companies that have operated for 200 years or more. There are 56 companies in this association across the world. Fifty-six companies that have operated for more than 200 years.

One of these Henokien member companies is Catherineau.

The company was founded in 1750. The founder Pierre Catherineau began making cartwheels. The business evolved and grew from generation to generation. Today, Catherineau designs and manufactures made-to-measure interiors for aircraft and yachts. Its customers are the rich, famous, and powerful – mainly in France. The company has now been passed down to the ninth generation of family members.

The family credits their business success and endurance to the following values:

- Constantly reinventing their business to survive.
- Constantly adapting to their environment.
- Meeting and exceeding customer expectations.

Does this sound like an old, slow-thinking company?

In fact, what you will find is that old companies are often the most innovative and adaptive companies.

I can't help but think about this Charles Darwin quote:

> It is not the strongest of the species that survives, nor the most intelligent that survives. It is the one that is most adaptable to change.

There have been over 100 significant global economic events since 1900. Wars, famines, recessions, and natural disasters. Layered on top of these events are consumer, technological, geopolitical shifts that reshape industries.

Businesses can't survive 50–100+ years unless they are both innovative and adaptive. They also must be conservative with their balance sheet. Ironically, it's the same thing I had to implement to be a full-time private investor. I was conservative with my personal finances so I could be aggressive with my portfolio.

In bull markets everyone focuses on the income statement and growth. In bear markets everyone focuses on the balance sheet and survival. A forward-thinking management team must do both.

If you are intrigued by the topic of business endurance, my favorite book is *Lessons From Century Club Companies* by Vicki TenHaken. It is a short and brilliant, 100-page book, filled with valuable lessons from studying century club companies. Vicki and her team studied, surveyed, and interviewed over 1,000 businesses in the United States, and 90 businesses in Japan, that have been in operation for more than 100 years.

Survival applied to microcaps

When you study enduring businesses, many of them aren't huge businesses. They are small- to medium-sized businesses that dominate small niche markets.

Peter Thiel talks about this in one of my favorite books, *Zero to One*.

> The perfect target market for a startup is a small group of particular people concentrated together and served by few or no competitors. Any big market is a bad choice, and a

> big market already served by competing companies is even worse. This is why it's always a red flag when entrepreneurs talk about getting 1% of a $100 billion market. In practice, a large market will either lack a good starting point or it will be open to competition, so it's hard to ever reach that 1%. And even if you do succeed in gaining a small foothold, you'll have to be satisfied with keeping the lights on: cutthroat competition means your profits will be zero.
>
> **– Peter Thiel**

Similarly, when you study microcap success stories most of these companies first dominated a small niche market that was expanding. After they dominated one small market, they used what they learned to enter complimentary markets.

These companies don't push into new markets – their happy customers pull them into new geographies, products, or services where they were being underserved. The growth is more natural and enduring this way.

When you study market leaders in niche markets they are often well-run, profitable businesses. I love to find these businesses in the public markets because it proves management is competent.

Management either created the market, or they took share away from competitors. Often these operators are potential intelligent fanatics that were able to create economic moats in these small markets. These types of leaders and small, dominant businesses are scarce in the public markets, but they can yield exceptional returns.

> Niche businesses find an area of the market that is not being serviced and in a short time dominates that area. Examples of companies that have exploited this type of opportunity can be found in almost every industry. Sam Walton founded Wal-Mart because he saw that the big chains, such as Sears, Kmart, and Montgomery Ward, were not servicing the small towns in the South. He created a much more efficient system of servicing small towns that caught them sleeping at the switch and built one of the largest companies in the world.
>
> **– Charlie Munger**

Most microcap companies go public too soon and are undercapitalized. They are thrown into the deep end of a pool without knowing how to swim. The consultants and investment banks that took them public abandon them. The management team must fight and claw and figure it out on their own.

All public companies have a public track record. I love to look through filings, press releases, earnings transcripts to see how management communicated in the tough times. I love to invest in management teams that grinded it out and did what was right for common shareholders. These leaders are proven survivors.

Quality is one of the most overused terms in investing.

Most investors' definition of a quality business or quality management has nothing to do with quality – it's simply the stock they own that is up the most in the last 12 months.

Quality is a label that can only be earned over a 10+ year period. The report card for any public CEO is a long-term stock chart. Quality shines through over time and mediocrity reverts to the mean.

Find a CEO and business that has outperformed the S&P 500 for 10+ years or more and those are the outliers that deserve recognition and the label of "quality."

These exceptional leaders are ultimately able to combine survival and growth. Owner management focus on the company's balance sheet, considering it an important indicator of durability and survival. At the same time, they value growth, not for growth's sake, but for deepening a competitive position and increasing market share.

My investor survival guide

Here is my four-part investor survival guide:

Part 1: Invest in businesses that can grow through a recession. The way to navigate any macro environment is to focus on businesses that can outperform in any macro environment. Only the highest-quality companies can make it over this hurdle. It will also eliminate entire industries. Extraordinary returns follow extraordinary discipline. Don't be afraid to say no to 99.9% of investment opportunities.

Part 2: Invest in businesses with a great balance sheet that can weather a storm and act with occasional boldness. A profitable business with a great balance sheet are the two key ingredients necessary for survival. A good balance sheet is filled with cash and assets, and few liabilities.

Peter Lynch said, "It's very hard to go bankrupt when you don't have any debt."

Morgan Housel said, "As debt increases, you narrow the range of outcomes you can endure in life (and in business)."

A great balance sheet gives to a business what a great personal balance sheet gives to an individual. Confidence and patience. When the time is right, when the valuation is right, they can act boldly when the competition is struggling.

Part 3: Invest at a valuation that can double in three years based on conservative fundamental assumptions with no multiple expansion. Multi-baggers are driven by earnings per share growth and multiple expansion. Value stocks that turn into growth stocks. If a company doubles its earnings per share over three years and the multiple stays the same, you make a 100% return in three years. This is a 25% CAGR and if you string together 20 years of this you become a GOAT stock picker.

Part 4: Invest in businesses with a leadership team and organization that show signs of intelligent fanaticism. Find management teams that are survivors and deserve to be running much larger companies. Find the businesses that dominate niche markets whose happy customers are pulling them into new underserved markets. In the end we are looking for adaptive management teams who are building for scale and endurance.

Finding intelligent fanatics is the key to everything.

CHAPTER 16

What Is an Intelligent Fanatic?

In 2014, I stumbled upon an idea that would quietly rewire how I thought about businesses, leaders, and conviction.

It came from William Thorndike's *The Outsiders*. At the surface, the book was about capital allocation. But beneath that was something far more interesting. A pattern of behavior. These CEOs weren't famous. They weren't flashy. They didn't fit the mold. They were iconoclasts that compounded capital at rates that bordered on the absurd. What struck me most wasn't what they knew but how intensely they believed. Each of them operated with a kind of calm obsession.

A year later, that pattern finally got a name.

In 2015, I heard the phrase *intelligent fanatic* for the first time, in a lecture by Professor Sanjay Bakshi. The term stopped me cold. It captured something I had sensed but couldn't articulate. The rare combination of deep rationality and almost irrational commitment. Not blind faith. Not stubbornness. But disciplined fanaticism that spread through their organizations to create a dominant culture.

Around that same period, Professor Bakshi and I crossed paths on X, almost by accident. He shared an article I had written called "The Conviction to Hold." It struck a nerve. The piece spread quickly, faster than anything I had written before. Within a week, my audience grew by 10,000 people.

The real benefit to me wasn't the followers, but the access to Professor Bakshi.

Despite living on opposite sides of the world and him a mid-cap investor in India and me a microcap investor in the United States, we discovered we were wrestling with the same ideas: conviction, temperament, and the qualitative side of investing. A friendship formed. He began sharing more of my writing with his students and followers. Doors that had always felt sealed suddenly opened.

In time, Professor Bakshi traveled to the United States to speak at a MicroCapClub event I hosted in Chicago. My audience and my investment maturity today would be a fraction of what it is without his generosity.

Intelligent fanatics and Charlie Munger

Charlie Munger said, "Occasionally, you'll find a human being who's so talented that he or she can do things that ordinary skilled mortals can't." He referred to such individuals as "intelligent fanatics."

Intelligent fanatic – *n (orig. from Charlie Munger)* – Founder, CEO or management team with unconventional ideas and fanatical drive to build a high-performance organization. A learning machine that can quickly adapt to change because he/she is "the change." Able to create a trust-based culture that aligns everyone to think like owners. Focused on acquiring, training, and motivating the best talent. Their time horizon is in 10-year increments, not quarterly, and they invest in their business accordingly. They own large pieces of their businesses. Regardless of the industry, they are able to create an impenetrable moat that competitors initially cannot understand and eventually fear.

I love the story of Sam Walton and Walmart. In 1962, at the age of 44, Sam Walton started with one store. In just 30 years, Walmart became the #1 retailer in the United States. At the time of his death in 1992, there were 1,735 Walmart, 380,000 employees, and annual sales approaching $50 billion.

The fact this was all accomplished in the second half of Sam Walton's life is staggering. This wasn't a present-day tech company that could scale effortlessly. Walton had huge tangible and logistical challenges. He was CEO until 1988, and Chairman until his death. Sam Walton was in charge. He was an intelligent fanatic.

Only an exceptional leader can successfully lead a company from hustle to super scale.

The smaller the company, the more important the CEO, founder, and management become. If you don't believe that founders and management are important to small businesses like microcaps, just wait a little longer. You will.

The moat of any small business is the management.

All great companies started as small companies. And so it follows that if we want to find great companies early, we must find intelligent fanatics early. Intelligent fanatics are the world's greatest business builders. They create companies that grow to dominate their niche, geography, or industry. These are the exceptional leaders we must find early and hitch our sidecar to.

Sean Iddings and I spent a few years studying the world's best business builders. Over a three-year period, we co-authored two books on intelligent fanatics and oversaw the research and writing of a third book.

1. *Intelligent Fanatics Project* (2016)
2. *Intelligent Fanatics – Standing on the Shoulders of Giants* (2017)
3. *Intelligent Fanatics of India* (2019)

We studied hundreds of intelligent fanatics that have built dominant public and private businesses and that operated in different industries, continents, and time periods. Perhaps the most fascinating thing we encountered was even though they were all quite different, their business philosophies were relatively similar. There was a blueprint for success. Intelligent fanatics possess similar attributes, characteristics, and behaviors.

As a stock picker, my main goal in researching intelligent fanatics was to fine tune my lens for finding great leaders running small microcap companies.

Finding intelligent fanatics early can be a tall task. Some might say it is impossible. I would say it's more like climbing Mt. Everest.

In 1980, climbers had a 3% success rate in reaching the summit on Mt. Everest. Today, due to more guides and better gear, the success rate is 50%. One thousand people climb Mt. Everest every year and around 500 make it to the summit. One thing is for certain. You can't reach the summit if you don't try.

You can't find intelligent fanatics early unless you can first identify the smoke signals of greatness.

CHAPTER 17

How Do You Find Intelligent Fanatics Early?

In 1959, Columbia Records was a sinking ship. Young Americans were done with jazz and classical music, Columbia's bread and butter. The company's talent scouts didn't understand the new wave of artists shaping the next generation.

Columbia's president, Goddard Lieberson, needed a miracle.

Lieberson made an odd decision. He brought back John Hammond, a man with an ear for hidden genius.

John Hammond had already rewritten the rules of music discovery once before.

At just 22 years old, during the depths of the Great Depression, he unearthed an unknown jazz singer named Billie Holiday. She went on to revolutionize jazz. Her voice cut across the rigid racial lines of the time.

Hammond's gut instinct had produced a who's who of jazz legends: Benny Goodman, Count Basie, Charlie Christian. He didn't just find talent, he spotted the ones who would change music forever.

But now, in 1960, John Hammond didn't look like a sure bet.

At 50 years old, he was considered out of touch. A relic. A man with an ear for yesterday's sound. Jazz was fading, rock was rising, and Columbia needed new blood to adapt their business to the 1960s, not the 1930s. Yet to count John Hammond out meant you didn't understand the man, or his process.

By 1961, Hammond was back in the hunt. But this time, instead of speakeasies and Harlem jazz clubs where he had spent his youth, he was lurking in the coffeehouses of Greenwich Village, soaking in the raw, unpolished energy of the folk music scene.

He quickly signed a young singer-songwriter named Carolyn Hester.

At a rehearsal for Hester's third album, her first for Columbia, that's when Hammond saw him.

Hammond couldn't take his eyes off a skinny, scruffy Midwestern kid in a peaked cap, playing a harmonica that wasn't particularly good. But there was something about him.

"I was taken with him," Hammond later recalled.

The executives at Columbia thought Hammond had lost it. But Hammond knew what he saw.

Despite their protests, he signed the kid anyway.

And then, disaster.

The young man's first album flopped. It sold an average of one copy per store. The Columbia top brass were furious with Hammond. They called the artist "Hammond's folly" and wanted to drop him immediately.

Hammond wouldn't budge.

"As soon as I got him into the studio, I knew that I was going to stick with him no matter what happened."

The kid's name? Robert Allen Zimmerman.

Doesn't sound familiar?

Guess again.

You might know him as Bob Dylan.

By 1966, Dylan had sold 10 million records. By 2008, 120 million. He became one of the most influential artists of the 20th century, a musician so revolutionary that in 2016, he became the first artist in history to be awarded the Nobel Prize in Literature.

Imagine investing in Sam Walton after Walmart's IPO and selling after the first dip, only to watch Walmart become the world's biggest retailer.

Imagine investing in Jeff Bezos after the Amazon IPO – Bezos was basically Sam Walton born again, 50 years later, applying Walton's lessons with physical retail to online retail. Most people sold out of Amazon during the 95% drawdown when the dot-com bubble crashed.

That's what Columbia almost did with Dylan.

John Hammond saw what no one else could. He didn't just spot talent, he saw the future before anyone knew it was there. He was the living proof of Schopenhauer's line: *"Talent hits targets no one else can hit; genius hits targets no one else can see."*

Hammond didn't just do it with Dylan, he saved Columbia Records.

He brought in artist after artist who would define the next generation: Aretha Franklin, Leonard Cohen, Bruce Springsteen, Stevie Ray Vaughan.

But how?

What gave him this uncanny ability to recognize world-changing talent before anyone else?

The answer lies in his insane standards and pattern recognition, and his relentless, obsessive study of excellence.

Hammond didn't stumble upon greatness; he trained himself to see it. By the time he met Dylan, he had developed a hunch for genius that no one else could see.

And this is exactly what separates the best investors from the rest: pattern recognition, high standards, and conviction.

Right now, there's an intelligent fanatic running a tiny, overlooked microcap company that Wall Street couldn't care less about.

In a decade, they'll have built something massive.

The question is, will you be like John Hammond and see them before almost everyone else does?

Here's how to do it, in five lessons.

Lesson 1: Build pattern recognition by immersing yourself in the greats

The best investors don't just stumble onto greatness. They live in it, surround themselves with it, study it relentlessly. They watch, listen, absorb until they can recognize brilliance before anyone else. Their ability to spot the best companies isn't luck. It is earned through years of immersion.

Great businesses aren't built by average leaders. They're built by intelligent fanatics who refuse to accept the status quo. They don't just chase profits; they redefine industries. If you want to find them before the rest of the world wakes up, you must understand what makes them different.

There are patterns. If you pay attention, you'll see them.

Some fanatics saw what others ignored and seized an opportunity no one else recognized. John H. Patterson wasn't just selling cash registers at NCR. He was building the modern sales force, setting standards for training, quotas, and customer service that still shape businesses today.

Herb Kelleher looked at the airline industry and saw something broken. Instead of following the bloated, inefficient legacy carriers, he created a low-cost, no-frills airline that remained profitable while his competitors collapsed.

Peter Kiewit understood that construction companies rise and fall on the strength of their workforce, so he built a culture of employee ownership, turning his firm into an institution that outlasted rivals.

Others were relentless product innovators, refusing to accept mediocrity. James Dyson spent five years and 5,126 prototypes refining the bagless vacuum while everyone else settled for outdated, ineffective designs. He refused to quit until he had something revolutionary.

Costco didn't chase margins, it chased trust. By slashing prices, capping markups, and treating employees like assets instead of costs, it built a fanatically loyal customer base and a culture of efficiency that turned warehouse shopping into a retail juggernaut.

Les Schwab built a tire empire not by marketing, but by demanding a customer service experience so obsessive that his employees literally ran to greet customers in the parking lot. Where others thought it was unnecessary, he saw an opportunity to dominate through fanaticism.

Ingvar Kamprad didn't just design furniture, he changed the way people bought and built it. His belief that great design should be affordable led him to pioneer flat-pack manufacturing, vertical integration, and ruthless cost efficiency, transforming IKEA into a global force.

Then there are the forward thinkers, the ones who took an idea to the next level. Howard Schultz wasn't selling coffee, he was selling a ritual, a third place between home and work, embedding Starbucks into the daily lives of millions.

Phil Knight didn't just manufacture shoes, he created a movement, embedding Nike into the DNA of elite athletes and weekend warriors alike.

Mary Kay Ash didn't just sell cosmetics, she rewrote the rules for women in sales, proving financial independence wasn't just for men, and built a culture that rewarded ambition instead of punishing it.

And then there are those who refused to lose. Bernie Marcus and Arthur Blank were fired from their own company, so they built Home Depot from scratch and obliterated their former employer.

Sam Walton lost his first successful business when his landlord refused to renew his lease and took over the store for himself. Instead of quitting, he set up shop across the street and led to building Walmart, a company that didn't just beat his old competitor, but wiped out entire retail chains.

Ken Iverson took over a failing steel company, reinvented the mini-mill model, and built Nucor into an unstoppable force.

The common thread is clear. They saw what others didn't. They executed relentlessly. They had something to prove.

You don't need to reinvent the wheel. You just need to study the right people.

Hammond didn't spot Dylan by chance. He trained himself to recognize genius by spending years around the best musicians. He built his instincts by living inside the world of talent before he ever dared to judge it.

You need to do the same in business. Read everything about these leaders. Study their decisions. Learn how they think.

Because somewhere out there, right now, an intelligent fanatic is running a tiny, overlooked company that no one cares about.

And if you've trained your instincts, you'll find them before the world does.

Lesson 2: Bet on leadership, not just numbers

Look for leaders who have something to prove

When evaluating small companies, I want to know the CEO's story.

Did they face hardship growing up or early in their careers? Were they passed over, disrespected, or overlooked? Do they have a chip on their shoulder?

The best leaders aren't born into success, they fight for it.

In 2023, I invested in a small obscure $12 million market cap company. The CEO took over after the previous management team ran it into the ground. He had been passed over for years. He wasn't wealthy when he stepped in as CEO. He could only afford to buy 3% of the company, but that stake meant everything to him.

And he turned the business around.

I asked him: Who or what is responsible for the company's turnaround?

His answer?

> An Olympic athlete becomes weak. Diagnosed with cancer. He goes to a surgeon who removes the cancer. The athlete heals fully. Then, after all that is over, he trains hard and wins a gold medal. Was the surgeon responsible for the gold medal? Of course not. I am just a surgeon who removed a cancer, but the success this company has enjoyed is due to the hard work and dedication of the people here.

Then he added:

> The most important thing I did was shift the focus to profit – not revenue. Old management, and most people who don't understand business, focus on revenue and run into problems trying to achieve it. The people leading our product development, sales, and marketing – they were responsible for the turnaround. I

could be replaced by a decent financial person, and this company wouldn't miss a beat.

I haven't told you the company, the industry, or the valuation.

You want to buy this stock because you want to bet on this kind of CEO. This is the type of leader you would work with.

Spotting an intelligent fanatic isn't just about recognizing talent, it's about recognizing conviction. The best leaders don't just have a vision; they bet everything on it.

John Hammond didn't just see raw ability in Bob Dylan. He saw a young artist willing to risk everything for his music. Dylan wasn't chasing a quick payday or trying to fit into the industry mold. He played in smoke-filled coffeehouses for pennies, writing song after song with no promise of success, refusing to conform to what labels thought was marketable. He had something to say, and he was willing to stake everything on it. Hammond went all-in too.

That's skin in the game.

Skin in the game: The only CEOs worth betting on

If a CEO doesn't have real ownership, both internal and external, in the business, why should you trust them?

Hammond recognized that Dylan wasn't hedging his bets. He was all-in, betting on himself before anyone else would. That same principle applies to business. The best CEOs don't play for salary, they play for equity.

Bob Kierlin (Fastenal) and Ken Iverson (Nucor) took the lowest salaries in their industry while running two of the most profitable companies in their sectors. They built their fortunes by making employees and shareholders richer, not by siphoning cash into personal compensation.

Compare that to the frauds running bloated corporations today, executives who:

- Issue millions in stock options while failing to generate real profits.
- Raise capital like beggars, constantly diluting shareholder value.

- Cash out before the business ever delivers results.

John Swallow, CEO of Idaho Strategic, summed it up best:

> Looking rich at the wrong time can be a disaster.

If a CEO is cashing in while the company is struggling, how can employees trust them? How can investors? When employees see their CEO rolling up in a new Cadillac Escalade while salaries are frozen, they check out.

The best CEOs don't drain the company, they bet on its future.

That's how real CEOs operate.

Mitch Rales, co-founder of Danaher, put it simply:

> Everybody told me I was too concentrated, and I needed to be more diversified. Thank God I didn't listen to any of them.

CEOs who think like owners don't hedge their bets. They commit. They don't raise unnecessary capital. They don't pad their own pockets at your expense.

Hammond bet on Dylan because Dylan bet on himself.

As an investor, you should be doing the same.

When evaluating a company, ask yourself: Is the CEO all-in?

If the answer is no, walk away.

If the answer is yes, and the business is solid, when challenges inevitably arise, you'll have the conviction to stand by them, just like Hammond stood by Dylan.

Lesson 3: Constraints breed greatness

John Hammond didn't just find talent, he found artists who thrived under constraints.

Bob Dylan wasn't handed success. His voice was called "terrible."

Columbia executives wanted to drop him because he sounded like a dying dog. No budget, no industry backing, no commercial appeal.

Dylan knew how to turn limitations into advantages.

His voice wasn't polished but he leaned into raw, unfiltered storytelling. No studio budget? He recorded fast, capturing urgency without overproduction. No industry support? He built an audience that didn't care what the industry thought.

Hammond saw it. Dylan wasn't waiting for perfect conditions, he created his own path.

Intelligent fanatics in business do the same.

Jeff Bezos built Amazon on frugality as a strategy, because constraints force better decisions. Ryan Pape took over a dying microcap company called Xpel Technologies and refused to dilute shareholders. Instead of raising capital, he focused every dollar on brand and execution. The result? A 1000X stock.

Pape explains it best:

> I believe that having constraints on a business makes it stronger. It's like if you're growing tomato plants in your garden, you don't want to give them too much water. They need a little struggle to be their best. And I think a business is the same way. I think there's a good argument that constraints make the business better.

The best leaders don't just survive constraints, they weaponize them.

When a CEO owns a large stake and takes a low salary, it's not just discipline, it's a signal. They aren't cashing in, they're betting on the future. They don't waste money on flashy offices, bloated payrolls, or useless software. Every dollar spent must return something, whether it's in talent, product, or customer loyalty.

Dylan didn't succeed despite his constraints, he succeeded because of them. The best companies are the same.

Find a CEO who knows how to turn limitations into leverage, and you've found something rare.

Lesson 4: Culture builders

Charlie Munger once said that the best operating companies aren't great because of their product. They're great because of their culture. A company's culture is what keeps it thriving long after a visionary leader is gone. It's the only sustainable competitive advantage, because it can't be copied.

You see this across industries. Costco, Kiewit, and Glenair don't sell anything remarkable. Yet their cultures are so strong that competitors know exactly what they're doing and still can't duplicate them.

Intelligent fanatics build cultures where employees think and act like owners. They create incentives that drive buy-in at every level, not just at the top. Their companies aren't built on charismatic leadership, they're built on deeply ingrained values that trickle down to the front lines.

You can fake culture at the top. You can't fake it at the bottom. The best leaders know this. They spend their time on the ground, not in a corner office.

Jim Casey, founder of UPS, was that kind of leader. He didn't just sit in boardrooms. He was in warehouses, in trucks, talking to drivers, listening to their ideas. When Ron Wallace, a young UPS employee, found himself struggling to start a delivery truck late in the day, Casey didn't walk by. He stepped in, held the cables, and helped get the truck running. Then, instead of leaving, he sat down and asked Wallace what he thought about "our" company.

That's culture. It isn't words on a mission statement. It's leaders who listen. Leaders who show up. Leaders who make people feel like their voice matters.

Hammond did that for Dylan.

Jim Casey did that for his UPS drivers.

And intelligent fanatics do it for their companies.

They don't build layers of bureaucracy. They create flat, decentralized organizations where ideas flow freely and employees are trusted with real responsibility. They drive decision-making closer to the customer so the company can adapt faster than its competitors. They promote from within, developing future leaders instead of hiring outsiders who don't understand the culture.

And they don't just create good workplaces; they create leadership factories.

The best cultures aren't about perks, flashy offices, or empty slogans. They're about alignment.

Everyone knows the numbers. Everyone has skin in the game. Everyone understands how their work contributes to the company's success.

That's why the best-run companies pay attention to details others overlook.

Roger Penske, who dominated both auto racing and business, believed that "cleaner cars run faster." He applied that same philosophy to his businesses: A well-run operation is an efficient operation.

Gustavus Swift (meatpacking), Frank Perdue (poultry), and Tom Monaghan (Domino's Pizza) were obsessed with cleanliness not because it looked good, but because details matter.

John Swallow, CEO of Idaho Strategic, told me he gauges company culture by how clean employees keep their equipment. When machinery starts looking neglected, it's a red flag. If people don't care about the small things, they won't care about the big ones either.

So how do you spot a great culture?

It's not about what the CEO says, it's about what the employees do.

- Check job review sites.
- Buy the company's product. Call customer service. See how they treat you.
- Talk to employees at different levels. Do they have real enthusiasm for their work?
- Ask them what they think about leadership – do they feel empowered or just another cog in the machine?
- See if they have authority to handle issues within their department.
- Find out if they can see real performance metrics or if transparency is just a talking point.
- Ask if they're incentivized beyond base salary because the best cultures create owners, not employees.

Great culture isn't a perk, it's the *most* durable competitive moat.

It's why companies with deep, ingrained cultures win over decades, while others burn bright and fade fast.

Hammond gave Dylan the right conditions to become legendary.

The best companies do the same for their people.

Lesson 5: The right people make the difference

Warren Buffett had Charlie Munger. Steve Jobs had Jony Ive. John D. Rockefeller had Henry Flagler. Bill Gates had Paul Allen. Bill Hewlett had Dave Packard. The best leaders aren't just visionaries, they build teams that multiply their strengths and cover their weaknesses.

Justin Ishbia, one of the greatest microcap investors in the world, attributes his success to this exact principle. Justin is the founding partner of Shore Capital Partners, a $9 billion private equity firm utilizing a systematic approach to acquire hundreds of private microcap businesses.

Since 2009, Shore Capital has acquired 800 small businesses, which makes them the #1 most active private equity firm in the world.

More importantly, Shore Capital is ranked in the top 1% of all private equity firms globally by performance. They have compounded investor capital at 50% net per year since inception. The firm's success has made Justin Ishbia a billionaire.

When Justin Ishbia was asked about the secret sauce of the firm he said, "The most important part of our thesis is recruiting the right board members."

Weak leaders build weak teams. Strong leaders seek out people who can make them better.

They don't just build great teams internally, they build great boards. Intelligent fanatics see their board of directors as an asset, not a liability. A great board isn't just there for oversight, it's there to add value, challenge assumptions, and accelerate decision-making.

Dylan had people around him who pushed his creativity, just like intelligent fanatics in business surround themselves with mentors, partners, and operators who push them to execute at the highest level.

That's why they win.

Ken Langone (co-founder of Home Depot) once said, "We have 3,000 people still working for us that got started pushing carts that are now millionaires. Those are our culture carriers."

That's what intelligent fanatics do. They build businesses that compound talent, culture, and capital over decades. They create systems that don't just win in the short term but dominate over the long haul. And just like great artists, great businesses can't fake it forever.

Investors always want to find the next Amazon, Google, Costco, Berkshire, Constellation Software, or any other monster winner. Copycats emerge, but it's the originals that create the highest returns. There are 30,000 Elvis impersonators, and their combined income is far less than the original.

Every public company CEO has a report card, it's called a long-term stock chart. You can fake it for a year or two. You can ride a lucky trend for three years. But you can't fake it for a decade. If a company has a strong 10-year track record and is still under the radar, that's when it's worth serious attention.

The great thing about microcaps? They can 10x and still be a small undiscovered opportunity to 99.9% of the investment universe.

Intelligent fanatics don't chase hype. They build enduring businesses. They focus on profitability, reinvestment, and long-term execution.

The best-performing microcap stocks weren't flashes in the pan. They were profitable growth companies that could self-fund their own expansion, which meant their CEOs weren't wasting time begging for capital or managing short-term expectations. They were too busy executing.

This is what makes intelligent fanatics so rare. They don't need Wall Street. They don't chase analyst approval. They ignore short-term investors because their business performance and ownership stakes give them the freedom to focus on what actually matters.

This obsession and total commitment to their company, their team, their product is what makes them unrepeatable.

Hammond didn't wait for approval to sign Dylan. He just knew.

Great investors don't wait for the market to tell them a company is great. They see it before anyone else does.

If you've studied intelligent fanaticism, if you've built your own pattern recognition, when the next great one crosses your path, you won't hesitate.

You'll know.

In the next section I'm going to reflect on some lessons of stock picking. The battle scars, drawdowns, bad management teams, emotional baggage, and the mental wear that accumulates over 20+ years of concentrated investing. This next section is about the inner game, the parts of investing that spreadsheets can't model.

SECTION 3

The Reflections of a Stock Picker

CHAPTER 18

Judas Goat

One of the strangest stories in agricultural history involves goats addicted to cigarettes leading sheep to their deaths. These animals were called *Judas goats*, and they were trained to guide sheep to slaughter. For each group of sheep they led to the killing floor, they got a reward: one cigarette.

Old slaughterhouses were huge buildings with several floors – sometimes five or six stories tall. Each floor had a different job in the process of turning animals into butchered meat. The top floor was where the animals were killed, and then their bodies were moved down to lower levels for further processing.

Moving large numbers of animals to the top floor took planning and skill. Cows could be pushed. Pigs could be guided. But sheep were much harder. They were nervous and didn't like moving toward places that smelled of blood and fear.

That's why the Judas goat was so important.

It strains credulity to envision the surreal parade of a lone goat leading sheep across a meatpacking facility, coaxing the flock up concrete ramps, delivering the herd beyond the point of no return, and then seeing the goat hustling toward a nicotine fix and a repeat performance. However, Judas goats were part-and-parcel of livestock slaughter, and their history sheds a fascinating light on a bygone era. Betrayal by bleat and tobacco.

An old-time meatpacker once explained how it worked:

> The only way to calmly get them [sheep] on the killing floor was a goat. We'd take the goat and put him in front of the sheep. Up the ramp they'd go, following Judas. If the sheep hesitated, Billy would bleat to keep them moving. If they didn't come, he'd stop, turn around, bleat more, and wait for them to catch up.

At the very top, on the sixth floor, was a single doorway the sheep passed through before they were killed. Once they were gone, the goat would walk back down the ramp for his reward.

The goat's craving was no joke.

> The goat was trained on unfiltered cigarettes, particularly one Camel or Lucky Strike per trip. He ate it whole. He loved it because he was addicted to nicotine.

It sounds unbelievable, but it was once a real part of the meat industry – a strange mix of habit, training, and betrayal.

In every industry there are people that knowingly and unknowingly lead sheep to slaughter. The financial industry is filled with them. Judas goats seem to multiply during bull markets. The worst part of bull markets is the rise of inexperienced people educating other inexperienced people. The thing that exacerbates the problem is the human desire for stock recommendations and to buy into them blindly. Most people are wired to be sheep.

Don't be a sheep

One of the most painful lessons is following people, even high-profile investors, into stocks you don't understand and losing money. Don't worry, everyone has done this at least once. If you don't do your own work, you will get slaughtered, especially in microcaps.

!WARNING! – I'm about to make a controversial statement that is 100% true.

Most microcaps you buy must be sold within 36 months. Even the winners. Only a small fraction of the winners will have management teams and businesses that can evolve and grow into something truly sustaining. This is a bitter pill for the buy-and-hold-forever crowd to swallow, but it is microcap reality.

When the crowd buys into an illiquid stock it is fun watching it go up. When the crowd decides to sell an illiquid stock, sheep get slaughtered. If you don't do your own work, you don't know when to sell. If you are waiting for someone else to tell you when to sell, it is already too late.

On the rare occasion a sheep buys a monster stock they will never be able to reap the full reward. Every monster stock that ascends 1000%+ over a three-, five-, or 10-year time frame goes through seasons where the stock is loved, hated, cheap, and expensive.

If you can't form your own conviction, you will get run over by your emotions. You must put in the work to earn the right to 10–100x stocks.

Sheep are followers. They get slaughtered either way. Don't be a sheep.

Don't be a Judas goat

If you're a young stock picker and looking to build a reputation, find a great company early, before institutions. Do the work. Be public about it. Be the axe in the name. Be right. People, employers, investors will find you. Then do it again and again. It's the only resume that matters. This is how I built my early reputation on public stock message boards.

But it's easy to take things too far. I know I did. When I was young and naïve I would pound on a specific company, and post on the message boards with the consistent drum beat of bullishness. Oftentimes as the stock would rise, my ego would swell, and I would pound that drum even harder.

As my early mentor Skip once told me, "Ian, you can get them up [the stock price], but the business needs to keep them up."

Building your reputation in illiquid stocks with short shelf lives can be problematic as your reputation grows. When the crowd piles into an illiquid thing, not everyone will be able to get out. Some portion of your followers will be left holding the bag and feeling used. Especially if they saw you bleating and luring the sheep higher into the slaughterhouse as the stock rose.

The hardest part of influence is knowing when to stop.

If you are building your reputation publicly, be thoughtful and disciplined with how you communicate to your audience.

- Give your audience unique situations with supporting evidence. Educate people so they can make decisions themselves, so when the next material event happens, they can think for themselves. Communicate to them that they own their own buy and sell decisions.
- Don't talk in absolutes like "X stock is going to Y price." You can't predict the future with certainty. Talk in if/then statements: "If the business does X, I think the stock can do Y." Tie the stock price to the business performance, so you never look dumb.
- As stocks rise, expectations rise, but keep yours grounded. A good rule of thumb is to be quieter than you want to be when you are right. Stop reaching for reasons the stock can go even higher. Don't pound the drum at the top. Your audience already knows you found it early. Control your ego.
- Don't talk bullishly about a stock unless you own it and would buy it at the current price.
- Don't ever talk bullishly about a stock you are selling.

If you want to gain followers, talk about your winners. If you want to gain the respect of your peers and keep your followers, talk about your losers. Postmortems are where the real learning happens.

Talking about your losers once per year shows your audience what you and they can learn from your mistakes. It also reinforces the right lesson – you aren't going to be right all the time. Microcap success is batting average + slugging percentage. You can make a lot of money being right half the time, but you will still be wrong half the time.

When you are building your reputation, the way you communicate matters. Be thoughtful. Don't be an amateur. Future investors, employers, business partners are watching you.

Most of the network I have today is because I play a long-term game. If you want to attract quality into your life, whether that is relationships, customers, or opportunities, then project quality with your actions and words.

The world doesn't need more sheep. The world doesn't need another Judas goat, either.

The older you get, the less you care about convincing others they should invest like you. After you become successful, the younger and opinionated version of you isn't necessary anymore.

We all think we are invested in the best stocks. Nothing you say will prove you right. Only time can prove you right. Insecurity is loud. Confidence is quiet.

Whether it's in stock picking or business, the more problems you solve, the more you get paid, and the higher you will rise. The higher you rise, the bigger the problems. The easiest way to stagnate is to complain and blame.

CHAPTER 19

No One to Blame

You will sell winners too soon. You will hold losers too long. You will buy stocks you shouldn't.

Don't blame others. When you blame others, it proves you didn't do the work you should have done. Fully own your investment mistakes so you learn from them.

Whether you watch American football, European football (soccer), cricket, baseball, or basketball – these are team sports. The team may have important players, but the credit and blame get cast over the entire team. Yes, you can blame the kicker that missed the game winning field goal or the player that missed the penalty kick or the goalie that allowed it, but even in these situations everyone knows it was the team that put the individual in that position in the first place. The team is to blame.

Individual sports like tennis, boxing, or golf are different. In individual sports the best players might have coaches, trainers, agents, and others supporting them, but in matches or tournaments it's one player versus another, or one player versus the world. The player gets the credit for the win, and the player gets the blame for the loss. It's why individual sports are agonizing even for the best in the world. Eight-time major tennis champion Andre Agassi said,

> It's no wonder that tennis causes more divorces among players than any other sport. It's so solitary, so cutthroat, it's Darwinism in a pair of shorts. You're always at the edge. There's no middle ground in tennis, like life itself. You're either winning or losing. You're never safe. Tennis is a psychological and physical war, one that never ends. It's gladiatorial. You're out there all alone, with no one to help, no place to hide.

Stock picking is an individual sport. It doesn't matter if you're a small retail investor or a portfolio manager of a $10 billion fund. As a portfolio manager, it doesn't matter if you have a team around you. Your investors don't care. You get the credit and the blame. You have no place to hide.

Winning is intoxicating. During bull markets you can't wait to journal, self-reflect, or write your annual letter and replay your achievements and humblebrag to the world. Bull markets are fun. Stocks go up four out of five days, and your last buy decision takes 4.3 seconds to be positively reinforced. Everyone sees the upside in everything. You're a great stock picker.

Losing is excruciating. The bull stops running, and the bear starts clawing at your returns. Market drawdowns are a cascade because investors sell stocks that are down 5% to buy more of the stocks down 10%. They do this over and over until everything is down.

When stocks go down, our self-confidence evaporates. Everything flips. Stocks go down four out of five days. The market reverts to longer feedback loops when it takes a year or more to be proven right on a thesis. Small stocks stop positively reacting to news because everything becomes a reason to sell. The "catalyst" you've been waiting for hits, and the stock still doesn't go up. The same stocks you loved 100% higher you now hesitate to buy lower. In bear markets everyone only sees the downside in everything.

When stocks go down, we stop looking in the mirror and start blaming everything and everyone else.

We blame others

When you are an amateur investor, you like to blame others. You blame other investors, talking heads on CNBC, analysts, recommendation services, your friend's boss who gave you the hot stock tip. Amateur investors consciously or subconsciously self-sabotage themselves. They weren't serious when they made the investment, so they aren't serious with the outcome. They must justify the loss so they blame others.

Are you an amateur investor?

We blame the stock market, market conditions, and geopolitics

> Investors who buy 'undervalued' small stocks have been punished for their prudence. People are wondering. How can the S&P 500 be up 20% and my stocks are down? The answer is that a few stocks in the S&P 500 are propping up the averages.

This quote is from Peter Lynch in 2000. You probably thought it was from 2010, or 2020, or 2025.

Investors have been complaining and blaming the same things for decades.

When you are a sea captain, you don't blame the tides and the weather. When you are a stock picker, you don't blame market conditions or macro forces. Bull markets, bear markets, recessions, interest rates, inflation, presidential elections, wars – they are all part of the journey. It's your job to pick stocks and navigate through any environment.

Never blame market conditions for underperformance. We are all dealing with the same circumstances. Losers take credit in the good times and then blame the market in the bad times. Winners take responsibility regardless of the outcome.

We blame management teams

Many management teams overpromise and underdeliver, but we investors are not completely innocent. We all want management to grow the business faster to help justify not caring about valuation. Far too often we let the bullish echo chamber in our minds build up an unrealistic view of a business. When our unrealistic expectations aren't met, we sell and blame management for not hitting targets they never endorsed.

When we lose money, we like to nit-pick. We say "management wasn't aligned!" They didn't own enough of the company. Whether a CEO owns 1% or 40% of a business, no one wants to fail.

We forget that running a business is hard. It's a daily knife fight with hundreds of other competitors vying for the same market and customers. When things don't work out, we like to tell ourselves management were negligent, incompetent buffoons. It lets us sleep better at night with our investing mistake to point the finger of blame.

Sometimes management is to blame, but most often they tried their best and it didn't work out. Sh!t happens.

We blame the lack of ideas

"I can't find ideas in this market."

"Everything is too expensive."

There are 60,000 public companies in the world. If you can't find a handful of great investment opportunities you aren't trying, you aren't evolving, or both. Every time I have complained about the lack of investment opportunities, it was because I wasn't working hard enough to find them.

We blame the lack of resources

If I just had [**insert anything**] I would be successful.

You don't need another computer screen, another newsfeed or datafeed, another opinion, another self-proclaimed guru, another crutch to replace thinking. You have what you need between your ears. Develop it.

The issue with blame is it keeps us from growing and becoming the stock picker we were always meant to be.

Blame is a sin that transcends investing and business and flows into our personal lives

In 2013, my mother was killed in a freak accident. She was walking across the street to get the mail at dusk and was struck by a car and killed instantly.

As you can imagine this was an emotional time for our family.

The police did a full investigation. They wanted to see if the driver was impaired, distracted, or speeding. Was the driver negligent?

The driver was a young woman.

If I'm being completely honest, deep down in that moment I wanted the driver to have been speeding. I wanted her to have been drunk. I wanted another excuse to hate her so I could justify the pain I was feeling.

During the investigation we learned the driver was in counseling for depression. Looking back, I can't imagine the pain she was feeling.

A week after the funeral the police finished the investigation. They found that the driver wasn't under the influence of drugs or alcohol. She wasn't speeding. She wasn't on her phone. The police found nothing.

To this day I still don't know what happened. I don't know if it was the sun at dusk that clouded the driver's vision. I'm not sure if my mother just didn't see the car coming for some reason. I imagine it was a bunch of random things leading to a tragic outcome.

Twenty-four hours after the accident I hated the driver. Two weeks after the accident our family had time to reflect. We contacted the driver and told her we forgive her.

We needed to move on, and I hope it helped her move on.

Whether it's in life, or business, or your portfolio, sometimes we get punched in the gut by events we don't see coming. Sometimes life hits us so hard it would even bring Superman to his knees. We look around for something or someone to blame, but oftentimes there is no one to blame even when there is someone to blame. Sometimes sh!t just happens.

The worst thing you can do is let these challenging events change who you are, from a happy person into a bitter person. Changing you from a person of values and principles into a person that doesn't care anymore. Changing you from a person of action into someone that gives up on their dreams and sits back and criticizes people that win.

The lesson is to keep moving forward. Blame and hate anchor us to the past.

A few years after my mother died I wrote this mantra.

Rise early.

Work hard.

Slow to anger.

Quick to forgive.

No one to blame.

Blame and comparison are two deadly investment sins that ride together. Let's look at comparison next.

CHAPTER 20

Comparison Is the Enemy

In 1996, a 29-year-old PGA Tour Pro named Steve Stricker won two tournaments and had seven top 10 finishes to finish fourth on the PGA Tour money list. In one of the first rounds of the 1997 season, Stricker was paired for the first time with a 22-year-old phenom named Tiger Woods. Stricker said:

> Several times, I would really connect with a drive only to be stunned to see that Tiger's ball had landed 40 to 50 yards beyond mine.
>
> After the first round had ended, I told Nicki, my wife and caddy, what I had been thinking since the moment we left the course: 'I can't compete with that type of game. I just can't compete with that.'

When he played Tiger, he saw a cyborg.

How could he compete against someone that could drive the ball 50 yards further than him? Then after a drive Stricker would have a 200-yard four-iron, while Tiger would have a 150-yard pitching wedge. How could he compete against him? How could anyone compete against him?

Stricker points to that round of golf with Tiger as the start of a

10-year slump that resulted in him losing his PGA Tour card. Thankfully this wasn't the end of Steve Stricker's story. He made a comeback.

Stricker decided to refocus on his strengths: his accuracy and putting. He stopped comparing his weakness, his driving distance, against someone else's strength. He stopped watching the playing field and focused on his own game.

In 2006, Steve Stricker won comeback player of the year. He went on to win nine more times on the PGA Tour and 18 more times on the Champions Tour.

Comparison among stock pickers

Stock pickers love to look at the leaderboard and compare themselves. We all say we love reading fund manager letters.

No, you don't. You love comparing.

What is the first thing you do when you read a fund manager's annual letter?

You skip to the performance table and compare your returns and track record. You focus first on the most recent 12 months or YTD performance.

Why?

YTD always feels the most important. These present emotions, accomplishments, and failures are still fresh in our minds.

If your performance is better, you feel superior. If your performance is worse, you feel envy.

The worst of comparison is felt after a year or two of underperformance. You are already questioning yourself and your abilities. It's in these times you pay closest attention to those that are outperforming.

Researchers call this "confirmation bias in comparison." When you selectively compare yourself to others in ways that reinforce negative self-perceptions. This is Steve Stricker comparing his driving distance to Tiger Woods.

This is toxic. In these moments you are comparing the worst of who you are against the best of everyone else.

Competition and comparison can be good, but not when it comes at the expense of self-mastery and focusing on your own game.

Tiger Woods loved watching the leaderboard. He trusted in his game enough to reach for more, press for more, to win tournaments. The difference is that in golf tournaments, or any sport, there is a beginning and an end. But in stock picking there is no end. Watching the scoreboard in investing isn't beneficial. Having the investing leaderboard influence your game can be detrimental.

It's all quite silly too. Each stock picker is unique. Our strategies are unique. This means our short-term performance will be unique. We will win at different times and lose at different times. We will all go through stretches where we outperform in bad market environments, and we will go through stretches where we underperform in good market environments.

We love to compare like we all invest the same way and it results in a feeling of isolation. Stock picking is one of the few professions where the wins can feel as lonely as the losses. When an investor is losing, lift them up. When an investor gets a big win in the portfolio, congratulate them and help them celebrate their victory. Your time will come. Investing is hard.

In 2019, Terry Smith, CIO of Fundsmith, gave a presentation highlighting how successful investing is like the Tour de France.

> The largest and most prestigious cycle tour in the world is the Tour de France. It has been run for over 100 years. There are 21 stages spread over 23 days. The Tour de France has never been won by somebody who won every stage. It's never going to be won by somebody who wins every stage.
>
> In fact, on several occasions it was won by riders who never won a single stage. The first time they ever stood on the podium was when they were getting the race prize.
>
> There are three different types of stages – There's the time trial, which is where people are set off individually, wearing a skintight suit and funny shaped hat. And they can't get within 20 meters of each other to get any aerodynamic assistance or they're disqualified.

It's a pure test of the ability of the rider on their own to supply a very high wattage in terms of power output for an hour unassisted.

In contrast, in the Peloton stages where everybody rides together, you can get about a 30% reduction in your effort by being in the middle of the Peloton and cutting the amount of work you must do. When I did the London/Paris race for the first time I mistakenly thought that meant it didn't hurt as much. But it does. They just go faster using that particular feature.

Towards the end of these Peloton stages, within 300 or 400 meters of the finish line, they let their sprinters go. It's going to be won by a sprinter.

A sprinter cannot win a time trial. For a time trial, think of someone like Sir Bradley Wiggins. Six foot three, something like 68 kilos with 7% body fat. He's got a shape like that. Basically that's a time trial winner.

Whereas when you're looking at Peloton stages with sprinters, you're talking about somebody who's probably a foot shorter with a thigh circumference bigger than their waist. A powerhouse basically. And the mountain stages have a combination of this.

So the reason I'm telling you all this: I think when people are looking at investments they seek a fund manager who can outperform in all market conditions and all reporting periods. There is no such human being. Good luck. If you find one let me know because I'm going to give him some money as well.

We're trying to win the Tour de France for you. We are not trying to win every stage. Any rider who tried to win every stage would fail and fail to win the Tour as a result. You must be good at something and then get your colleagues and the team to carry you through the bits that you're not so good at to get the best long-term result.

Stock picking is a deeply personal pursuit. Each one of us is unique because what we've gone through can't be duplicated.

There are so many different flavors of stock picking – deep value, value, growth, microcaps, large caps, resources, life sciences, cyclicals, and many others. In addition, we all have different time horizons, valuation frameworks, risk and volatility tolerances. We are all so different.

Bobby Jones, Arnold Palmer, Tiger Woods, Jack Nicklaus, Lee Trevino all took great pride in how their golf swings were not conventional. You could tell it was Lee Trevino 100 yards away from how he swung the golf club. Their swings were a highly personal expression of their art. They had the confidence to learn from the greats but to swing in their own way.

Warren Buffett invests his way while Walter Schloss did it another way. Carl Icahn does it his way while Peter Lynch did it another way. David Tepper does it his way while Marc Andreessen does it another. Some are long term. Some are short term. Some are value investors. Some are growth investors. Some are activist investors. Some bet on change. Some bet on things that won't change. The greatest investors ever have opposing strategies. Within the world of "value investing" alone, there are hundreds of successful iterations. Great stock pickers do it their own way.

The hardest part of achieving a great long-term investment track record is over half the time your returns will look average. Especially if you are a concentrated stock picker like me. You can go years where it feels like you are working hard for mediocre returns. You wait for business fundamentals to grow, fundamentals to backfill, and multiples to compress. You wait for that coiled and compressed multiple to eventually springboard the stock back to new highs.

If you're invested in solid businesses that are growing, earning more money, and not diluting then time is your friend. If you're invested in mediocre businesses "hoping" something changes, time is your enemy.

I love to compete. I love to win. But I don't watch the leaderboard. My competition isn't other investors. I'm competing against two things:

- **The previous version of me**. Stock picking is the pursuit of self-mastery. Don't compare yourself to others. You aren't running their race. Compare yourself to yourself two years ago.
- **The status quo**. For me, it's the 10-year performance of the S&P 500. The S&P 500 is a formidable adversary. Only 10% of active managers can beat the S&P 500 over a 10-year period.

When I was a full-time private investor, I didn't care what other investors were doing. I never even tracked my own performance.

Why? There was no reason to do so.

I had no clients or investors. I didn't need to share my performance to try to gain attention. I had no one to impress but me. I had no one to disappoint but me. I had no one watching but me. I was playing my own game.

When you are a full-time private investor, success is straightforward:

Winning = paying bills and growing your portfolio.

Losing = paying bills and shrinking your portfolio.

A new challenge

In 2018, I was 37 years old and winning as a full-time private investor. MicroCapClub.com was seven years old, and I had just finished co-authoring two books on intelligent fanatics. I was ready for a new challenge.

I had always said no to managing other people's money. I mainly said no because I always said no. Then I started to meet small business owners that wanted to take a small fraction of their net worth and invest with me. These were the perfect investors for my strategy.

I could have continued to manage my own portfolio out of the corner of my basement, but I kept feeling God's nudge. I spent several months thinking about it and talking to other fund managers I respected. I spoke to my wife countless times and prayed about the decision countless more. Many of my friends were fund managers, and I learned from their mistakes.

I felt it was time.

In late 2018 I passed my series 65 exam, filed the appropriate filings and formation documents and hung up a shingle for Intelligent Fanatics Capital Management (IFCM).

I posted a letter on our website which read:

Dear Investor,

I am soon celebrating my 10-year anniversary as a full-time private microcap investor.

Successfully supporting oneself on your own capital is one of the most fulfilling and challenging occupations on Earth. It is the ultimate test as it forces you to answer the question: Can you survive and thrive on your own capital and expertise? I have for almost 10 years. It is an amazing feeling. Now I'm ready for more.

In the past I have always dismissed the idea of managing other people's money. It certainly sparks the question: Why now?

Here is the short answer: I have been a full-time private investor for a long time and have developed a unique set of skills and resources. I'm still young. I want to do more. I want to help others. I'd like to build a team. The microcap arena is incredible. The investment opportunity is far greater than my personal net worth. Lastly, I think we can kill it.

A true microcap focused strategy should be built for performance, not scale. It should be focused on the greatest area of inefficiency in the public equity universe: the smallest microcaps. In doing so, the strategy will be capacity constrained.

Ultimately a strategy such as this is not an institutional product offering. It is an entrepreneurial product offering, and it must be managed by a person or team that has the discipline to say 'no more' when it reaches capacity.

Some of the best things in life don't scale very well.

I'm excited to announce the launch of Intelligent Fanatics Capital Management (IFCM). Looking back, this firm is the product of over a decade of work. Only in hindsight does the journey look crystal clear. Over the past year, I've spent countless hours in thought while connecting with individuals I respect to help me structure and navigate the process of launching an investment strategy. The time is finally here.

I'm the first money in and am seeking a small number of individuals to invest alongside me.

As a full-time private investor, I needed my lifestyle and portfolio to be in harmony. To manage other people's money, I needed my investors and me to be in harmony. This is difficult when your strategy resides in the most dangerous and volatile arena of the public markets. Every investor says they can handle volatility. What they really mean is they can handle the upside volatility, not the downside volatility.

When you manage other people's money you better put as much effort into picking your investors as picking your stocks. One bad investor will make your life miserable. If you must hard sell someone on your strategy, they aren't the right investor.

I needed to be extremely disciplined with the type of investor and the amount of money invested. My strategy was legitimately capacity constrained. You can only shovel so much capital into a handful of small stocks. The goal with my disciplined approach was to make what looked fragile into something antifragile.

What fund manager ever puts a maximum on how much people can invest?

When I launched, I had a $100,000 minimum and a $200,000 maximum. Limiting the amount of money a person could invest was important for these reasons:

- First, I would always be the largest investor. I didn't want any investor to influence me, or exert control over me through the amount of money they were investing.
- Second, all investors had to be qualified investors which at the time meant a $2.2 million net worth, not including their home or residence. By capping investment to $200,000, I knew they were only investing a small fraction of their net worth. This would allow them to stomach the volatility and stay invested for a full business cycle. It would also give them the capacity to add more capital during the drawdowns and maybe even outperform the average performance of the strategy.
- Lastly, if an investor wanted out, I could get them out without pushing down the entire portfolio. I viewed the strategy as the tabletop, and the investors as the legs of the table. A table with four legs will collapse

> if you pull one leg out. A table with 50 legs will be just as stable if you pull one leg out. I wanted many small smart investors.

The best investors for my strategy were small business owners, not institutional investors. They gravitated to my style of investing. Why? Microcaps are small businesses that just happen to be public companies. The businesses I invest in remind small business owners of the businesses they own or sold.

I was brutally honest with every investor. I tried to scare them away. "If the market goes down 30%, we'll probably be down 45%, are you okay with that?" Small business owners understand volatility more than institutionally minded investors.

I must also mention I was blessed in that I had a relatively large private and public following. I had already built a good reputation. This allowed me to be disciplined. I could have grown my assets under management much quicker, but it would have been a big mistake. The wrong investors were easily turned off by my approach, and the right investors self-selected in.

I had 25 investors join the first year. Most were small business owners or principals at private equity and venture capital firms.

In 2019, our first year, we were up 98% net.

In Q1 2020, when Covid rocked the markets, we were only down 8.95% while the iShares Micro-Cap ETF was down 32.34% and the S&P 500 was down 20%.

In 2020, we were up 92% net.

At the 2024 Berkshire Hathaway Annual Meeting Warren Buffett said, "I like being trusted." This is such a simple yet powerful statement. It feels good making yourself money, but it feels even better making money for people that trusted you.

Avoiding comparison

From the beginning, I decided not to publicly share my performance or fund letters. I wanted to manage capital like I did when I was a full-time private investor. I didn't want the extra pressure of comparison. I didn't want other investors to compare themselves to me. I also asked my investors to not share my letters.

In fact, those first two years I didn't even share my performance with prospective investors.

Why?

When investors see great performance, they chase it. They don't do the work that they should researching the manager. Every investor that came in those first two years saw no historical performance. They came in because they did a lot of work and trusted me.

Another reason I didn't share my letters publicly is I invest in a concentrated portfolio of illiquid stocks. We aren't investing in Google or Apple. I'm not going to give my best ideas to anyone for free. I feel it's disrespectful to my investors that pay me. I view my investor letters as intellectual property. If someone wants to read them, then let's have a conversation to see if we would be a good fit and make a minimum investment.

I also believed the tone and messaging of my letters would change consciously or subconsciously if the public could read my letters. I would slowly start writing like a salesman instead of a missionary. Family business is meant for the family. I want my letters to be for the family. My partners.

In 2021, 2022, and 2023 we had average to below average performance.

In 2023, we were down 21.95% while the S&P 500 was up 24.23%. We looked like idiots. It certainly tested the patience of some of my investors. I encouraged investors to add funds. I personally added more capital.

Then in 2024, we were up 54% net and looked like heroes again.

In any one- or two-year period, we could look like Tiger Woods in his prime or some amateur that shouldn't even be playing in the tournament. In reality, we are Steve Stricker. We know our strengths and our weaknesses. We aren't going to win every tournament, but we will win our fair share over our career. Steve Sticker actually won more tournaments as he grew older.

My goal is self-mastery and continuing to refine my artform. I don't compete against other investors. I'm competing against the 10-year average return of the S&P 500. I intend to crush my opponent.

If you intend to make stock picking a lifelong pursuit, you must prepare yourself to go the distance.

CHAPTER 21

Going the Distance

Great investment careers can span five years to an entire lifetime. Stock picking reputations are normally built by stepping away after a hot streak, evolving and adapting to stay in the game, or by making sure you have the duration to grind through the bad years to get to the good ones.

When a stock picker's performance is public record, it adds even more pressure to perform and the ability to go the distance becomes even more difficult. Survival is the ultimate performance measure of any stock picker, just like it is for any business.

In every sport, occupation, or endeavor you can find examples of the best of in their craft retiring at the top of their game while others kept going way past their prime. I've always enjoyed studying the greats in different areas and seeing how they navigated success.

On July 5, 1989, *Seinfeld* first premiered on NBC in the United States. It ran for nine seasons until its final episode aired on May 14, 1998. Jerry Seinfeld was offered $110 million to produce one more year. An astounding amount of money at the time that few if any would ever decline.

He said, "No."

In 2013, Jerry Seinfeld was on the *Howard Stern Show* and was asked about the decision to end the show and not reach for more:

> To be honest – the love affair with the people making the show and the audience was so intense, so white hot. I had to respect that. I could not let the show get to the point where it started to age and wither. It doesn't take long. You go see a comedian and at 60 minutes you love the guy but at 70 minutes you are like 'ehhh' and walk out with a whole different feeling. It's a small amount of 'too much,' too much cake, too much anything, and it changes the whole feeling. I wanted the show to end with 'it was never bad.' As a comedian, I have a sense for timing. I knew it was time.

Also in 1989, *The Simpsons* debuted. The animated show revolves around the Simpson family, consisting of Homer, Marge, Bart, Lisa, and Maggie, residing in the fictional town of Springfield. The show has been in production for 36 seasons.

The first nine years of the show were historic for ratings – each episode pulled in over 15 million viewers. Then it declined. And declined. Now new episodes struggle to get one million viewers. Why doesn't it get canceled? Between licensing, streaming, and merchandise sales, *The Simpsons* is still a money maker for 21st Century Fox (now Disney).

For Simpsons fans it's painful to watch its owners try to shake every last penny out of the piggy bank. With every passing bad season, you forget about the great seasons.

Greatness has a shelf life.

In 1999, at the age of 30, Barry Sanders shocked the National Football League (NFL) and fans by announcing his retirement. Despite being in the prime of his career and coming off a season where he rushed for over 2,000 yards, he decided to step away.

Barry Sanders is widely considered one of the greatest running backs in NFL history. He played his entire nine-year career for the Detroit Lions. He rushed for 15,269 yards, which ranks him third in all-time rushing yards in the NFL. He led the NFL in rushing yards four times and won the MVP in 1997.

In Sanders' autobiography, he writes, "Physically I knew I could still perform at a high level, but mentally I just wasn't as sharply focused... I lost my edge, and I wanted to stop before that started to show."

There is something beautiful about seeing an athlete retire at peak performance. It's the ultimate sign of discipline.

In the 1990s, no one sold more albums than Garth Brooks. In fact, Brooks has sold more albums than Elvis Presley and is second only to the Beatles in total album sales.

Billboard recently ranked Garth Brooks the greatest male solo artist of all time. By the late 1990s he was on top of the world. In 1999, Garth Brooks took a break from country music, and created an alter-ego for himself around a fictional pop-rock artist Chris Gaines.

Brooks even came up with a storyline and developed a movie, *The Lamb*, around Chris Gaines which was supposed to debut in 2000. He recorded a pop-rock-rap album called "Chris Gaines Greatest Hits" which was meant to build an audience for the character and gain momentum for the film.

The album hit #2 on the charts but fell flat with Brooks's core audience. The movie was never released. I don't know whether it was a God complex, boredom, subconsciously wanting to fail at something? What made him think this was a good idea?

Whether it's Michael Jordan quitting basketball to play baseball, or Garth Brooks quitting country music to do a rap album, sometimes people self-sabotage by reaching too far.

It's a balance for all of us. To grow you must reach past your limits. It's hard to know when you should risk who you are for what you can be.

Peter Lynch ran the Magellan Fund from 1977 to 1990. Under his leadership the fund delivered a compounded annual return of 29.2% compared to 15% for the S&P 500. His assets under management ballooned from $20 million to $14 billion. Lynch said:

> When the fund reached a billion, critics said it's too big, stop managing it, then $3 billion, they said get out now. In the last five years I managed the fund we beat 99% of all funds and it was the largest fund in the country. That's what I'm most proud of.

In May of 1990, Peter Lynch retired at the age of 46 and said, "One of the reasons I left Magellan was that I wanted to retire while I still had a good record. I left the party when the cake and champagne were still being served."

I love Peter Lynch. We all love Peter Lynch. Why? We never saw him decline. We never had to make excuses for him. Four years after he retired, he gave a speech at the National Press Club. He oozed wit and charisma. He looked like he could step back in the game and crush everyone. This is how we want to remember our investment heroes.

In 1985, Joel Greenblatt started a hedge fund, Gotham Capital, with $7 million, most of which was provided by "junk-bond king" Michael Milken. During his tenure at Gotham Capital, Joel Greenblatt established one of the most impressive 10-year performance records in the industry.

From 1985 to 1994, Gotham Capital produced a blistering 50% CAGR (34.4% net) return for partners. Following this extraordinary run, Greenblatt returned all the capital to his partners.

Greenblatt said of this time that he was "young enough to pursue other interests and old enough to realize what a great run we had."

He was also burned out by the run and stress of trying to beat the market while managing a larger AUM. He stepped away for a few years and wrote, *You Can Be a Stock Market Genius*, taught some classes, and then stepped back into the ring again.

It's like Roger Federer said, "If you look at the big picture, sometimes you have to step away to come back stronger."

From 1991 to 2005, Bill Miller achieved the impossible. His Legg Mason Capital Management Value Trust outperformed the S&P 500 for 15 straight years. The fund had an annualized return of 15.8%, compared with 11.9% for S&P. In 1999, Morningstar named Miller the mutual fund manager of the decade and the fund's AUM grew from $750 million to $20 billion.

From 2007 to 2011, he underperformed the S&P 500. Miller stepped down from managing the Legg Mason Capital Management Value Trust and parted ways with Legg Mason in 2016.

In 2017, Miller completed a deal to buy out Legg Mason's 50% stake in his boutique LMM LLC, and changed the name to Miller Value Partners, and managed it until 2022. He's now a billionaire.

His personal portfolio is mainly two or three massive core positions.

He was the largest individual holder of Amazon for a time. In 2014 he started to buy bitcoin at $200. He forms deep conviction and swings hard.

Howard Marks once said, "There are old investors, and there are bold investors, but there are no old bold investors." Not true. Bill Miller is 76, making bold bets. He hasn't let father time scare all of the risk out of him.

From 1986 to 2007, Robert Auer turned $100,000 into $32 million using an investment framework developed by his father. An astounding 31% CAGR over 21 years. A track record that beat most of the greatest investors ever.

In 2007, Robert Auer started the Auer Growth Fund by rolling the $32 million into a public fund. I interviewed Robert Auer back in 2012 when the fund had reached $100 million. The Auer Growth Fund has underperformed since inception.

During this underperformance they have not budged on their investing principles and strategy. They keep playing their own game. 21 years of massive outperformance followed by almost 20 years of underperformance. However, they have outperformed the last few years. In 2025, the fund was in the top 1% in the category and had a 5-star Morningstar rating. I'm rooting for them. They are good people.

How does Jerry Seinfeld know when to say no to one more episode?

How does Barry Sanders know when to say no to one more season?

How does Peter Lynch know when to say no to one more year?

Discipline is having the strength to say no to a lot of money.

Jerry Seinfeld knew the show's "white hot" intensity wasn't sustainable. Barry Sanders knew that NFL running backs have a shelf life father time catches up slowly and then all at once. His legacy meant more to him than his bank account. No one worked harder than Peter Lynch. How else do you stay on top of 1,000 stocks in the portfolio? He burned out. Warren Buffett started out with a high-turnover cigar-butt strategy and ended as a longer-term quality-focused investor. The latter allowed him to play the game for a lifetime.

If you love to invest and pick stocks like me, you want to be Peter Lynch, but if you want to go the distance you must evolve, build a team, or both.

For me this means leaning into my strengths and using technology, tools, or people to fill in my weaknesses.

For me this means prioritizing my investing and my family and saying no to a lot of distractions.

For me this means embracing an imbalanced life at times, but setting up boundaries, so I don't lose the people I love the most.

Albert Pujols retired in 2022 and is considered one of the greatest hitters in Major League Baseball (MLB) history.

He played 22 seasons, and his career statistics are impressive: .296 batting average, 3,384 hits, 703 home runs, 2,218 RBIs and 1,914 runs scored.

Pujols had a distinguished career that straddled two distinct phases.

From 2001–2011 he played for the St. Louis Cardinals. Pujols put up blistering offensive numbers, hitting .328, 445 homers, and 1,329 RBIs. He won three MVP awards and two World Series titles.

From 2012–2022, Albert Pujols' played for the Los Angeles Dodgers, and finished his career with the St. Louis Cardinals. During the second half of his career, he had six seasons where he hit below .250, the league average.

In fact, from 2017– 2021, Pujols OPS+ was 13% worse than the league's average hitter. What made matters worse was Albert Pujols was a great human being. He deserved to go out better than this. It's painful to see immortals become mortal on a grand stage.

Most of us remember the story of Samson.

Samson, a biblical figure from the Book of Judges, was gifted with extraordinary strength. He performed great feats like killing a lion with his bare hands and slaying a thousand Philistines with a donkey's jawbone.

He fell in love with Delilah who found out the secret to his strength. While Samson was sleeping Delilah cut his hair which depleted his strength. The Philistines were able to capture him and gouged out his eyes.

Soon after, at a party, the Philistines brought Samson out to mock him. They stood him between two pillars and bound him in chains.

Samson prayed to the Lord, "Please, God, strengthen me just once more."

God granted him strength one more time. Samson pushed with all his might and down came the temple on the rulers and all the people in it.

Fans were excited when Albert Pujols announced the 2022 season would be his last. Everyone was sick of seeing him decline.

But then something happened.

In his final 51 games, Albert Pujols batted .313, hit 15 home runs, and had some of the best offensive numbers of his career.

Pujols was given his strength one last time.

It's the way we all deserve to leave the game.

If you plan to go the distance. You must become unbreakable.

CHAPTER 22

Unbreakable

In rising markets, it's easy to nonchalantly talk about risk, patience, and the conviction to hold through volatility. In rising markets, the stock market's job is to make you forget about valuation.

But you will eventually be tested.

There will come a period when something you have high conviction in quickly drops 40%, 50%, or 60% due to internal or macro forces. You will question your conviction, your strategy, your process. In falling markets, the stock market's job is to find your breaking point.

This will be your test.

Few things test your conviction like falling stock prices.

Successful investing is hard work because it means disciplining your mind to do the opposite of human nature. Buying during a panic, selling during euphoria, and holding on when you are bored and crave action.

It takes strength. It takes courage. You must be a rock. You must be unbreakable.

Stock picking is a serious game with serious consequences. When I was a full-time private investor supporting my family, I couldn't ever be broken. Now that I run a fund with 70 partners it is even more important.

Unbreakable in market drawdowns

Since 1950, the average drawdown in the S&P 500 has been 14% in a calendar year, and 10% drawdowns of at least 10% have occurred in 37 of the past 75 years.

20%+ corrections have occurred in 11 out of the past 75 years.

30%+ corrections have occurred in four of the past 75 years.

You never know when the big corrections are coming because it's the surprise factor that breaks the market. This is when the big money is made. The greatest opportunity is always at the depths of uncertainty. You get one or two of these big opportunities per decade.

I'm old enough to have invested through three 30%+ drawdowns: the dot-com crash, Global Financial Crisis, and Covid pandemic. I'm lucky in that I'm still young enough to take advantage of the lessons learned.

Whenever you experience a drawdown it feels like an outlier event, when in reality the outlier is not having a drawdown every couple of years. When you haven't had a correction in a few years investors forget what they feel like and overreact when the next one occurs.

In early 2020, the markets were collapsing due to the Covid pandemic. In hindsight we realize it wasn't that bad. But in the moment, investors, governments, and markets were losing their minds.

From February 19, 2020 to March 23, 2020 the S&P 500 fell 34%.

On March 18, Bill Ackman came on CNBC to say, "hell was coming" and the US needed to seal off the border to protect the population.

No one was talking positively about stock prices. When you see the best investors in the world throw in the towel you know the bottom is close. There were so many investors sitting on 50–75% cash waiting and hoping for the world to get even worse. Warren Buffett was no different. He waited to see how things would turn out.

In early March, I started to post on social media to help people gain some clarity. Here are some of my posts:

March 12: "This is becoming an incredible opportunity for anyone that has more than a one-year time horizon."

March 14: "Stop trying to pick the bottom. You just have to buy a little as it drops and not worry about looking wrong in the short term. You'll be right in the long term."

March 16: "It can happen over days, weeks, or months during drawdowns. Investors sell the weakest positions first. Then they sell whatever is doing best/hasn't fallen yet. Then they concentrate into higher risk plays to make money back. Then they are broke. Don't do it."

March 17: "The worst part of bear markets is people trying to pick bottoms instead of slowly nibbling on the stocks they've always wanted to buy."

March 18: "Investors love to look for new opportunities when times are good. But the best times are when most investors are too afraid to look."

On March 20, two days after Ackman's famous "hell is coming" tirade, I felt we were close to a bottom and posted:

> What you do over the next few months will likely decide the next five to 10 years of returns. Everyone looks back and wants a shot at buying in 2008–09. You might get it now. Do you have the stomach for it?

The post was shared thousands of times. 90% of the replies were negative. It's interesting to go back and read the comments. Investors screamed at me that I didn't understand how bad things were going to get.

March 23 was the low in the market.

Everyone says they are ready for a correction. Some even say they want a correction. Very few will have the stomach or the cash to follow through on their intentions and buy when others are selling.

Drawdowns can last for weeks, months, quarters, even years. The longer a drawdown, the more painful they become. Market drawdowns are a cascade because investors sell stocks that are down 5% to buy more of the stocks down 10%. They do this again and again until everything is down and there is nothing left to sell.

I can't help but laugh during drawdowns when investors constantly post, write, scream about the great buys they are seeing – obviously all of these ideas are positions they are down in.

It reminds me of a time I messaged my mentor Skip during the panic of 2008–2009 and he responded, "Stop showing me stuff to buy. I have plenty of stuff to buy. I need something to sell."

When the market moves higher it makes you want to buy. When it moves lower it makes you want to sell. The market never screams at you to do the right thing, only the wrong thing.

In significant corrections, the market turns even great investors into average ones. What saves great investors is they can find cash quicker than you.

What is the worst-case scenario?

We hit a market environment like 2008. The stock market drops 50% and your stocks are probably down 60%. This was the scenario for 90% of professional investors at that time.

At that moment, what can you control? You can't control stock prices. The answer is cash. Drawdowns are a reminder that cash is a position.

If your portfolio was down significantly but you had cash to deploy, how bad would it be? Half as bad. A quarter as bad. It wouldn't be that bad, right? Drawdowns are only bad if you can't take advantage of them.

When you have cash during a drawdown you hope it drops. When you don't have cash, you pray it stops. You must find the right balance.

I don't believe in holding a large cash position.

In bull markets, everyone tries to become long-term investors. In bear markets everyone turns into macro strategists, geopolitical experts, and market timers.

The larger your cash position becomes the more you become a market timer instead of a stock picker. You are trying to time a drawdown.

Peter Lynch famously stated, "Far more money has been lost by investors in preparing for corrections, or anticipating corrections, than has been lost in the corrections themselves."

When you sit on a significant cash position it's easy to become too bearish. I witnessed this during the Covid drawdown of 2020. Investors let their large cash position and negativity control them. They only look for confirming evidence that supports their belief the world is getting worse.

Trying to time a market bottom is a mistake. The stock market usually bottoms before earnings bottom. During Covid, S&P earnings bottomed 13 months after the stock market bottomed.

Too large a cash position clouds your judgment. You wake up hoping the markets crash, and your negativity paralyzes your common sense. Instead of timing a bottom, you should be slowly adding to the businesses you love.

If you invest in small stocks that aren't broadly owned by institutions and ETFs, your portfolio can zig when the markets zag. During the one-month Covid drawdown, one of my positions went up 300% and my strategy was only down single digits when many were down 20–50%. Small stocks surprise you in good and bad ways.

The amount of cash you hold is a function of your temperament and strategy. I like to only hold enough cash to buy half of a new position and then be forced to sell an existing position to buy the other half. It forces me to sell my weakest convictions to add new convictions.

If you can deploy even a small amount of capital during a market drawdown it can be a life saver. The ability to at least feel like you took advantage of lower prices even in a small way can't be overstated. I hold enough cash to safeguard my emotions.

When you have cash, you have confidence. When you don't have cash, you are just like everybody else.

Every so often the market throws us a gut punch we didn't see coming. Don't panic. Don't lay down in the fetal position. Stand up, step into the fear and lead your portfolio. It takes strength. It takes courage. You must be a rock. You must be unbreakable.

Unbreakable when your stocks drop

Most declines in my portfolio occurred outside of general market corrections. The decline was triggered by an earnings miss, negative event, or simply a large seller.

At least once per year I'll wake up to a position trading down 30% pre-market. I never know when it will happen. I always imagine some large holder wakes up grumpy and decides today will be the day to sell their entire position in an illiquid stock as quickly as possible.

I always wonder what sparks this rage-filled seller. Did they wake up on the wrong side of the bed? Was it a nightmare about the stock? Did the seller find out the CEO flirted with his wife at a cocktail party?

Did the seller get back from a meditative retreat where they became enlightened? Do they hate me personally?

Fat finger sellers always sell in the worst possible way. They decide to hit some bids in pre-market trading. Indiscriminate pre-market selling scares all the longs.

Longs are thinking:

Is the company about to announce a dilutive equity raise?

Did they lose a large customer?

Is the annual report delayed due to accounting irregularities?

Did a newsletter or fund put out a short report?

The market freezes. Everyone becomes paralyzed thinking the same thing, "someone knows something."

By the time the regular session opens for trading there is no bid support. The bid–ask spread is a mile wide and Level 2 market depth looks literally like Level 2 – only two levels of support to zero.

While pointing at yourself in the mirror you say some positive words of affirmation, "I'm a professional stock picker. I'm knowledgeable. I can do this."

You swallow the throw up in your mouth.

You place a buy order below the market hoping it doesn't get hit. Ten seconds later your order gets hit. As you stare at the executed trade notification, you throw up in your mouth again. "Well, I don't need breakfast."

The opportunity presents itself for seconds, minutes, hours, or maybe days. While most investors freeze, you are decisive. You buy the pain. The only reason you can find the courage is because you did the work others didn't do and you trust management.

Ninety-nine percent of the time you must be a stoic investor. The other 1% you must be a savage.

Then the madness stops. The stock recovers. Everyone that wasn't buying near the lows now starts to buy 30% off the lows so they can tell themselves they bought the dip even though they didn't really buy the dip.

The art of catching falling knives is determining whether the stock crash is business or non-business related. If it is non-business related you buy. If it is business related you don't buy or maybe even sell.

Microcap stocks become more illiquid the longer the duration of the drawdown. Why? Because the long-term holders run out of money or conviction to buy lower.

It isn't a drawdown until you start hesitating to buy something you believe in at a lower price. You loved it 20% lower, but not 50%. When you are down 50%, doubt starts to creep in. You start thinking, "Let me see how this shakes out first."

If you loved buying stocks 30%, 50%, or 100% higher and now you hesitate when the price is lower, you didn't know what you owned in the first place.

Nonetheless, when you are down 50% you can't handle being any more wrong than you feel at that moment. That feeling of complete mental and emotional exhaustion – that is the low in the stock.

This was written in 1930:

> The day you sell is reasonably certain to mark the end of the decline, because you are not the only one who was finally scared into selling. You, being an average man, were merely representative.
>
> **– Fred Kelly**

My largest positions are the management teams I trust the most. To be unbreakable you must know what you own and trust what you own at all times.

But it's also a function of valuation.

Instead of making your largest stock position the one you think can go up 500% in the next six months, your largest position should be the one where you can't lose over the next few years. Ironically, often it's the latter where you find the next multi-bagger.

Most investors are fragile. When you apply pressure to an object that is fragile it shatters. I believe the best investors are antifragile. They become stronger under pressure and stress.

Great stock pickers weren't born this way, but their lives and philosophies were built on a solid foundation that wouldn't crack under pressure. They cared little for public opinion. They learned from mistakes and drew strength from every success.

Mr. Market could never connect with a knock-out punch because the investor wouldn't stand still long enough. They were always learning, moving, and evolving. Their resources accumulated as the result of prudence, patience, and occasional aggression when the odds were in their favor.

They were decisive. They were fearless. They were unbreakable.

I've been a stock picker for over 20 years. It doesn't matter your flavor of stock picking. I've learned that we are all fighting the same battles.

CHAPTER 23

We Are All Fighting the Same Battles

In 1951, at the age of 21, Warren Buffett put 53% of his portfolio into GEICO and wrote up his thesis in *The Commercial and Financial Chronicle.*

Buffett would make a quick 50% return in a year – turning $10,282 ($122,000 in today's dollars) into $15,259 ($180,000). Not bad for a young 20-something.

He sold GEICO and put the proceeds into a cheaper stock. This was part of a five-year run where Buffett would average ~50% annual returns, growing his capital 10x and breaking the $100,000 mark, equivalent to $1.2 million today.

I think about this story quite often. Not the GEICO part. Not the big bet and concentration part. Not the first million part. I think about Buffett writing up GEICO and publishing an article after he bought a position. Even the Oracle of Omaha talked up his book. He is the same as us.

Whether it's in social gatherings, presentations, blogs, social media, MicroCapClub, or 1950s newspapers, we stock pickers love to talk our book.

Our stock positions and convictions are like our children. We must promote them. We feel it's our duty to be the change agent that unmasks a wonderful opportunity to the world.

We must help nudge, push, force the stock price closer to our estimate of intrinsic value.

We prefer to have tomorrow's gains today and not wait around for time to prove us right.

As we accumulate a position, we curse the stock for moving higher, and as soon as we are done acquiring the position, we curse the stock for not immediately moving higher.

It's humorous because we all still say, "I am a long-term investor."

We are all long-term investors that prefer our gains come as quickly as possible.

We do exhaustive research and analysis to find that one company where we can form a one to three-year variant view. We take a position and wait. When the stock doesn't move for six months, we start questioning everything.

But we are long-term investors.

Holding winners is difficult because you keep looking back at your cost basis instead of looking forward at the business. When you are standing on top of Mount Everest all you can see is what is beneath you. Your cost basis, naysayers, emotions are all screaming at you to sell.

But we are long-term investors.

Microcap management teams that execute are rare. We spend 95% of our time looking for any excuse to sell our winners instead of selling our losers. Capital flows to the management teams that are proven to be good stewards, and yet the investors that find them first are also the first to leave.

But we are long-term investors.

We love to trade in our positions. Add a little bit here and sell a little bit there and, in the end, we conclude we would have been better off focusing on making fewer bolder decisions instead of a hundred smaller ones. We love to think that activity equals productivity. We hate being bored.

But we are long-term investors.

We do a ton of work identifying a wish list of businesses we would buy if they were cheaper. The stock market finally has a correction, and we hesitate. We sit on our hands analyzing macro data, trying to pick a bottom. In an instant the market turns and we join the crowd paying up for positions again.

But we are long-term investors.

When a microcap stock moves against us in the short term, we like to blame management. Management isn't telling the story correctly. Why hasn't the investor relations page been updated with the latest investor presentation? Why aren't insiders buying? Normally nothing fundamental has changed. The stock is down 20% because someone decided to sell $50k worth of stock to pay for a wedding, tuition, any number of reasons. Short-term volatility in life, business, and markets brings out who we really are and our true convictions. Apply a little pressure and our façade crumbles.

But we are long-term investors.

We see a CEO sell some stock after the stock appreciates 200%-500%-5000%. We get alarmed and start questioning them. We forget they have children in college. We forget they have new memories they want to make with their kids and grandkids with a new boat or lake house. We forget that winning as we go and being able to enjoy life makes us more productive, not less productive. We investors forget that we would also sell if we were in their shoes.

But we are long-term investors.

The investor that worries about "next quarter" will sell at any sign of imperfection. Since no company is perfect, it means we always sell winners too soon. More importantly, it's a bad sign whenever you start worrying about "the next quarter" because it proves you don't have enough conviction to look past "the next quarter."

But we are long-term investors.

As longer-term stock pickers, we are all faced with these situations hundreds if not thousands of times. What has helped me is being self-aware of my own emotional and psychological delusions.

Human nature can be hilarious. We love to do the wrong thing at the wrong time. Sometimes I just sit back and laugh at what I'm feeling. Over time the thing that has changed is how I react to what I'm feeling.

It's often how you react to the same situations that show you how much you've grown.

The irony is even if you knew the future it wouldn't help you.

What if you knew in early 2022 that the United States Federal Reserve was going to raise interest rates 11 times in a row? The cost of capital was about to skyrocket.

What if you knew in early 2022 that the United States 30-year fixed mortgage rate was going to rise from 2.8% to 7.3%?

Before the rise of interest rates, 35% of US households could afford a $450,000 home. 18 months later 20% of US households can afford a $450,000 home.

What if you knew in early 2022 that Russia was going to invade Ukraine and disrupt energy and fertilizer markets?

If you knew these three things were going to occur, how would you position yourself?

Short home builders, short technology, short consumer discretionary, long energy, long fertilizer.

What would have happened?

Over the next 18 months, the largest residential home builder in the United States, D.R. Horton, went up 5%. The Nasdaq went down 12%. Consumer discretionary stocks were down 15%. Oil went down 18%. Fertilizer prices went down 25%.

You knew the future and you only got two out of five right.

Even if you knew the future, you would still be mostly wrong.

Even. If. You. Knew.

In Chris Mayer's book, *How Do You Know?*, he gives another great example from an article written by O'Higgins Asset Management:

> Suppose that on January 31, 2006, you knew with certainty that the price of gold would more than triple over the next five years,

> from $569 per ounce to $1,900 per ounce. Knowing that, might you have invested in Newmont Mining, the world's second-largest gold producer? Odds are high that you would have gladly bought Newmont Shares. With that kind of surge in the price of gold, buying in one of the world's largest gold companies would seem like a no-brainer. Yet, the share price of Newmont fell 5% over that time.

O'Higgins gave another example: "Suppose that at the start of 1973 you knew that the earnings of the Dow Jones Industrial Average would rise 50% over the next two years. Seems you would bet on the Dow, right? Well, the Dow was cut in half."

If I told you there was a country whose GDP would rise 500% over the next 17 years and the country had a liquid stock market where you could participate, what would you do?

Not only would you buy this stock market, but you would over allocate to this stock market.

From 2007–2024, China's GDP rose 500%. The main stock market in China was down 35%.

From 2007–2024, United States GDP rose 75%. The S&P 500 was up 440%.

Investing is hard.

When Covid hit in early 2020, I quickly sold off the one stock in my portfolio I knew could be crippled by restrictions.

I sold a company called ClearPoint Neuro (CLPT) at $4.00 per share. It pained me to sell it. I had just met the CEO in New York City. I admired the company, the CEO, and the important role they were playing in advancing gene therapies.

I was right. The business was hampered, but I was wrong on the stock. The stock closed 2020 at $16.00 per share, up 300%.

The only stock I sold during Covid was the one that went up the most. My reasoning was right, but the result was all wrong.

Isn't playing the short-term macro game such madness?

The way you handle the macro is to handle the micro. Find companies that can grow, earn more money, and not dilute you. Buy them at good prices and wait. The returns will come to you. Don't get distracted by how the macro winds are blowing.

Even if you knew the future, it wouldn't help you.

The encouraging thing is we are all fighting the same battles. Riding a winner, deciding if you should hold it. Holding a loser, deciding if you should sell it. Sticking with a stock that has gone nowhere for quarters or years questioning your thesis. You aren't alone.

The main reason stock picking can feel so isolating is your short-term and long-term report card is staring at you in the face.

The mind games are real. Investing is 5% intellect and 95% temperament. It's a test of how well you can sit quietly when your emotions are screaming at you to do the wrong thing.

When stocks go up, all you see is the upside. When stocks go down, all you see is the downside.

Winning blinds you to risk. Losing blinds you to opportunity because you are focused on surviving today.

Holding losers is easier than holding winners. Why? Because losers always look cheap.

Holding winners is hard in small stocks. Why? The moves can be fleeting. The shelf lives shorter.

At your highs, you double down on what was working last year at peak valuation or chase into a new area where you lack competence.

At your lows, you keep averaging down into your losers or sell stocks that aren't working to buy into hot stocks at highs only to get cut in half again.

Stock picking can be polarizing because we all invest differently, and our wins and losses come at different times. This can bring out the worst in people. Certain personality types can't stand seeing other stock pickers make money in ways they don't agree with. The financial media loves to throw gasoline on the fire.

Every day is a reminder to play your own game. Focus on your own game or the stock market will take aim at you next. It loves to destroy egos. There is a reason the best investors are the quietest. The best investors keep their heads down.

A good rule of thumb is to be quieter than you want to be. Don't give people a reason to root against you. It's an asset when people can't tell whether you are winning or losing.

You see it most vividly in how we treat those closest to us.

How often do you let your portfolio direction dictate your mood? I know I've been guilty of this.

If I had a good week: "Family, we are going out for steak tonight!"

If I had a bad week: "Family, here is a pack of saltine crackers to split amongst yourselves."

How much precious time has been stolen from you even after the markets closed for the day? You are thinking about the markets instead of living in the present with your family.

The worst part of investing is wishing time goes faster so you can get to your returns quicker only to be disappointed when you get there that you didn't fully live in the present with the time you had. Live in the present. No one that loves you cares about your returns.

I am guilty of all of this and more. We are all fighting the same battles.

Every year you get better at dealing with these situations and emotions. Every year you realize it isn't about predicting, but preparing. Every year you realize you aren't getting that year back so focus on what is important.

Every year we must grow and guard our self-confidence.

CHAPTER 24

Self-Confidence

In 1831, William Kirkpatrick agreed to compensate a 22-year-old Abraham Lincoln to move some saw logs.

Kirkpatrick refused to give Lincoln the equipment he needed, but Lincoln still completed the job. Kirkpatrick then paid Lincoln $2 less than the agreed upon rate. This was $75 less in today's dollars. Kirkpatrick stiffed him.

A few months later Governor Reynolds of Illinois called for volunteers to join a militia against a Native American named Black Hawk.

Black Hawk was a Sauk leader who led raiding and war parties. The Sauk and Fox tribes ceded their lands in 1828 and were relocated west of the Mississippi river to the newly formed Iowa Indian Territory.

In 1832, Black Hawk became frustrated and moved 1,500 of his people back to Illinois, which sparked local militia groups to band together to force Black Hawk back to the Iowa territory.

Among the companies that responded was one from Menard County, Illinois. Abraham Lincoln was still seeking work and doing odd jobs, so he was the first to enlist, and it didn't take long for the quota of men to be met.

An election was held among the company for who was to be the captain. A few men wanted Lincoln.

Lincoln didn't want the leadership position but finally consented to be a candidate.

The only other candidate was William Kirkpatrick, the man who previously mistreated Lincoln, and who was one of the most influential men in the area.

The election process was simple. Lincoln stood on one side of the room and Kirkpatrick stood on the other side. Each man in the company was to choose their leader by standing beside either Lincoln or Kirkpatrick.

Immediately, 75% of the men stood beside Lincoln. When it was obvious Lincoln was going to win, the few standing next to Kirkpatrick left him, and stood next to Lincoln.

Kirkpatrick was left all alone. Lincoln the wronged laborer was now his ex-employer's captain.

Later in life, Abraham Lincoln said no other success during his entire lifetime had given him half the satisfaction he felt that day.

The early self-confidence he gained would power him through the next round of struggles. In fact, later in 1832 Lincoln lost his first political race for Illinois State Legislature.

Many people say early success is a horrible thing because it gives you misguided confidence in your abilities. I disagree.

I often think about how lucky I was that my first experience in the stock market was a big win. It didn't matter that it was 100% luck. It didn't matter that I mistook a bull market for brains. The experience gave me self-confidence.

The early win proved to me "I can do this," and that's all that mattered.

If my first investing experience was a big loss instead of a big win, I would have likely moved on to some other money-making endeavor – worked for my family business, started my own business, or started a career.

But I did have a big win.

A couple years later, when the dot-com bubble burst, I lost 90% of my money. This loss didn't destroy me because I still had self-confidence. Why? I made money before. I knew it could be done. It didn't occur to me that it couldn't be done again. I eventually made the money back.

Abraham Lincoln was 7-5 in elections during his career. Seven wins and five losses. His last two elections were wins in 1860 and 1864 for the President of the United States.

An election is a popularity contest. How crushing it must be to lose. Your entire state or even country chooses the other person over you. Everyone knows you were the loser. An election loss must crush your self-confidence.

In 1858, Lincoln lost in a Senate race against Stephen Douglas. This was only two years before his historical presidential win.

In a letter to a friend after the loss, Lincoln expressed determination rather than discouragement:

> The fight must go on. The cause of civil liberty must not be surrendered at the end of one, or even one hundred defeats.

Battle scars

The longer you pick stocks, the more wins and losses you accumulate. Battle scars start to form.

In stock picking your biggest opponent is you. You look for reasons to sell because the stock isn't moving. You buy something else. The thing you sold immediately goes up. Then you realize you are just like everybody else.

Nothing screws with your head more than watching something you used to own outperform the things you own. It's the stocks you used to own that could have and should have changed your life. They haunt your soul.

Have you ever bought and held a stock and made 100-500-1000%+? When you look back at the win you realize the catalyst that propelled the stock wasn't even part of your thesis. The win was all luck. You start wondering, "Am I good or am I lucky?"

Have you ever bought and held a stock and made 100-500-1000%+? The win was 10 years ago. If you went back in time with today's wisdom you would never buy that stock. You realize how much you've grown. You start questioning yourself, "Am I evolving in good ways or bad ways?"

Have you ever bought a stock too early? You hold it for a year and nothing happens. Investing is hard because in the moment we don't know if holding is patience or stupidity. Sometimes being too early is the same thing as being wrong.

Have you ever been 100% convicted in a position that goes nowhere for years? The business tracks "close enough" to your thesis to keep you invested. The stock acts like a piece of driftwood in the ocean. It has no direction – floating around between -30% and +30% from your cost basis. Sometimes the most painful positions aren't the ones that go down but the ones that go nowhere.

Have you ever bought a stock and held on too long? Let's wait another quarter. Those "wait another quarter" stocks can drive you insane. You hope the business inflects. You hope the business accelerates. You hope they sign the partnership management keeps alluding to on earnings calls and private conversations. You hope they get the financing done.

In the meantime, you accumulate so much meaningless knowledge on the business trying to justify holding that it becomes your prison. You can't let the position go. You can't move on. You want to be right so bad. Being right becomes more important than making money.

Have you ever bought and held a stock and you find out later the CEO lied to you or embellished the truth? You thought you knew them. You thought they were better than that. It's painful when trust is broken. It makes it harder to trust the next one.

Have you ever built a position in a stock and, as soon as you buy your full position, the stock drops? You paid full price right before the stock went on sale. It's frustrating seeing new investors getting a better price than you. These new investors did half the work you did and now they are getting the stock half off. They don't deserve it. You held on when no one else would. You deserve to gain the most for what you've been through.

Have you ever bought a stock and then told the world about it? You attach your name to it. You write about it. You tweet about it. In fact, that stock becomes your identity. It's like the symbol is tattooed on your forehead. Worse yet, you tell friends and family. Then the thesis changes, the stock drops, and you feel humiliated. You lose money, but worse yet, people you care about lose money. You don't even want to go to the next family gathering.

Battle scars.

As stock pickers you will accumulate battle scars. Especially in microcap and smallcap stocks where the spectrum of outcomes are wider and more violent. The more battle scars you accumulate, the more courage gets scared out of you. You hesitate instead of acting instinctively.

Research has shown that negative events impact us more than positive ones. Negative emotions generally involve more thinking, and the information is processed more thoroughly than positive ones. In addition, bad events wear off more slowly than good ones.

Daniel Kahneman and Amos Tversky first coined this phenomenon as loss aversion. You are more upset about losing $100 than you are happy about gaining $100. In fact, in many cases you are two to three times more upset about losing $100 than you are happy about gaining $100. We then go out of our way to avoid negative events and outcomes, even if there is a greater probability of a positive outcome.

In *Moneyball*, author Michael Lewis chronicles the life of Billy Beane, a Major League Baseball General Manager of the Oakland Athletics. Beane utilized sabermetric principles to run the financially strapped team in an extremely effective way. Prior to his general manager career, Billy Beane was a professional baseball player.

In 1980, Billy Beane was drafted in the first round by the Mets. Beane looked like Mr. Baseball. He was 6 foot 4 inches tall and perceived as having an extreme amount of talent. He never lived up to the hype, hitting just .219 with three homers in 301 at bats across eight seasons.

Here is a highly entertaining excerpt where Billy Beane compares himself to teammate Lenny Dykstra and why he (Billy) failed as a baseball player:

> Physically, Lenny didn't belong in the same league with him. He was half Billy's size and had a fraction of Billy's promise – which is why the Mets hadn't drafted him until the 13th round. Mentally, Lenny was superior, which was odd, considering Lenny wasn't what you'd call a student of the game. Billy remembers sitting with Lenny in a Mets dugout watching the opposing pitcher warm up. Lenny says, 'So who's that big dumb ass out there on the hill?'

> And I say, 'Lenny, you're kidding me, right? That's Steve Carlton. He's maybe the greatest left-hander in the history of the game.' Lenny says, 'Oh, yeah! I knew that!' He sits there for a minute and says, 'So, what's he got?' and I say, 'Lenny, come on. Steve Carlton. He's got heat and also maybe the nastiest slider ever.' And Lenny sits there for a while longer as if he's taking that in. Finally, he just says, 'Shit, I'll stick him.' I'm sitting here thinking, that's a magazine cover out there on the hill and all Lenny can think is that he'll stick him.'
>
> The point about Lenny, at least to Billy, was clear: Lenny didn't let his mind screw him up. The physical gifts required to play pro ball were, in some ways, less extraordinary than the mental ones. Only a psychological freak could approach a 100mph fastball aimed not all that far from his head with total confidence.
>
> 'Lenny was so perfectly designed, emotionally, to play the game of baseball,' said Billy. 'He was able to instantly forget any failure and draw strength from every success. He had no concept of failure. And he had no idea where he was. And I was the opposite.'

I've come across a lot of investors whose past battle scars and experiences knocked them out of the game. They weren't necessarily knocked out financially, but they were knocked out mentally.

I love this statement from investor Marc Cohodes:

> I've been doing this since 1982. When you go at it that long – you're like Nolan Ryan. You set the record for wins. You set the record for losses. You set the record for strikeouts. You set the record for walks because you've been doing it so damn long.

I've been picking stocks for over 20 years, and the wins and losses keep piling up. The older I get, the better I get at forgetting the losers and drawing strength from my winners. I'm extremely self-confident. When I had three below average years at my fund, I had zero doubt I would bounce back.

In the final year of Roger Federer's playing career, he said:

"It is always in my mind that I can still crush anybody. That's not an issue. If you don't believe you can win tournaments anymore, then you can't do it."

Stock picking is a game of self-confidence. Whether you win or lose today, you must know with 110% confidence that another big win is right around the corner.

In the book, *Golf Is Not a Game of Perfect*, Dr. Bob Rotella tells the story of Stuart Anderson.

Anderson was professional football player that attended one of Dr. Rotella's seminars on building confidence in athletics. Dr. Rotella asked Stuart to tell the class about a time he was confident.

Stuart thought for a minute and told a story about when he played high school basketball. He was a 50% shooter, and his team was in the state playoffs.

He had the worst night of shooting in his whole career – 20 missed shots in a row.

The team kept it close, and it came down to the last play of the game. Stuart asked to take the last shot of the game. He made that final shot and his team won.

After he told the story to the class, a student in the class asked, "How did you stay confident after you missed all those shots?"

Stuart replied, "I've always been a 50% shooter. After I missed one, I figured the next one would go in. After I missed two, I was overdue. By the time I missed five, I figured the next one absolutely had to drop. Every time I missed, I figured the odds were increasing in my favor."

The student replied to Stuart, "Okay, if that's how you think when you miss your first shots, what do you think if you make your first six or seven in a row?"

"That's totally different," Stuart said. "You decide that tonight's your night, and you're on a hot streak, and you're going to make everything you look at."

"That's ridiculous," the student said. "You can't have it both ways."

"Of course you can," Stuart said.

Stuart Anderson properly illustrated a winner's mentality. Every failure was reframed in his mind as one step closer to success. Whether it's sports or investing, 90% of success is determined by your mental approach to the game.

Self-confidence is built on the bedrock of skill, which is a topic for the next section of this book. If your confidence isn't built on self-mastery and skill building, your results will start to unravel under stress.

SECTION 4

The Skills of a Stock Picker

CHAPTER 25

The Skills

John Danaher is arguably the best Brazilian jiu-jitsu (BJJ) and mixed martial arts instructor in the world. He is a sixth-degree black belt in BJJ. He's coached some of the best athletes in the sport, including Georges St-Pierre, considered the greatest mixed martial artist of all time, and Gordon Ryan, who is considered the greatest submission grappler of all time.

John Danaher grew up in New Zealand. His father was an Air Force pilot. Danaher was born with deformed patellas, making him prone to knee injuries throughout his early years. He had multiple surgeries on his legs that left one leg slightly shorter than the other. But his physical issues didn't stop him from learning Muay Thai and karate when he was young.

Danaher was always a cerebral human being. He enjoyed thinking about thinking. He received his bachelor's degree in philosophy and then received his master's in philosophy. In 1991 he came to the United States to pursue his PhD in Philosophy at Columbia University in New York City.

While studying at Columbia, he became obsessed with weightlifting. He was only 5 foot 9 inches but was 240 pounds of solid muscle. He knew some Muay Thai and could defend himself, so he made extra money in the evenings as a bouncer at a night club.

Danaher's life mission changed one evening on the floor of his apartment. His roommate, who was 60 pounds lighter, challenged him to a wrestling match. The first man to tap out loses. Danaher was defeated in less than a minute. He had never been beaten so effortlessly. He was stunned.

He asked his roommate where he trained and it was at a new gym called the Renzo Gracie Academy in New York City. The next day Danaher walked into the Gracie Academy and later devoted his life to the mastery of BJJ.

Today, Danaher is called the Einstein of BJJ because of how deeply he thinks about combat, innovation, and finding new ways for his students to dominate their opponents. Listening to Danaher is like listening to Warren Buffett, Charlie Munger, or anyone that is considered a GOAT (Greatest of all Time) in their chosen field.

Danaher is a multi-disciplinary learner and educator that just happens to focus all his mental horsepower on martial arts. He has studied relentlessly all fighting styles. He even studies fighting tactics of animals.

In an interview Danaher was asked, "In a fight between a gorilla, a lion, and a bear, who wins?"

His answer is 37 minutes long and has received two million views on YouTube.

Danaher cites research and academic studies. He talks about the hunting patterns of each animal. The aggression and behavioral tendencies of each animal. The bite force, stamina, and fighting experience that each animal faces in the wild.

Danaher talks about why a lion is the most ferocious and how male lions fight to the death for the right to lead their pride. When two male lions fight it doesn't end until one of them dies. They aren't just fighting for their own lives, but the lives of their sons.

The winning male lion will also kill the male offspring of the losing lion, and so when two male lions fight, they are fighting for their entire bloodline.

Half of all male lions will die in their first year of life because their fathers lost a fight. This is why male lions fight with such fury.

You think the question is a joke, but you are stunned when Danaher delivers a serious answer. Danaher didn't know this question was coming. The only reason he could answer so fluently and effortlessly is because he already did deep research into each animal so he could be a better coach to his students.

Isn't this what a master does? They think so deeply about their craft and study areas that others would only laugh at. They are extremely curious human beings that can find inspiration anywhere and can go 10 miles deep into any topic or skill related to their craft.

From 1969–1978, John Madden was the head football coach for the Oakland Raiders. In nine seasons, the Raiders made the playoffs eight times, won seven division titles, and won a Super Bowl. Madden still holds the highest winning percentage among NFL head coaches who have coached more than 100 games.

John Madden wasn't always fanatical about coaching. From 1964–1966, he was an assistant coach at San Diego State. He found out that Vince Lombardi was giving a coaching clinic in Reno, Nevada. Lombardi was in peak form. At this time, Lombardi had won two NFL championships with the Green Bay Packers. Madden said he spent all his savings to go to this coaching clinic.

"I went up there and Vince Lombardi spoke on one play for eight hours. One play. Eight hours. I couldn't speak on any subject for more than two minutes. I realized at that moment I didn't know a damn thing. I was a phony. My knowledge was just surface knowledge. I knew nothing about the game of football."

This experience changed John Madden's life forever and he started truly studying the game and he became fanatical about football.

Frank Perdue took Perdue Farms from a single chicken farm to one of the largest chicken producers and brands in the world. Frank died in 2005, and Frank's widow Mitzi Perdue wrote a great book about her late husband, *Tough Man, Tender Chicken: Business and Life Lessons from Frank Perdue*.

When Sean Iddings and I were writing our books on intelligent fanatics, we reached out to Mitzi Perdue and we had an enlightening conversation. Frank Perdue was the Sam Walton of chicken. He had the rare combination of attention to detail today and vision for the future tomorrow. He was a man that thought 10 levels deeper than the competition.

Mitzi said people often asked Frank how he became so successful. She told us he first told people he was in the right place at the right time. If someone pushed him further he would say it was the great people he had around him. On a few occasions when someone wasn't satisfied with these two answers, Frank would point to a picture framed up on the wall with a quote from Alexander Hamilton.

> Men give me credit for some genius. All the genius I have lies in this; when I have a subject in hand, I study it profoundly. Day and night, it is before me. My mind becomes pervaded with it. Then the effort that I have made is what people are pleased to call the fruit of genius. It is the fruit of labor and thought.

Whether it's John Danaher, Vince Lombardi, Sam Walton, or Frank Perdue, the greats study the game they are playing at levels that are miles below the surface of the competition.

When you hear John Danaher provide an articulate answer to a ridiculous question about bears, gorillas, and lions, you know he's probably thought even deeper about more applicable questions.

In an interview John Danaher was asked, "How do you become the best in the world at what you do?"

He replied, "Any sport or profession has five or six core skills that are necessary to participate. To be the best in the world you must be good at all the skills, and best in the world in at least one, preferably two, of those skills."

A talent is a gift or strength you were born with. A skill is a strength that can be developed.

This got me thinking: What are the skills of stock picking?

Stock picking is the active management of a portfolio of individual stocks. Whether you're an individual investor or professional investor, whether your portfolio consists of five or 200 stocks – stock picking means YOU are making the buy, hold, and sell decisions.

There are hundreds of variations of stock picking. From day trading to coffee canning. From fundamental to technical analysis. From market generalists to industry focused. From deep value to hyper growth. From shorting to long only to activism. In the end, I don't think it matters.

I believe there are five universal skills to stock picking:

1. **Identifying** – Finding actionable ideas before others and the pursuit of active patience.
2. **Analyzing** – Due diligence and valuation.
3. **Buying** – Sizing your conviction.
4. **Selling** – Limiting losses and capturing gains.
5. **Holding** – Maintenance due diligence.

Each skill is unique. A stock picker might be exceptional at identifying, but the curiosity, energy, and drive to discover something new doesn't always translate into being good at the other skills. When Columbus first discovered America he wasn't also the best person to set up trade routes and infrastructure – these were separate distinct skills and so is each skill of stock picking.

Conviction is the lifeblood of a stock picker and it flows through each one of the skills of stock picking.

Conviction means doing independent research to form an independent view on a business.

Every multi-bagger journey is filled with the corpses of loud opinionated naysayers. You must do the work, so you know what and when to buy. You must do the work, so you know when to sell before others. You must do the work, so you can hold longer than others. You must do your own work, so you can stand alone in your conviction.

In the following chapters we will review each skill and then outline what it takes to be good, great, or even a GOAT stock picker.

CHAPTER 26

IDENTIFYING
Finding Ideas Before Others

When Robert Ballard found the *Titanic* in 1985, he was officially on a classified military project to find the wrecks of two sunken nuclear submarines, the USS *Thresher*, and the USS *Scorpion*.

Ballard had long been fascinated by the *Titanic* and its mysterious fate since it sank in the North Atlantic Ocean in 1912. He had previously led an expedition in 1977 to find the ship, but came up empty handed.

Apart from his interest in the *Titanic*, Ballard was also heavily involved in underwater robotics and deep-sea exploration technology. The military agreed to fund one of his projects. Ballard designed the *Argo*, a 16-foot (5-meter) submersible sled that could be towed by a ship at depths of 20,000 feet. The sled was equipped with a remote-controlled camera that could transmit live images back to the ship.

Ballard made an agreement with the US Navy that if he successfully completed his primary mission of locating the two submarines early, he could use the remaining time and resources to search for the *Titanic*. After completing the submarine surveys, Ballard had 12 days to find the *Titanic*. It took eight days.

On September 1, 1985, after a week of searching the seafloor, the team's persistence paid off. The *Argo* camera captured the first images of the *Titanic*'s boiler, a key piece of debris from the wreck, lying on the ocean floor about 12,500 feet (3,800 meters) below the surface. At these depths the water is 1–2 Centigrade (34–36 Fahrenheit) with low light, and low oxygen. The water acts as a time capsule. This initial finding was quickly followed by more discoveries, including large sections of the ship and a vast debris field.

We can picture Ballard and the crew on the ship in celebration watching the live video feed. First the boiler. A few minutes later they see china plates and cutlery. A few minutes later a child's leather shoe. At that moment the excitement starts to fade.

Ballard described the emotional impact of the find: "When I first saw the *Titanic* through the porthole, the impact was overwhelming. It took my breath away. Then, in the next moment, I realized that what I was seeing was also a grave site. It was a very sobering moment."

Just a few years earlier, Texas oilman Jack Grimm backstopped the expense of three expeditions to find the *Titanic* with no success. Later it was found the sonar used in his 1980 expedition passed right over the *Titanic* but didn't detect it. He was so close.

When we are kids, we are amazed by everything, and as we age, we are amazed by nothing. Today as adults we read this story and think to ourselves, "What took so long?" We forget that only 5% of the world's oceans have been explored and how difficult it is to find something two miles underwater in the pitch black.

It took 72 years of studying, searching, talking to past search parties, and the invention of new technologies, to find the *Titanic*. It also took the funding of a separate, unrelated exhibition to lead to the discovery of the *Titanic*. The search for one thing led to finding another.

I often think about this story and the parallels with stock picking.

After 20+ years in the game, it's still exhilarating to stumble upon a new opportunity that makes me stop everything I'm doing – those "clear the calendar" moments that happen a couple times per year. The thrill of discovery. There is no greater high in the world.

Identifying and finding ideas before others is one of the five core skills of a stock picker.

The common element in every great stock picker is relentless curiosity and persistence. A stock picker must use all the tools at their disposal to find actionable ideas before others.

Sometimes it's serendipity, luck, or fate that lead you to find something great, but even then, it's the result of a consistently applied search plan.

How do you find actionable stock ideas in an ocean of stocks?

There are 60,000 public companies worldwide and half are microcaps.

Microcaps are small companies with little to no analyst coverage. They aren't being spoon-fed and sold to you by the Wall Street (United States), Bay Street (Canada), the Square Mile (United Kingdom), and Dalal Street (India) financial machines. You must leave the comfort of the crowd and go find them.

Where do you start? It can be overwhelming unless you know what you are looking for.

What flavor of investor are you? Are you deep value, GARP, inflection, special situation, hypergrowth, momentum, short-term, macro, technical analyst? Perhaps you are a combination of a bunch of things?

Depending on the type of investor you are and what you are looking for will determine how you find opportunities.

I find actionable ideas like a spider builds a web. A spider can't catch a fly by singling out one fly. It makes a web and waits. It's the same for finding ideas.

You must build out your web through brute force, screening, researching, networking, and relationships. You must be diligent in maintaining your web and keeping it free of debris so you can feel the tremor. It might be once every two years or 10 times per year, but eventually something will hit your web, and you will feel the vibration. Then you go see what you caught.

I've found there are three main ways you find ideas and two ways ideas find you.

Here are the ways you find ideas.

How to find ideas

Brute force: *the only way you know you aren't missing something is to look at everything.*

A big advantage can be the fact that you are willing to sift through a mountain of sand to find a small diamond. Your willingness to look at hundreds of uninvestable ideas to find one. This will put you in the top 5% in finding ideas. Many say they do it, but most don't.

I regularly go through the list of companies on the London AIM. This means going A through Z on 1,100 stocks. You can't just do it once. You must do it every year. I also do this once per year on the OTC markets here in the United States. It takes a lot of work, but the more you do it the better you get at deselection. If you know what you are looking for, it only takes a few seconds per company. You might be left with 20 out of 1,100 that are worthy of additional time.

How many times have you looked at a stock that went up 100%, 500% or 1000% and went back to see when the first clues were visible that it was something special? The clues are usually found in a press release, transcript, filing, or insider transaction.

Set up key word searches. Perhaps it's a PR headline or verbiage in the body that states "record results," "accretive acquisition," "record backlog," or any number of things that alert us to a transformation.

Set up insider buy screens, or simply review all press releases for all companies under a certain market cap.

Every great opportunity left us clues before it showed up in the financials and propelled the stock.

Are you willing to do the work?

Screens: *narrowing down the investment universe based on what you value.*

Screening is a tradeoff between being specific and being comprehensive. Specific screens are screening for fundamental criteria. For example, I want to screen all stocks on United States and Canadian exchanges, sub $100 million market cap, TTM revenues >$10 million, growing >20%, insider ownership >20%, and ROE > 20%.

Initial universe 23,698 stocks; output after this screen = three stocks.

Is this useful? Not really.

Every other microcap investor is doing this exact same screen. I also don't find screening for specific attributes like ROE to be helpful. When you do so you're screening for the perfect company. Often an opportunity is an opportunity because the business isn't perfect yet.

Given my flavor of investing, I'm more interested in comprehensive screens and event-driven screens.

An example might be screening by market cap (sub $100 million) and TTM Net Income > 0.

Initial universe 23,698 stocks; output after this screen = 1,294 stocks.

Is this useful? Yes, you aren't screening for perfection. It's going to give you a lot more companies to sift through, but you will potentially find some interesting situations that others would have screened out.

Examples of event-driven screens are screening for rights offerings, management changes, or insider buys over $100,000. In this screen you are looking for substantial skin in the game and transformations.

Technical analysis is also a way stock pickers screen for stocks and identify trends and shifts in investor psychology.

Researching: *company and industry research leads to finding ideas.*

Robert Ballard discovered the *Titanic* because he was searching for something else. When you consistently do the work, great things happen in life, business, and stocks. The seeds you plant today analyzing companies and industries is what bears fruit today, tomorrow, and in the years and decades ahead. Your ongoing initial diligence and maintenance due diligence in one company can compound into discovering other opportunities that are even better.

And now here are the ways ideas find you.

How ideas find you

Networking: *proactively engaging with others.*

Successful microcap investors are independent thinkers, but they also share ideas and reciprocate with other investors they trust.

When I was getting started in the early 2000s, most microcap discussion and networking occurred on public stock message boards. Over time many of these public forums died off and the conversations shifted to private forums like MicroCapClub or blogs, reddit, X, Substacks and other places. You supercharge the power of serendipity by sharing your ideas.

As you build out your network you start to form relationships, and those relationships will become your biggest asset as a stock picker.

Relationships: *the greatest asset of a stock picker.*

As I mentioned earlier in the book, as you mature as a stock picker your relationships become your greatest assets. These relationships will be with investors, CEOs, industry experts, and others you've built over years and decades through reciprocity. It's the gold plating on your reputation.

This is when opportunities find you. Investors and operators want you involved because they see the value add in having you as a shareholder. The absolute pinnacle of this is, "You're the first call."

Over time you realize finding ideas before others often means finding ideas with others. Stock picking isn't a zero-sum game.

Your flavor of investing will influence how you find them, but every stock picker finds ideas in these five core ways.

As you develop into a stock picker, you will fine tune your idea generation and identification process. The key is applying it consistently.

Finding ideas before others is a skill you develop over years and decades. You find mastery with this skill when you achieve active patience.

CHAPTER 27

IDENTIFYING
Active Patience

The longer I invest, the more I realize you get one or two great opportunities every few years. The rest of the time is spent wondering if you will ever get another great opportunity again and convincing yourself to own mediocre opportunities while you wait. Mediocrity is the price you pay for impatience.

Great investors develop active patience.

Active patience means knowing what you are looking for and doing nothing until you find it.

I mentioned active patience to Anthony Deden and he responded:

> Active patience, yes. Think of an art collector wishing to add to his collection. He mostly sits around reading auction catalogs.

His comment reminded me of this great quote by memorabilia collector Darren Rovell:

> I want to be in a market where a specific collectible hasn't sold for three years but there are 11 people total in the world who want it and I know I can name my price.

Active patience is not an inborn ability or skill. It is developed over years and decades in the following stages:

1. **Developing Your Temperament** – Finding out who you are.
2. **Finding Your Principles** – Finding out what you believe.
3. **Committing to Your Principles** – Living out what you believe.

Many investors never find out who they are. Even fewer figure out what they believe. Only a select few live out what they believe.

Let's look at each of these in turn.

Developing your temperament

Temperament means developing your views on risk, time horizons, volatility, position sizing, and value. It means determining what flavor of investing aligns with your natural inclinations so you can apply it consistently and successfully over time.

Your temperament is first formed by how you were raised, your relationships, your circumstances, and your life experiences. They shape how you view the world.

I often think about how formative the first few investment decisions are in an investment journey. Whether your first investments were big wins or losses. The outcomes can send you up or down the risk tree permanently. They shape who you are.

If you took risk and won in your early years like I did, even if you suffered big losses later like I did, you likely feel more comfortable taking risk today because you already proved to yourself it could be done.

The opposite is also true.

If you took risk in your early years and lost, you likely have spent more time thinking about protecting yourself from ever feeling that way again.

The feedback loops with investing are long. Developing your temperament and determining the type of investor you are takes time and reps. It takes loss. It takes overreaching in risk, position sizing, trusting management, and many other factors. You must push yourself to find your limits.

You must live through, trade through, and invest through many scenarios and circumstances to understand how you will react.

You must experience the emotional highs and lows of greed and despair, several times, before you know how, and in what ways, to exploit these emotions in others for your own benefit.

Investing is 5% intellect and 95% temperament. It means finding the strategy that will allow you to sit quietly when your emotions are screaming at you to do the wrong thing.

Only after you develop your temperament and figure out who you are, can you find your principles.

Finding your principles

Anthony Deden also once told me, "Ian you aren't a microcap investor. You invest with a certain set of principles."

Principles are what guide us. They are what make us unique.

It took me 15 years to develop my business principles around scarcity, survival, tailwinds, and discovery.

It took 15 years of investing with different types of leaders, founders, CEOs – speaking with them regularly, having dinner with them, truly knowing them – until I started seeing patterns in personality and character.

Your principles are the qualities of a business that are mandatory. Principles allow you to say no to entire swaths of the investment universe.

Your principles are the qualities of men and women that are mandatory in someone you can partner with and trust. Your principles allow you to say no to certain types of people.

Principles allow you to say "Yes" very quickly because you know what you are looking for. Sometimes within 10 minutes you know this company is the one.

Principles allow you to sell in an instant when trust is broken in a business or person.

I've found over the years that value is completely subjective. Your principles are the things YOU find valuable. They are the must haves that are necessary for you to buy and hold an investment.

You can't expect others to completely understand your principles. It's how you can be in a room with 100 successful investors and each person is horrified at the next person's best idea. It's how you can be in a room with 100 investors that own the same stock, and each investor is holding for slightly different reasons. Your principles are your uniqueness.

It takes time and reps to find your principles.

It took Buffett two decades to go from deep value to quality.

It took Nick Sleep and Qais Zakaria almost a decade to go from "we will go anywhere in the world to find deep value" to only investing in business models that represented scale economics shared.

It took Reece Duca at IGSB two decades to develop the expertise and insight to only invest in vertical software companies. Reece said in an interview:

> The first decade, we would look at and invest in all kinds of industries and all kinds of models within the industry. And I would say with hindsight, that was good, because it gave us an understanding of how things worked in manufacturing and how they worked in retail and how they worked in oil and gas, and... But what happens is you're not an expert in anything. In fact, your knowledge is pretty superficial of any particular model. And as I would say today is the single most important thing in determining whether a company is an exceptional company or not is going to be their business model.
>
> By the time we got to the end of the second decade, we were focusing on essentially software companies. And over the next two decades, we essentially went from the combination of looking at consumer software companies and businesses software companies, basically to business B2B companies, then SaaS-based companies, then – we didn't distinguish between horizontal and vertical SaaS, but then we focused more on vertical SaaS than we did horizontal SaaS. And one of the byproducts of that was that we really developed expertise in how these models work.

Every investment you make ends up teaching you something about yourself. You can't rush it.

Pastor T. D. Jakes put it so beautifully:

Many people cannot find success because they lack the patience to go through the process to become who they want to be.

It takes time to find out who you are and what you believe. After you find your principles, you must commit to them.

Committing to your principles

> Until one is committed, there is hesitancy, the chance to draw back, always ineffectiveness. Concerning all acts of initiative and creation, there is one elementary truth the ignorance of which kills countless ideas and splendid plans: that the moment one definitely commits oneself, then providence moves too. All sorts of things occur to help one that would never otherwise have occurred.
>
> **– William Hutchison Murray**

You are the happiest when you are the most focused. You are the unhappiest when you are the most distracted.

If you want to be miserable, be halfway committed to things.

Halfway committed to your business, halfway committed to your spouse, halfway committed to your faith, halfway committed to your kids, halfway committed to your process, halfway committed to your principles.

The world wants us to believe "halfway committed" is freedom of choice. You are simply keeping your options open – the ability to change course. It seems more productive to have multiple options. It's quite the opposite.

Halfway committed is misery because no one ever sees your full potential, least of all you.

Total commitment is freedom. Total commitment is happiness. Once you find your principles, you must fully commit to them. Anything less is a waste of time.

Distractions come in many different forms.

The shiny new ideas that tantalize us but are missing our core principles for investment. The mind games our emotions (greed, fear, boredom) play on us, making us sell positions or buy new ones that we shouldn't. The opinions and criticisms we internalize from investors that haven't done the work. Distractions are anything that causes us to lose focus.

Discipline means having the strength to say no to the thousands of things that distract you.

Courage means having the strength to say yes to the few things that matter.

Commitment means having unwavering confidence in yourself and your principles.

I'm a Christian, but I enjoy learning about other faiths. Swami Vivekananda was an Indian Hindu monk, philosopher, and social reformer. He is best known for bringing Hinduism to the West and raising interfaith awareness.

Vivekananda traveled to the United States in 1893 to give talks at the World's Parliament of Religions in Chicago. He was a popular speaker and presented Hinduism as a scientific and universal religion. His talks led to the spread of Hindu spiritual ideas and yoga in the West.

Vivekananda promoted the notion of *daridra narayana seva* which means "serving the poor is the same as serving God." He believed that reducing human suffering was essential to spiritual practice. In 1896, he published a book called *Karma Yoga*. Here is a beautiful passage:

> Take up one idea. Make that one idea your life; dream of it; think of it; live on that idea. Let the brain, the body, muscles, nerves, every part of your body be full of that idea, and just leave every other idea alone. This is the way to success, and this is the way great spiritual giants are produced. Others are mere talking machines. If we really want to work, we must get rid of this idea of nothingness. We are but tools in the hands of the Lord, and what can tools do without Him? How can we accomplish anything if we lack the constant presence of the Almighty?

No matter your faith or occupation, it's hard to disagree with this passage. There are many takeaways, but one is that great achievements come from great sacrifice and concentration of effort. Ordinary results come from aimless distraction and talking without action. Great things occur through commitment.

I love this quote from Hall of Fame professional golfer Raymond Floyd:

> Patience means knowing that your practice and hard work will pay off, and understanding that improvement often comes from plateaus rather than at a steady rate.
>
> A scorer is patient because he has faith in himself and in his approach. A golfer who believes in himself doesn't panic or lose his composure when things go wrong. He calmly rights the ship, bears down, and waits for things to go his way. Jack Nicklaus has often been admired for his patience on the golf course, and it's no coincidence that no player I've ever seen has believed in himself more than Jack.
>
> The kind of confidence doesn't just happen. But to develop patience, it's important to have a plan for yourself that you believe in – whether it's for the way you want to swing or the strategy you want to employ. If you're truly committed to your plan you won't abandon it so easily when things go badly - especially if you accept that there will be shots and holes and rounds when things go badly. When you believe in your plan and believe in your ability to carry it out, patience is your ally.

Patience is an asset for those that know it's only a matter of time.

The longer you commit to your principles, the more you naturally set up your life, network, and habits to find ideas for you.

It might be months or maybe even years depending on your strategy before you find something new and actionable, but you remain confident because you know what you are looking for.

Charlie Munger famously said:

> If you took our top 15 decisions out, we'd have a pretty average

> record. It wasn't hyperactivity, but a hell of a lot of patience. You stuck to your principles and when opportunities came along, you pounced on them with vigor.

When you fully understand active patience, you become an art collector. You see your portfolio as a collection of prized assets. Your intention with every purchase is to never sell unless your principles are broken, or you get your price.

Most new ideas can be quickly discarded within one to 10 minutes of surface due diligence. But the inversion of this is also true. A few times per year you will know within a few minutes you found something special. Then you clear your schedule and dive into due diligence.

CHAPTER 28

ANALYZING

Due Diligence

In 2025, Toomas Laarits and Jeffrey Wurgler, two New York University Stern School of Business professors, published a study on individual investors and the amount of time spent on stock research. They collected data from 484 households using web scraping tools to analyze 2,911 stock trading decisions. They studied eight million clicks and 60,000 hours of internet use.

The results were alarming but at the same time unsurprising to those of us that are students of the markets and investor psychology.

They found the median individual investor spends six minutes on research prior to placing a trade. The mean was a little better at 30 minutes. Individual investors spent most of this time reviewing short-term stock charts followed by analyst recommendations.

The study also showed that market cap explained 19% of the variation of the breadth of research interest across stocks. A one-standard deviation increase in log market cap from $775 million market cap to $5.4 billion doubles the percentage of investors conducting some research. Put simply, the smaller the company, the less research that was done.

This makes logical sense since smaller stocks have less third-party reports and analyst recommendations. Microcap investors don't have the crutch of analyst coverage to lean on. You can't rely on others. The astute microcap investor must do the work that professional analysts do, and more.

The two schools of stock analysis

Several years ago, John Huber from Saber Capital Management wrote an article on quantitative analysis versus qualitative analysis. He outlined the two schools of analysis – quantitative analysis and qualitative analysis – as follows:

Quantitative analysis

- Analyzing income statements, balance sheets, cash flows.
- Comparing current valuations with historical valuations.
- Comparing valuations and company financials with other companies in the same industry.
- Rarely talk to company management.
- Studies the stock, but not the company (not overly concerned with the company's products or services).
- Doesn't rely on anything other than publicly available data.
- Doesn't put much weight on the industry or sector, nor the trends of those sectors.
- Doesn't rely on macro-economic trends or overall top-down analysis.
- Usually run diversified portfolios since they don't analyze each company in depth.

Qualitative analysis

- Talking to management.
- Relies on "scuttlebutt": i.e., talking with a company's competitors, vendors, and distributors to gain legal information that others might not have.
- Analyzing in depth the company's products or services.
- Determining the capability of the company's management.

- Determining the competitive advantages a company has or doesn't have.
- Making judgments on the prospects for the industry or general line of business the company is in (sustainable, growing, etc.).
- Often concentrates the portfolio in a select few positions that have been thoroughly researched.

Quantitative analysis is surface due diligence. This information is readily available, like SEC filings, financial statements, industry reports, and press releases. Being good at conducting surface diligence is table stakes – the starting point.

Most stock pickers start as value investors. They dive into stock picking after taking their first accounting course. Next, they read *Security Analysis* by Ben Graham, and they start screening for cheap stocks.

After several years they realize most cheap stocks stay cheap, so they transition to a GARP (growth at a reasonable price) style which means looking for cheap stocks that could evolve into growth stocks. When a stock picker makes this transition, they start down the path of qualitative analysis.

Qualitative analysis is below the surface due diligence. Ninety-five percent of variant perception is found looking below the surface. The search for exclusive public information. It takes time and effort. It can be expensive. It can be uncomfortable. This is the informational edge.

Here is a story that will help solidify the importance of qualitative analysis.

The importance of proper qualitative analysis

In the weeks following the September 11th attacks there was immense political pressure "to do something." Pete Blaber was part of a special forces unit that was the first to touch down in the Persian Gulf to prepare for retaliation in Afghanistan.

The order from the top was simple. Find something to attack – a terrorist training camp, some tanks, Osama bin Laden's house, anything. The US government had to make a statement.

The best they could find was an old airfield in the middle of the desert and an abandoned house of one of the Taliban leaders.

To reach these empty targets they would have to go through or around the city of Kandahar, which was known as the "ring of fire." Satellite imagery showed enemy tanks were positioned around the city. It was also believed the city was protected by rockets, missile launchers, anti-aircraft guns and thousands of capable Taliban soldiers.

In addition, it was assumed the Afghan people were helping and supporting Al Qaeda and Taliban forces. Winter was approaching in Afghanistan, which added to the rush to do something before it got too cold for ground movement.

To make matters worse, the newly constructed mobile US military base was stationed on a small desert island and the only way to reach these empty targets were large CH-47 helicopters. It was an eight-hour journey (1,000 miles) to the targets.

This would be the longest wartime helicopter mission in history. The problem with the CH-47 is that it is loud, and the enemy can literally hear them coming from miles away. The mission sounded like insanity – especially given the targets were duds.

Blaber and his team were dumbfounded. He said: "For my comrades and me in the Unit, we were beginning to understand a stark new reality concerning our role in the global war against terrorists. Instead of rolling up our sleeves, immersing ourselves in the mission, and developing out of the box concepts and ideas for our country's most sensitive missions, we now found ourselves on the receiving end of the massive military decision-making hierarchy."

Blaber was frustrated. Other units were frustrated. They decided to come together to formulate a plan and do real work into the situation.

The goal was to convince headquarters to drop the empty target plan. Instead of relying simply on satellite imagery, they needed on-the-ground input from Afghans and input from someone who understood Al Qaeda. Blaber knew he wasn't going to find the answers sitting inside a tent.

He said, "I had to take action to make action."

Blaber and the other units started reading everything they could find about Afghanistan and the current situation. He reached out to some old friends that used to be high ranking officials in the government, asking if they knew of anyone stateside with local knowledge of the situation in Afghanistan.

One of Blaber's contacts replied that he had some Afghan American friends he met with weekly at an Afghan restaurant just outside of Washington D.C. One of these friends was an ex-Afghan general who had fought against the Soviets in the mid 1980s.

Pete spoke to the old general over satellite phone the next day.

This is what he learned:

1. There were tanks surrounding the city but "very few, if any, were operational." In fact, most of the advanced technologies they thought the enemy had they didn't. Al Qaeda wasn't preparing defenses around the city.
2. The Afghan locals hated Al Qaeda.
3. The "harsh Afghan winter" averages mid-30s Fahrenheit; not exactly harsh.

Blaber explained, "Slowly but surely, a different picture was beginning to form for me and my comrades as we accrued more and more on-the-ground information. We began to challenge everything we thought we knew about the reality of the situation on the ground in Afghanistan.

"Back in D.C both the secretary of defense and the president were expressing well-earned frustration with the dearth of intelligence being fed to them from a trillion dollars' worth of space-age intelligence technology. Ironically just a few miles away from the White House, across the Potomac River in Virginia, there were men sitting around a table in an Afghan restaurant who had better, and more accurate, intelligence."

When Blaber and others presented their findings to senior officers they were immediately dismissed. No one wanted to listen to the truth. The helicopter mission moved forward. The empty targets were destroyed.

The parallels with investing

When I heard this story, I couldn't help but see parallels with investing. We love to come to quick conclusions by analyzing what is on the surface like satellite imagery. But reality is more nuanced. Sometimes what is easily seen is meant to distract us. All investors can see what is on the surface. Only 1% are willing to dig below the surface to find the truth.

Here are four things we can learn from Blaber when doing reconnaissance into a business:

Read everything – When you are analyzing a company, competition, and industry, read everything. But you must also realize this is what everyone else is doing. Don't fool yourself into thinking you know what is happening on the ground by reading secondary sources instead of talking to primary sources.

Utilize your network – We like to lie to ourselves by thinking, "I don't want to talk to other investors about my ideas because I don't want them to know what I'm looking at." We would rather be first and naïve than second and educated. It makes no sense. Don't be afraid to ask your network, "Does anyone know anything about company XYZ?" We underestimate the power of our networks.

Talk to people on the ground, but not just one – Talking to on-the-ground experts is incredibly important. The rise of expert networks is making this easier for stock pickers, but don't be afraid to reach out to individuals. When you are locating an expert or paying a firm to do this for you it's important you are finding the right expert. Your goal is to find experts with direct knowledge of an industry in addition to decades of tacit knowledge that can only be expressed through long, in-person meetings.

Not all "experts" are created equal. Some experts come into the conversation with certain motivations. For example, ex-employees or previous management might be negatively biased towards their former employer. In addition, if an expert is being paid by an expert network it's in their best interest to talk to you and look important. You must be able to spot these biases. When you talk to experts it's important to talk to five or more.

In-person interviews are an order of magnitude better than phone or video interviews. Ninety-five percent of investors don't do interviews. Ninety-nine point nine percent don't do in-person interviews. If you do what other investors aren't doing you will get the returns you seek.

Get on the ground – Visit companies. Don't let the fact you are a retail investor stop you. Go with a few other investors that have deep knowledge of the company. Make the effort to get on the ground yourself and talk to people. You can only pick up on the nuances, subtleties, emotion, and body language in person. Most investors won't make the effort to do this, so this is a real difference maker.

I'm reminded of this great quote by pastor Craig Groeschel: "It's often the small things no one sees that result in the big things everyone wants."

Pete Blaber concludes, "Until we get on-the-ground input, we should expect that most of what we think we know will likely turn out to be incorrect or incomplete. This mindset allows us to maintain our most prized freedom, the freedom of choice to change our minds and liberate our thinking from the commonsense blocking emotions of pride and hubris."

I can't tell you how many times I thought one thing about a business, and then after talking to management, I realized I was completely wrong. One conversation unearthed a differential insight that gave me a variant perception which led to a multi-bagger outcome.

Don't be lazy. Don't be like everyone else.

In 2016, portfolio manager Paul Lountzis gave a wonderful presentation on his qualitative research process at our MicroCapClub Summit. Lountzis outlined his framework for drilling 10 miles deep into a company to find differential insights. When asked why most investors don't do the work that he does, he explained, "Most investors either don't concentrate enough and hold too many stocks to devote the time, or they don't hold stocks long enough to warrant the time and investment."

He is correct. Most professional money managers aren't trying to be right; they are trying not to look wrong. They default to diversification instead of extreme focus and knowing a few positions better than most.

Fred C. Kelly was an amateur psychologist, writer, traveler, and even worked as a special agent for the FBI. Kelly was also a trader and active market participant in the late 1920s. In 1930, he wrote a book called,

Why You Win or Lose: The Psychology of Speculation, and in it he sums up this topic perfectly:

> Another group, and it is a large group, who should stay away from Wall Street, is made up of those who expect the good things in life to come too easily and therefore are unwilling to put forth proper effort to find out which stocks are good. Only a few of us are naturally so lazy that we are willing to study and work desperately hard at times, in the hope of working less hard later on. I have often gone on a long railroad journey to investigate a corporation whose stock I am thinking of buying. Anybody with a reporter's instincts, and plenty of curiosity, can keep asking questions until he satisfies himself that a thing is good, or not quite so good.
>
> But most people are not willing to go to all this bother and prefer simply to accept the advice of a stranger sitting alongside of them in a broker's office. Indeed, I know of only one kind of commitment that people make with less investigation than when they buy stocks, and that is when they get married. A man who would spend an hour shopping for a shirt, may select a stock or a wife after only the most casual inquiry. Likewise, the same person who would seek expert advice before investing $10,000 in a home, will invest that much in a stock of an unknown corporation as readily as he would buy a collar button. The type of person who is bored with the idea of having to look before he leaps should let the stock market stay right where it is.

If you want above-average returns, you must do what average investors aren't willing to do. You must gain perspectives that average investors aren't willing to gain because it's just too hard, too uncomfortable, and takes too much time. It's far easier to sit in an office and crunch numbers than it is to get on a phone or plane and talk to people. If you aren't willing to do so, then don't complain about being average.

The longer you dig into a company the more you will look for confirming evidence that supports a buy decision. It's important to stay anchored to reality, and that reality is valuation matters. A solid foundation for any new investment is a low valuation.

CHAPTER 29

ANALYZING
Valuation

In 1970, Lawrence See, the oldest son of See's Candies founder Charles A. See, died at the age of 57. By 1972, the See family was looking to sell the business for $30 million to pay off substantial death taxes.

Robert Flaherty, an investor in Blue Chip Stamps, found out See's was for sale. He told William Ramsey, an executive at Blue Chip Stamps. At the time, Berkshire Hathaway owned 19% of Blue Chip Stamps. Ramsey did some due diligence into See's and concluded he should show the idea to Warren Buffett and spoke to him over the phone.

"The candy business?" Buffett initially responded skeptically. "I don't think we want to be in the candy business."

Ramsey followed up by sending Buffett the financials on the company.

In 1972, See's Candies generated approximately $30 million in revenue and less than $5 million in pre-tax earnings, with net tangible assets around $8 million. The $30 million sale price represented a multiple of roughly 13 times after-tax earnings and almost four times net tangible assets, a valuation considered high for Buffett at the time.

But after studying the financials, Buffett changed his tone. "Yeah, I'd be willing to buy See's at a price."

Buffett and Munger offered $25 million. This was still well over 10 times after-tax earnings. Buffett was used to paying 3x earnings for businesses and stocks.

Why did he stretch so far for a candy business?

See's is considered a turning point in Buffett's investment philosophy, marking a shift towards valuing businesses with strong intangible assets.

Buffett, heavily influenced by Munger, believed See's offered operating leverage through pricing power. If they could raise the price of a box of candy from $1.96 to $2.25 earnings would increase by $4.8 million.

See's accepted Berkshire's $25 million counteroffer. Over the next decade the number of See's stores and volume grew by 2–4%, while Buffett raised the price 11% per year. Buffett and Munger looked below the surface and saw the potential of a wonderful business. They were right.

In the 2007 Berkshire Hathaway letter, Buffett stated, "Last year See's sales were $383 million, and pre-tax profits were $82 million. The capital now required to run the business is $40 million. This means we have had to reinvest only $32 million since 1972 to handle the modest physical growth and somewhat immodest financial growth of the business. In the meantime, pre-tax earnings have totaled $1.35 billion. All of that, except for the $32 million, has been sent to Berkshire."

Gary Mishuris, CIO at Silver Ring Value Partners, did an analysis of Berkshire's acquisition of See's Candies. He concluded that from 1972 to 2007 See's Candies produced a 20% internal rate of return (IRR) for Berkshire. A phenomenal outcome.

This outcome only occurred because Berkshire purchased See's for a fair price. If Berkshire stretched and paid 25x earnings, the IRR would have dropped from 20% to 12%. A good but not great return.

The lesson is the price you pay matters even when purchasing a wonderful business.

Look down before you look up

All successful investors have two things in common. They are extremely disciplined, and they understand the downside of their investments even more than the upside.

They look down before they look up.

"Look down before you look up" is a phrase articulated by Steven Scruggs, portfolio manager at FPA Queens Road Smallcap Value Fund. The phrase is so brilliantly simple, and I wish I had said it first.

Of course, other famous investors have said similar things in different ways. Warren Buffett said, "Investing is all about protecting your downside. The upside will take care of itself," and "Price is my due diligence."

Most investors forget about valuation in bull markets. All they see is more upside to justify paying up.

At the time of writing, the S&P 500 trades at 25 times earnings and I can feel the Ben Graham value investors nodding your heads in unison. Perhaps even shaking their fists towards the heavens as they've watched the magnificent seven, artificial intelligence stocks, bitcoin, and sh!tcos outperform the last several years.

Nothing is more toxic than watching other investors outperform you in things you don't like or believe in.

But valuation is like a great balance sheet – eventually it matters.

In 1999, Microsoft (MSFT) hit a high of $58 per share. It took 17 years to surpass that high even while revenues grew from $19 billion to $90 billion, and EPS grew from $0.71 to $2.56.

But it's actually much worse than this.

If you bought MSFT at $58 in 1999, it would have taken you 21 years to get back to even with the S&P 500 return. Twenty-one years!

Here is another example.

From 1999–2024, Costco (COST) grew revenues from $32 billion to $254 billion, and net income from $630 million to $7.4 billion. Costco's stock was up 2100% (13.2% CAGR) over this period compared to 609% for the S&P 500.

Costco's price to earnings ratio was 20–25 in the 2000s, 25–35 in the 2010s, and 35–45 in the early 2020s. In early 2025, Costco was trading at 61 times earnings.

I think even Charlie Munger would agree the valuation is a little rich. The crowd loves Costco. It's a crowded trade.

If Costco's PE ratio re-rated back to 40 times earnings, a more reasonable valuation, it would take five years for Costco's stock to get back to the current stock price. Five years!

In extreme cases, even a great business can't save you from a bad entry price.

Multiple expansion is a beautiful thing when you buy before the multiple expands.

No one wants to wait five, 17 or 21 years to be right. You don't want this. Your investors don't want this. Your spouse doesn't want this.

It's better to buy companies before the multiple expands. Before they are discovered by institutions. Before they are priced for perfection.

By the time everyone calls it a great business the exceptional returns are usually in the rearview. The time to buy is when a company is misunderstood, undiscovered, and underappreciated.

You want to find uncrowded trades.

Your entry price matters. Valuation matters. It's why valuation is one of the five core skills of stock picking.

When you buy at a low valuation it provides a better base to grow from. You don't need as much to go right to make money.

If you want to find good businesses trading at low multiples you will be focused on unknown or unloved stocks. The intersection of unknown and unloved is microcap.

The next big winner is a company that is quietly executing under the radar that most investors don't know about or believe in.

Many misinterpret investing in microcaps as risky. It can be if you don't care about valuation and profitability. Eighty-seven percent of 10-baggers in global equity markets started as microcaps and were profitable.

Multi-bagger investing would be best described as getting a good entry price on a small business that can consistently grow revenues and earnings with limited dilution.

Depending on the industry, businesses are valued on one of the following ratios: enterprise value to sales, price to earnings, enterprise value to EBITDA, price to book, or some variant of each.

To find a 10-bagger, first find a stock that can double in three years with conservative fundamental assumptions and no multiple expansion.

What is the key to this?

For a stock to double in three years, you need 25% annual organic growth in the denominator of the valuation metric used, with little dilution.

Let me give you two examples.

Example 1

Company X is a consumer products company. They make industry-leading food products in a small but growing product category. In this area companies trade between 1–4 EV/sales. The higher the organic growth rate, the higher multiple. If the company is at EBITDA breakeven or better, it is additive to the multiple.

- Company X is organically growing sales 25%.
- Company X is cash flow positive.
- Company X is confident the current growth rate will continue.
- Company X doesn't need to raise money.
- Company X is trading at 1x EV/sales. At the low end of valuation.

Company X is a wise purchase. The equity return should match the organic growth rate over a three-year period. One hundred percent in three years. If the multiple expands to 2x EV/sales, it supercharges the return to 300% in three years.

Heads you win. Tails you win even more.

Example 2

Company Y is a debt-free, profitable, growing company in an unloved industry. A current example of unloved industry would be cannabis or oil and gas. All your peers say you're an idiot for investing in this industry, which proves it's an uncrowded trade.

- Company Y is organically growing sales and earnings 25%.
- Company Y is confident the current growth rate will continue.
- Company Y doesn't need to raise money.
- Company Y is at an eight PE.

Company Y is a great setup. You can double your money in three years without any multiple expansion or operating leverage.

If the company does grow 25% for three years in a row, chances are they will show significant operating leverage, i.e., 25% revenue growth produces 50%+ earnings growth. It's also likely that by year two or three the multiple will expand from eight to 15.

Then all your peers will pile in after it triples and call it a wonderful business.

In both examples, heads you win with no multiple expansion and tails you win even more with multiple expansion.

A solid foundation is buying at a low valuation.

Your purchase price matters. Valuation matters. When you combine low valuation with double digit organic growth and a company that doesn't need to raise money, you get market-beating returns.

Peter Lynch wrote in *One Up on Wall Street*:

> These are among my favorite investments: small, aggressive new enterprises that grow 20–25% a year. If you choose wisely, this is the land of the 10 to 40 baggers, and even 200-baggers. With a small portfolio, one or two of these can make a career.

Let's say you find a great opportunity at a low valuation, when should you buy?

CHAPTER 30

BUYING
The Best Time to Buy

The roller coaster has a long and surprising history that stretches back several centuries. Its origins trace to 17th-century Russia, where "Russian Mountains" were popular winter attractions. These early rides were massive wooden slides covered in ice, reaching heights of 70 feet and speeds up to 50 miles per hour. Riders would climb stairs and descend on sleds made of wood or ice. Catherine the Great was reportedly a fan, and even had one built on her estate.

In the early 1800s, the concept spread to France, where it evolved into wheeled carts on tracks. One of the first was the "Les Montagnes Russes à Belleville" in Paris. These rides used guided rails to keep the carts on track – setting the stage for modern roller coaster design.

The roller coaster took a major leap forward in the United States. In 1884, LaMarcus Thompson opened the first successful gravity-powered coaster in Coney Island, New York. Called the Switchback Railway, it ran on a wooden track and carried riders at six miles per hour. It was a major success and helped spark a golden age of coaster building across America.

I was recently at Hersheypark in Pennsylvania, and I went on the Comet which is the oldest roller coaster in the park. It was built in 1946 and it's made of wood. It's a rather tame roller coaster by today's standards.

The Comet starts in a slow ascent up the 96-foot main camelback hill. Anticipation builds as the roller coaster slowly climbs the hill. At the top, the roller coaster feels like it almost stops. Then momentum shifts forward, and you plunge into the descent, hitting 55 mph at the bottom, and that momentum takes you through the remainder of the 3,300-foot ride.

Small stocks aren't smooth train rides through the countryside. The path isn't carved through the landscape and tunneled through mountains.

Small stocks are old roller coasters. They are fast and violent. They go up and down, and sometimes upside down. You must hold onto your lap bar and anchor yourself to the business, so you don't get tossed out.

The best time to buy great microcaps is before discovery.

Get on the ride before the first big hill. When you buy before the initial discovery move it's just you and a few others that probably don't even understand what they own.

The first big discovery move in a microcap is always the easiest. Why? No one owns it to sell it. There is the least amount of friction. Just a few people with low expectations.

The catalyst could be a large contract win or series of small wins, legislation change, a competitor leaving the market, or any number of reasons that create a quick 20–100% growth spurt in the business over two to six quarters.

The first breakout quarter is like a siren going off to the thousands of retail and small institutions looking for such things.

The revenue growth flows through the income statement with relative ease, producing operating leverage on the bottom line.

The crowd gets excited. The stock moves up 100–500% in 12 months. The issue with discovery moves is expectations become too high.

Everyone projects out 50% annual revenue growth and 200% net income growth for the next 10 years. Smart retail buys first, small institutions second, and finally dumb retail pay the highest price at the top.

The stock trades for perfection. You've reached the height of the discovery move.

What most investors don't realize is the business is over-earning. Management is learning as they go and is late in making the necessary investments to support a larger enterprise.

Then management realizes they are behind the curve. They need more infrastructure and redundancies. C players must be replaced with B or A players. They must spend $3 million on a new Sales Force CRM implementation.

At the same time, growth gets harder.

Last year's 50% growth turns into this year's 30%.

200% earnings growth turns into flat earnings year-on-year due to the increased investment in labor, technology, and infrastructure.

Investors are shocked because they've never run a business before.

Expectations fall.

The stock made an elegant and graceful rise over a few quarters and now it plunges 50%+ in a few days.

Ryan Telford, head of Evidence Based Research at MicroCapClub, looked at the historical data of microcaps. He analyzed four categories of 12-month multibaggers – microcaps that went up >2x, >3x, >4x, and >5x over a 12-month period. He then analyzed the subsequent peak-to-trough 12-month drawdown. Essentially, the higher or quicker the rise, the larger the subsequent 12-month drawdown. The median drawdown of each category was 58%, 68%, 75%, and 85%. These declines are gut wrenching. Some stocks recover and continue their ascent, but most do not.

This is why selling is necessary and perhaps the most important skill in microcap investing. Those that sell the first wave of discovery are correct for doing so. The base rates are low for management teams proving they are more than a one hit wonder.

The valuation compresses. 50x forward earnings turns into 15x trailing earnings. Growth investors leave, and value investors start circling the company again.

The second-best time to buy great microcaps is after the discovery bubble bursts.

Investor sentiment flips like a light switch from extreme optimism to extreme pessimism. From nothing can go wrong to nothing can go right. From penthouse to outhouse. From high expectations to low expectations.

The opportunity is doing independent work and buying when nothing good is priced in. If the business is growing, profitable, and not diluting, chances are investors will come back to it.

But now the stock is a known company. It might even have an analyst or two that picked up coverage.

When a stock goes from $1.00 to $5.00 and back to $2.00, it will take a lot more time, volume, and fundamental progress to surpass $5.00. Unlike the initial discovery move, now you have a bunch of investors with a higher cost basis waiting to sell when they get back to breakeven.

The hardest part of buying the rebound is most stocks never surpass their discovery peak. The discovery move was driven by high expectations. It's a tall task for management because it will likely take 2–3x the earnings to surpass the old highs.

Short-term stock prices are driven by emotion, sentiment, and expectations.

Long-term stock prices are driven by fundamentals.

Morgan Housel brings it together brilliantly:

> The valuation of every company is simply a number from today multiplied by a story about tomorrow.

Small stocks are roller coasters. Learn when to get on the ride.

A critical component of buying is sizing your conviction.

CHAPTER 31

BUYING

Sizing Your Conviction

Warren Buffett owned five to 10 stocks at a time. Phil Fisher owned 30 stocks. Walter Schloss owned 100 stocks. Peter Lynch owned 1,000 stocks at a time. They all beat the market. You don't have to follow anyone. You can do it your own way.

Herschel Walker was a formidable running back in the late 1980s and early 1990s. He was drafted in 1985 by the Dallas Cowboys. The move created tension because Dallas already had future Hall of Fame running back, Tony Dorsett, who was eventually traded to the Denver Broncos. Walker was a multi-talented player who could run the ball and receive.

In 1988, he had the best season of his career with 1,514 rushing yards and 505 receiving yards. The following year the Minnesota Vikings decided they had to have him.

The Vikings believed he would be the final piece they needed to win a Super Bowl. They gave up a total of eight draft picks, including three first-round picks and three second-round picks, along with five players.

However, Walker was never able to live up to those expectations in Minnesota and was gone from the team within three seasons.

The Cowboys used the wealth of draft picks and trades to help build a dynasty in the 1990s. They drafted future Hall of Famers Emmitt Smith and Darren Woodson, as well as several other key contributors to their championship teams. The Cowboys won three Super Bowls with those players in 1992, 1993, and 1995.

Minnesota was thinking about one amazing player. Dallas was thinking about the whole team. The trade became known as "The Great Train Robbery" because of how one-sided the outcome was in Dallas's favor. It's used as a prime example of how focusing on a single player rather than the whole team can be a colossal mistake.

When I was a private investor, I was super concentrated in two or three stocks. All it took was one great player or one great stock in any given year to have a phenomenal year. I define a phenomenal year as a portfolio return of 75%+.

When you own a two- or three-stock portfolio, you have the time to go a mile deep into your positions. This can also become the biggest downside. The downside of super concentration is overthinking your positions. You have too much time to think about a few things.

As your capital grows it's important to grow yourself with your capital. It's a natural progression to add a few more positions. Why? You get better at active patience and knowing what you are looking for and waiting until you find it. You also get better at evaluating and tracking more positions than when you were younger. I feel today I can get similar performance out of four to six core positions with less volatility and risk as I did with two or three core positions.

I started managing outside capital in 2019. The four to six core positions total 60–70% of the portfolio. We also hold four to eight smaller positions that make up the remainder of the portfolio.

I view our large core positions in a similar way to veteran players on a professional sports team. Core positions have earned their right to their position size like a veteran player has earned their right to a higher salary.

I've spent considerable time getting to know my core positions. I've witnessed how the management and the business perform under pressure. They've proven themselves and have earned my conviction and trust. The stocks have rewarded me with good returns and I've rewarded the management and business with a larger weighting in the portfolio.

As the number of positions in my portfolio has grown, my initial position sizing has come down. In the first 10 years of my career it wasn't abnormal for me to take a 20–30% initial position size at cost. Today I normally take a 2–8% position size at cost. I will let positions grow into 20% positions, but not from mindlessly adding to them. They grow into 20% positions by the stock appreciating and earning the right to the larger position size.

The market will naturally concentrate your portfolio into your winners if you stop meddling. When you let a position naturally become larger instead of forcing a position to become large, it is much easier to hold. The best positions are the ones you don't have to justify owning. Management does it for you by executing and the stock appreciates.

For long-only, quality-focused stock pickers, your largest positions should be the businesses you've held the longest that have gone up the most. It never works out exactly this way, but directionally that is the goal.

If you are a concentrated investor that lets positions run, the larger a position becomes, the more it will lead the entire portfolio up and down. Every stock has its own bull and bear market cycle independent of the macro cycle. These cycles can last for months, quarters, or years, triggered by a good or bad quarter. Large positions can make your portfolio look like a hero in bad times, and an idiot in good times.

In 2024, I had a 30% position that was down 30% year to date, and I had two 5% positions go up 100%. I remember thinking to myself how hard I had to work to break even when my largest position pulled back. But this is the price you pay for concentration. It cuts both ways. I'm used to this, but every stock picker must find the right balance.

The more you pay your superstar, the less you can allocate to the other players. When you pay your superstar a premium, you better pray they don't get hurt. If you don't get production out of your superstar, the rest of the team must really step up.

In 2019, IFCM was up 98% net. We owned 10 stocks and seven of them returned 100%+ in the same year. I look forward to that happening again – in my lifetime!

When I looked at the attribution, I realized it now takes a team effort to produce a phenomenal return in the portfolio in a single year. I used to go all-in on one superstar, like the Minnesota Vikings did with Herschel Walker. Now I build winning teams.

I view my four to eight smaller positions as our farm team or minor league team. These businesses have most of the characteristics I seek to make an investment, but they are still young, immature, and unproven. I buy a little to put them on our team. I start to build a relationship with management, and I give them a little playing time in our portfolio.

A mistake amateur stock pickers make is over-sizing their initial position. If you invest in small stocks, there is no need to oversize any position. The larger the position size at cost, the more you are making a bet on timing.

Do you know which position is going to move up the most next? I never do.

I've found over the years that very few deserve an oversized bet at cost because my timing is normally wrong. When a microcap works, 4% versus 12% at cost doesn't really matter. The beauty of small stocks is they have a long way to run when you find the right one.

The best feeling is when a small position turns into a core position because it went up.

Today, I take smaller initial positions. If the management team and business perform, I don't think twice about averaging up.

Buy low and then buy higher

I've kept an investment journal for the past 15 years. When I read it, I see that all my winners had two things in common. I bought low, and then I bought higher. I averaged up.

Building conviction in a position is the same as building trust in a relationship. It takes time to develop. It can't be forced. The best relationships are built over time. The best positions are built over time. Every new investment is a new relationship.

When you start dating someone, it's normally because they passed your initial hurdle. The person has some combination of the right look, education, background, faith, and values. You make a small investment in time and money into a first date or two.

You know immediately if the person isn't the one, but it might take a long time to know if the person is the one. You must see the individual in different circumstances. You must see them at their highs and their lows to see how they treat you and others. Through all these shared experiences, you grow closer or fall apart. It takes time, shared experience, and reps to find the one.

It's the same for stocks.

Time is a very effective hurdle. With most microcaps, you will like the management, business, and situation less six months later. The special ones, the rare ones, are those you genuinely like more the longer you get to know them.

We small stock investors sometimes overemphasize the importance of discovery. We sprint at new ideas like they are the last cup of water in a desert. We feel the urge to beat the next investor to a new idea. Only on a few occasions over a 20-year career do I ever remember buying a stock where the stock immediately went up and never was buyable again.

We have more time to build conviction and build a position than we think. Almost every year I'm able to add to my core holdings at similar risk-adjusted prices. The market normally gives you an opportunity to buy the same stocks every year. You can buy some today and buy more later. It's a good thing if you must pay higher later. This means management is executing. Averaging up doesn't always mean you are overpaying.

Many investors have a mental hurdle around averaging up. They only think about a stock getting cheaper if it drops. This is misguided. A stock that ascends can also remain cheap as fundamentals backfill into higher stock prices. This occurs when the business fundamentals are growing faster than the stock price and the future operating leverage is underappreciated.

In addition, when a microcap gets larger it deserves a higher multiple. If you have two companies in the same industry and Company A is a $100 million revenue business growing at 30% and Company B is a $25 million revenue business growing at 30%, Company A should trade at a higher multiple.

This makes intuitive sense because as a business becomes larger, stronger, and more diversified, the business quality increases. A microcap then transitions from a speculation to an investment and deserves a higher multiple.

For management teams that are executing, the result is a stock that can be a better buy at higher prices. I've bought stocks two to three times higher than my initial purchase and it was just as "cheap" as it was when I first bought.

I'm more valuation focused on my initial buys and more execution focused on subsequent purchases. I love averaging up into situations as management proves themselves to be worthy of additional trust and capital. I like to scale into positions in smaller chunks as my conviction builds.

Whether it's averaging up or averaging down, the decision to add new capital to an existing position is like deciding to stay in a hand in poker. Playing poker and picking stocks might seem different, but they have a lot in common. Both involve making smart choices and understanding your probability of success. The probabilities are always changing.

In poker, there are four betting rounds at pre-flop, after the flop, after the turn, and after the river. Every time the dealer unveils more community cards, the probabilities change. The players are all evaluating their hand against what other players could have. If a player has a great hand, they might be more aggressive in their betting.

In stock picking, instead of a dealer unveiling community cards, the business or market environment gives you more information. The companies give you earnings reports, press releases, and periodic updates. My continuous maintenance due diligence might expose something good or bad. At the same time, the valuation of the company is constantly changing. Probabilities and conviction are always changing.

As a professional stock picker, I then assimilate all this information and standardize so I can make decisions. I calculate upside versus downside ratios for every position so I can formulaically assess when and where to allocate new capital inside the portfolio. You also have a similar spreadsheet for your watchlist of companies.

If you don't systematically track upside to downside ratios across your positions and watchlists, your biases will cloud your judgment.

In error you might:

- Buy more of your largest position because it's the one you think about most.
- Buy more of the position you are down the most in.
- Buy more of the position you are up the most in.

- Buy more of the position that issues a positive press release.
- Buy more of the position where there is insider buying.
- Buy more of the position where you most recently spoke to the CEO.

You let your most recent positive emotion dictate your buying instead of creating a systematic approach that can be done consistently. It's not what you do randomly that will produce long-term returns; it's what you do consistently.

When should you average down?

Averaging down is a skill. Done well it can be your greatest asset. Done poorly it can mean disaster.

When you find yourself constantly averaging down in a microcap, it's normally a sign your ego has taken over. Proving you're right has become more important than making money. You've forgotten that being broke and right is the same thing as being wrong.

John Hempton wrote a good article on the types of situations that are poor choices for averaging down. He cited:

Highly levered companies. The issue with highly levered companies is the market cap and stock price can go down significantly but the enterprise value doesn't go down that much. It's easy for equity holders to get wiped out figuratively and literally. Don't average down into highly levered companies.

Companies with obsolescence risk. These companies often look like they have a great brand, but they have declining market share. There are many examples of this in microcap. For instance, a small $10–50 million market cap owns a brand most people remember from 10, 20, or 50 years ago. We all think to ourselves that the brand must be worth more than this. Most times it isn't. Another category are companies that sell me-too products or services with little differentiation. The company's goal is to put marketing lipstick on a pig and hope someone accidentally buys the product. Don't average down into pigs.

I would add two more situations to Hempton's list:

Unprofitable businesses. A microcap investor's biggest risk is dilution. If a company has less than 12 months of cash, most of the time an equity raise is coming. Don't jump in front of the dilution freight train. The stock market is good at sniffing out a dilutive equity raise. When the stock market knows an equity raise is probable, the stock will be stuck in quicksand. In addition, after a company raises capital, it often takes months, quarters, even years to churn through the dilution and the negative taste left in investors' mouths. Don't average down into unprofitable businesses.

Underperforming businesses. One of my biggest mistakes has been averaging down after a company posts an unexpected bad quarter. Nine times out of 10, another mediocre quarter is coming right behind it. We all want to believe the bad quarter was a one-time event, we say "this time is different," but it rarely is. Most microcaps are turnaround stories in some way. We love to root for the underdogs. We all want to believe things will get better – that the proverbial frog will turn into a prince. It's easy to convince yourself to average down one more time. You average down again and again, and then you realize the frog is just a frog. No offense to frogs. Don't average down into losers.

I was interviewed several times over the last decade by Larissa Fernand from Morningstar India, who is now semi-retired somewhere in the Lakshadweep Islands. She asked me about averaging down into losers and this was my answer:

> If you personally lent someone money, and they only repaid you half of what they owed you, would you give that person more money? Of course not. Yet we continually do this with our investing, where we average down into things that have a history of disappointing us.

Averaging down can be a wonderful thing. In fact, variable pricing is the best thing about the public markets. Short-term stock prices are yanked like a dog on a leash by the madness of the crowd.

Investor sentiment is a pendulum that swings back and forth between extreme optimism and extreme pessimism and never sits still. It's on the extremes where the astute investor waits patiently buying or selling.

Even Berkshire Hathaway, one of the largest, most durable businesses in the world, trades in a 30–50% range every year. Every. Year.

Coincidentally, this is also why many successful short-term traders focus on trading the same two or three stocks every year. There is enough volatility in a couple stocks to make a living. These successful traders find the pulse of a company's stock. They know when the heartbeat becomes irregular.

Microcap stocks are inherently more volatile, which means you will have even more chances to average down.

It always feels like you'll never get another shot to buy a company you love, but almost every year the market gives you another opportunity.

This leads us to the most important question: **When should you average down?**

The answer is to invert the list of situations to avoid. You should only average down when:

1. The business is accelerating.
2. The business is profitable with no financing risk.
3. The business has a sustainable growth trajectory.
4. The business isn't highly levered.

Don't average down into losers. Average down into winners.

If a stock is dropping and the underlying business doesn't have all four characteristics above, let the stock drop. Let the position become a smaller portion of your portfolio. Don't try to catch the knife.

We all have losses in the portfolio. It's part of the game. Don't turn a loss into a mistake. Mistakes are when our actions or inaction turns a small loss into a bigger loss. It's when you are hurting your returns.

The most gut-wrenching and emotional times are when stocks fall. Remember the four characteristics you need to justify averaging down.

Sizing your conviction is an art and a science. I've always found averaging down is overrated, and averaging up is underrated.

The best investments are the ones where management executes, fundamentals accelerate, and the stock is a better risk-adjusted return at a higher price than it was at a lower price.

Often the best place for new capital is buying more of the companies that make it look easy.

This leads us to the next skill that is imperative to successful stock picking. Selling.

CHAPTER 32

SELLING
Limiting Losses and Capturing Gains

What if Warren Buffett would have bought 10 stocks in the 1950s, held onto them, and they all turned out to be monster winners? Like Moses coming down from the mountain with 10 stocks carved into stone tablets. Isn't this what we want our stock picking heroes to look like? A few great decisions. A punch card. 10 for 10. All winners. Perfection.

But this isn't reality. It takes the best stock pickers in the world a few decades of owning hundreds of stocks to find a handful that are worthy of holding for the long term.

Most stocks only deserve to be rented. A few deserve to be owned.

It takes time and turnover to find the few.

In 1988, Warren Buffett famously said, "Our favorite holding period is forever." Some people took the statement literally, meaning every stock he buys will be held forever. Most of us that are true students of stock picking knew what he actually meant. His intention is to find businesses he can hold forever, but reality is much different.

He finally got sick of people misrepresenting what he said, and in 2016 responded:

> Sometimes the comments of shareholders or media imply that we will own certain stocks forever. It is true that we own some stocks that I have no intention of selling for as far as the eye can see (and we're talking 20/20 vision). But we have made no commitment that Berkshire will hold any of its marketable securities forever.

Intentions are important in life and in stocks.

Here is the difference between trading and investing:

- **Investing** – your intention with every purchase is to hold.
- **Trading** – your intention with every purchase is to sell.

From 1980 to 2016 Warren Buffett owned 230 stocks in Berkshire's public stock portfolio. Of these, 60% were sold in less than a year. From 2015 to 2024, Buffett owned ~120 stocks total in Berkshire's public stock portfolio. He only owns nine stocks that pre-date this 10-year vintage.

Buffett's intentions were to hold forever, but the business or macro situation changed so he sold. He still made money on many of them.

This proves what we know to be true but don't like to admit.

All stocks have a different shelf life.

The difference between food and stocks is we don't know the shelf life of a stock when we buy it. There is no one-size-fits-all cookie cutter time frame because every business evolves in different ways. Some businesses will age like fine wine and others like raw fish left on a kitchen counter.

In an interview, Drew Dickson, CIO of Albert Bridge Capital, said:

> A lot of my good friends like Guy Spier and Chris Bloomstran want to buy good companies and hold onto them. We don't. We want to know where we are versus the street over the next two to three years. We might own some longer. That's our whole story. Is this company going to beat numbers.

I found the statement refreshing. Drew knows exactly who he is and what he's trying to do. He has fully developed active patience. He isn't trying to be something he's not. He isn't misrepresenting his strategy.

Most stock pickers define their strategy with some variation of the following: "I do exhaustive research turning over thousands of rocks to identify a handful of wonderful businesses to buy and hold for the long term."

Isn't it funny how we define our strategies by the exception and not the norm?

Like Buffett, maybe two out of 50 stocks you buy might be worthy of owning for 10+ years. These are the exceptions, not the norm. We define our strategies as finding the two, but our strategies are best described by how we've dealt with the other 48. We can still make a lot of money on the 48. You get a lot of nutrients from eating perishable foods.

Most winning stocks only deserve to be held for a few quarters to a few years. The ones you ultimately hold for 10+ years are wonderful, but they are the exception. Even for Buffett.

Few like to talk about the skill of selling because it's either an admission you were wrong, or that you don't hold stocks forever. Admitting you are wrong means you aren't perfect, and no one wants to admit they aren't perfect. Admitting you don't hold stocks forever just isn't *en vogue* and won't get you invited to "compounder bro" cocktail parties.

My intention with every purchase is to hold forever (five years plus), but less than 5% will earn that right. From 2020–2025, I've owned 90 different stocks, and I've owned one for five years plus. The natural shelf life on average of a small microcap business is shorter than mid and large cap businesses. They are smaller and more fragile businesses. My average holding period is a little over one year.

Most winning stocks in microcap have a winning season that lasts two to eight quarters.

Perhaps management got lucky with product market fit for a year. Maybe it was a new government program or regulation that drove demand for 12 months. Maybe a competitor had temporary supply issues. Maybe the VP of Sales wined and dined the right executive and got the big contract. But none of this was sustainable.

I've always thought the best definition of microcap due diligence is: Analyzing if management is lucky or skilled and how long it will last.

Robert Wilson was a legendary trader who turned $15,000 into $800 million over his 40-year career. He called himself a long-term trader. I like that term. He would sell positions after a few days, or after a decade. He just rode them as long as they were winning.

Isn't Wilson's strategy closer to our reality than we want to admit? Aren't we all just long-term traders masking ourselves as long-term investors?

Most micro- and smallcap stock pickers try too hard to fit into a buy-and-hold-forever style box of investing. Forever doesn't align with the shelf life of small businesses. Embrace reality.

Portfolio turnover is necessary to be a successful microcap investor.

Investopedia describes portfolio turnover as a measure of how frequently assets within a fund are bought and sold by the managers. Portfolio turnover is calculated by taking either the total amount of new securities purchased, or the number of securities sold (whichever is less) over a particular period, divided by the total net asset value (NAV) of the fund. The measurement is usually reported for a 12-month period.

In 2019 I launched Intelligent Fanatics Capital Management (IFCM). In late 2020, I reviewed our portfolio reports, and I noticed for the previous 12 months our portfolio turnover was 102%.

Per the definition above this doesn't mean we didn't hold positions for the duration; it means I was active in the positions I wasn't holding.

When I was a full-time private investor managing my own capital, I never bothered to look at such metrics. But now portfolio turnover and several other statistics were front and center when an investor would download their annual statements.

I couldn't help but worry what my investors would think when they saw 102% portfolio turnover.

"Are we investing or trading?"

"Isn't this supposed to be a buy and hold strategy?"

"Don't you do enough initial due diligence to hold for at least a year?"

I started to drill down into the topic of portfolio turnover and studied some of the great investors that I admired.

Peter Lynch had 300% turnover per year in the early years of the Magellan Fund. Joel Greenblatt had similar turnover at Gotham Capital. Even Warren Buffett's public company portfolio ranged from 50–100% turnover per year during his early peak-return decades.

In fact, contrary to what most believe, many of the greatest long-only investors had their best performance when they had higher rates of turnover in their portfolios. It's also worth mentioning that these were investors that invested in larger, more established businesses where low turnover is much more achievable.

The best investors aren't coffee can investors. They are conviction investors.

In 1984, Robert Kirby wrote an article for the *Journal of Portfolio Management* titled "The Coffee Can Portfolio." The coffee can term comes from a time in America when people used to keep their most valuable possessions in coffee cans under the bed. Today, a coffee can portfolio is a term used to describe a buy and forget, or never sell, approach to investing. The coffee can approach solves two primary issues investors face. Getting scared out of big winners while lowering transaction costs, commissions, and taxes to the lowest point possible.

Conviction investing is when you do independent research and analysis to know the underlying business better than the average investor in the stock. Conviction investors normally manage a concentrated portfolio of 30 stocks or less so they can focus on accumulating knowledge on their best ideas. The ultimate edge for conviction investors is their ongoing maintenance due diligence. They grow a deep connection to the business, and this is where conviction is formed. It also allows them to take advantage of manic short-term stock price movements when the market value gets too disconnected from intrinsic value.

Conviction investors do independent research to form independent conviction. They do the work, so they know when to buy. They do the work, so they know when to hold. But most importantly they do the work, so they know when to sell.

Coffee can investing and conviction investing are opposites. When you take the sell decision out of the investment process you don't need conviction. You hope for the best and move on to the next idea. Coffee can investing views selling as a liability. Conviction investing views selling as an asset. Selling is the skill of limiting losses and capturing gains.

The greatest advantage of public markets investing is you can sell. You don't have to continue holding companies you no longer believe in. Especially in microcaps, which are predominantly smaller, more fragile businesses where the spectrum of outcomes is wider. The risk of permanent capital loss is higher. Selling isn't just prudent, it is necessary. You can't coffee can microcaps.

It's romantic to think you can be the Terry Smith of microcap and smallcap, gloating about your low turnover, but this isn't reality. You can't say, "I'm going to hold this stock for one, five, 10, or 40 years." No – you are going to hold on as long as management executes. This could be three months, or it could be 30 years. This is what Buffett does with his public portfolio. Most of the companies you own today will only deserve to be rented. Ownership is earned.

If you invest in microcaps you will have turnover. You must have turnover. Less than 10% of what you own today will likely deserve to be owned five years from today. This means that 90% of what you own today will deserve to be sold. My intention with every purchase is to hold forever, but very few will earn that right.

Here are my four principles of selling.

Four principles of selling

Sell when a stock gets very overvalued

Microcaps overshoot to the upside all the time. They go up 200–500% in a 12-month period. They go up too far too fast. They go from unloved to loved. The multiple expands to levels that price the business for perfection. In 99% of cases the company will eventually post an imperfect quarter, and the equity falls 50%+ from the highs. You must sell some or all of your position before the imperfect quarter hits. The goal of investment is to find stocks that are undervalued that will get overvalued. This reason for selling is a time to celebrate. I would love for this to happen with every position. I define very overvalued as pulling forward the next three to five years' worth of returns.

Sell when you find something better than your least convicted position

A stock picker is like a coach on a professional sports team. You must always play your best players. The players might change throughout the season and year to year. A new opportunity can't have a similar upside to your stable of investments; it must have considerably more upside to replace the trust in an established position. A couple times per year you will likely find a rookie that is so talented it will force you to bench a veteran. Always play your best players. The team you win with this year might be different from the team you won with last year.

Sell when the business changes for the worse or doesn't change for the better

This is the most likely reason you will sell. The shelf lives of microcaps are always shorter than we think. We buy thinking the business will get better and it doesn't. We buy a company with a growing core business and many green shoots, but then the core stops growing. We hold onto losers far too long because they look cheap and then act surprised when they keep dropping. Sometimes the most annoying positions aren't the ones that go down but the ones that go nowhere. They keep pushing out the catalyst, inflection, or acceleration event. These positions string you along for just another quarter and just another quarter. These "just another quarter stocks" will drive you mad. You know you should sell them, but you don't. When you start rationalizing a position, you sell. You must spot the signs of the investment thesis cracking before others so you can sell before others. You can't wait. Don't justify holding on or waiting another quarter. You sell immediately when you spot the signs.

Sell when you see any sign that management is unethical, untrustworthy, or incompetent

Whenever I feel management can't be trusted, I sell immediately. When I feel I've been misled, I sell. When I feel I've been lied to, I sell. When management is aggressively telling the story right before a bad quarter, I sell. I don't care about the price. There is no price too low. I have zero patience for management teams I don't trust.

Ten percent of successful stock picking is picking great stocks. The other 90% is selling them at the right time. My selling principles and instincts have kept me in the game longer than most others.

Selling and holding are two skills that go hand and hand. If you aren't selling you are holding and if you aren't holding you are selling. Holding monster winners is the most difficult skill of them all.

CHAPTER 33

HOLDING
Maintenance Due Diligence

Extraordinary returns follow extraordinary discipline. Discipline in buying and selling, and maybe the most important one of all, holding. You will buy more stocks than you sell and sell more stocks than you hold. Yet, holding is the most difficult.

The Forbes 400 is a list of the wealthiest 400 American citizens who own assets in the US, ranked by net worth. Many of the people on the list are famous and well known, but many of them are not. It's fun and educational to go top to bottom and click on unrecognizable names and see how their wealth was accumulated.

Here are some people in the 2024 Forbes 400:

#1 Elon Musk –$244 billion
#5 Warren Buffett –$150 billion
#24 Phil Knight –$36.8 billion
#89 John Malone –$10.7 billion
#142 Paul Tudor Jones –$8.1 billion
#247 Steven Spielberg –$5.3 billion

Buried down at #347 is a gentleman named Stewart Horejsi (pronounced HOR-ish). His estimated net worth is $3.8 billion.

Under "Major Achievements" and "Notable Works" it lists:

"Early Investor in Berkshire Hathaway."

That's it. No brilliant startup. No flashy hedge fund. No revolutionary invention.

In 1980, Stewart Horejsi was having doubts that his business would survive. His company, Brown Welding Supply LLC, had been in business for 50 years, but they were slowly losing market share to the competition.

Horejsi heard about Berkshire Hathaway in John Train's book *The Money Masters*. He was frustrated with the growth prospects for his business, so he started buying Berkshire Hathaway with his company's shrinking earnings. He purchased 40 shares of Berkshire Hathaway at $265. Two weeks later he bought 60 shares at $295. A month later he bought 200 shares at $330 per share.

He started attending the annual meetings when there were fewer than a dozen people in attendance. He forced his friends to go too because he was worried the company would stop having them because attendance was so low.

"I kept running the [family] business, but I just kept buying Berkshire. I can't really believe I put so much into one issue, though," he said.

Eventually he accumulated 5,800 Class A shares. He sold about a quarter of them in 1998 at $78,000 per share. He still owns more than $1.5 billion of Berkshire stock.

Isn't it ironic that Horejsi likely accumulated as much wealth from Berkshire Hathaway as Charlie Munger?

It is incredibly humbling, inspiring, and a bit scary when you realize that one great investment can make your year, decade, and even career.

The work behind conviction

Consider the story of Jason Hirschman and Meredith Brill, two private investors and a tiny company called XPEL.

When they first got involved, XPEL was a microcap worth around $20 million. The company sold paint protection film for cars. It was small, profitable, growing rapidly and then it got hit with a lawsuit from a competitor more than a thousand times its size.

Most investors saw the headline, assumed the lawsuit was fatal, and walked away. The stock slid to about $1.

Hirschman and Brill reacted differently. Brill, as a patent lawyer, conducted substantial legal analysis into the case. They also hired an analytical chemistry lab that reverse engineered the formulations of each layer of the paint protection film so that Brill could perform a full infringement analysis from scratch.

No message boards, no rumor, no fear, just primary work. The conclusion was the lawsuit was weak. The risk of true catastrophe was low.

Armed with that work, they didn't run. They bought the stock other investors sold.

That's what conviction looks like in real time: buying when everyone else is certain you're wrong. It doesn't feel brave. It feels like standing out on a limb while the rest of the market is sawing at the base.

The lawsuit eventually settled on terms that were basically irrelevant to the long-term story. The business executed. Revenue grew. Profitability improved. The stock re rated. Over the next five years, XPEL went up 100x.

Crucially, they both held on. They didn't sell at 2x because it "moved too fast," or at 5x because it looked "expensive," or at 10x because they were "happy with the gain." They held most of their stake through the entire climb. The result was generational wealth and a legendary reputation.

Conviction isn't believing a story harder than everyone else.

Conviction is doing more work than everyone else so you can hold when everyone else can't.

Are you willing to put in that type of work?

The monster that took 11 years to wake up

In 1992, two South African businessmen, Rodney Sacks and Hilton Schlosberg, bought a struggling juice company called Hansen Natural for about $14.5 million. Each owned roughly 40%. The company had about $20 million in sales, was losing money, and had a market cap around $20 million.

It did not get better right away.

From 1993 through 1995, the company kept losing money. The stock drifted down until the whole company was worth only about $6 million. It was the kind of name you scroll past without a second thought.

In late 1995, Hansen launched a smoothie line. Within nine months, smoothies were roughly a third of revenue and about 20% of total cases sold. For the first time, Hansen posted a modest profit, around $357,000 in 1996, and the stock crawled back to a $25 million market cap. Still insignificant. Still ignored.

By 1997, sales grew to $43 million and earnings were $1.3 million. By 1998, sales inched up to $54 million, earnings to $3.6 million, and the market cap was about $40 million.

From 1998 to 2002, sales grew from roughly $54 million to $92 million. Earnings stagnated at around $3–4 million per year. The stock basically went sideways for five years. Nothing exciting, nothing obviously broken, just a small company grinding away, invisible to almost everyone.

From the day Sacks and Schlosberg bought Hansen in 1992 to the end of 2003, the stock returned about 50% in total. A 3.75% CAGR over 11 years. That's worse than T-Bills.

I often think about the first 11 years of Hansen under Sacks and Schlosberg's leadership. A mediocre-looking business with a mediocre-looking management team running a $40 million market cap.

This is the part we always edit out of the story. We imagine we'd have seen the magic early. More likely, we would have shrugged and passed.

In fact, we all have at least one of these companies in our portfolio. A company you've held onto far too long, hoping that a new product or strategy will completely change the trajectory of the company.

The PE ratio is a good sentiment indicator. When a PE is high, expectations are high. When a PE is low, expectations are low. From 2000–2002, Hansen Natural was trading at a 10 PE. No one was expecting anything. But then lightning struck.

In late 2002, Monster Energy was born.

The energy drink had edgier marketing, a bold logo, and a tagline, "Unleash the Beast," that had nothing to do with "natural" juice. The branding was loud. It worked.

They landed early sponsorships in extreme sports. Distribution improved. Within a couple of years, Monster had a meaningful slice of the energy drink market, which itself was booming.

By 2004, sales were around $180 million and earnings more than $20 million. By 2005, sales reached $350 million, earnings tripled to $60 million and the market cap soared into the billions. The stock went up about 30x in three years.

Here's the twist: during that first 3000% run from 2003 to 2006, the founders sold roughly 40% of their shares. It made sense. After a decade of pain, they finally had real money on the table and wanted to diversify.

The stock went on to rise another 16,000% after they sold.

If the people who knew the most about the business, who ran it, lived it, and had their whole identity in it couldn't sit perfectly still, what are the odds an outside investor would have?

What CAGRs hide

In 2012, Hansen Natural changed its name to Monster Beverage (MNST). The compounding continued.

From 1992 to 2024, Monster Beverage produced a 26.5% CAGR over 32 years. When you zoom out on the long-term chart this CAGR looks smooth, a rising line that wiggles a bit but marches steadily upward.

That's the lie behind compound annual growth rates. They compress decades of terror and boredom into one polite number.

Underneath that 26% CAGR were multiple 40%-plus drawdowns, a couple of 70%-plus plunges, and several stretches of 18 months or more where the stock went nowhere. There were headlines predicting doom, analyst downgrades, competitive scares, and product worries. Holding requires a stomach made of steel.

That's what a truly great long-term return feels like in real time: alternating episodes of "I'm an idiot for owning this" and "I'm an idiot for not owning more," separated by very long stretches of "why is nothing happening?"

Every real multi-bagger tells a similar story. The stock surges, then stalls while the business fundamentals catch up. Some shareholders get bored and move on to something "more exciting." New shareholders wander in. These stagnation periods are when we must dig deep and analyze the business to see if the wait will be worth it. All the while, you will be watching other stocks outperform.

Time and volatility always force out the weakly convicted. You don't deserve the upside unless you can stomach the volatility and boredom along the way.

The reward for holding monster stocks is enormous. The path to earning that reward is almost impossible to tolerate.

Even God would get fired

There's a wonderful thought experiment by Wes Gray titled, "Even God Would Get Fired as an Active Investor."

He asked: What if you had perfect foresight?

Imagine a portfolio that, every five years, magically knows which 50 stocks in the S&P 500 will perform best over the next five years, and then holds only those. That's omniscient stock picking. No mistakes. No uncertainty. Just perfection.

You'd expect the ride to be serene. It wasn't.

Yes, the long-term returns were 3x the S&P 500. But along the way, this "God portfolio" suffered gut-wrenching drawdowns, including a crash on the order of 70%-plus during the Great Depression and several smaller crashes of 30% or more. In the short term it often looked awful.

If someone ran that strategy in real life, I'm sure many investors would have fired them.

That's the uncomfortable truth: Even perfect stock selection doesn't spare you from brutal volatility.

So if a hypothetical omniscient investor would look incompetent half the time, what chance do you and I have of looking smart all the time?

None.

The only edge we can reasonably aim for is not superior prediction, but superior tolerance for looking wrong while being right over a long stretch of time.

What "sitting tight" really means

As Edwin Lefèvre put it in *Reminiscences of a Stock Operator*:

"After spending many years in Wall Street and after making and losing millions of dollars I want to tell you this: It never was my thinking that made the big money for me. It always was my sitting. Got that? My sitting tight!"

Many quote this passage but have no idea of its intention. Amateurs who don't want to devote the time to know their investments intimately deduce that Lefèvre is implying we must hold stocks forever.

No! Holding for the correct duration is where the big money is made.

Over the course of a stock picking career, you will own hundreds of stocks. Half will be winners and half will be losers.

Here is my 90–9–1 rule of winners:

90% of your winners will return 1–100%

9% of your winners will return 100–1000%

1% of your winners will return 1000%+

Those 1% positions are the ones that justify enduring the volatility and boredom.

To exploit them, you must live inside a contradiction: Nearly all your holdings should eventually be sold or trimmed because they will disappoint or mature, yet you must be prepared to hold a rare few for a very long time.

Managing that contradiction requires what I'd call productive paranoia.

It's not vague fear. It's focused anxiety, channeled into specific questions: Is this business getting better or worse? Are returns on capital improving or eroding? Is management executing or drifting? Are competitive advantages deepening or fading?

The best "sitters" aren't passive. They're intensely engaged with the business, but patient with the price.

Maintenance due diligence: Holding with eyes open

Successful holding doesn't mean your eyes are shut. It means your eyes are wide open.

If you invest in microcaps or illiquid small companies, surprise is your biggest enemy. You don't have the luxury of waking up to a blow-up and easily moving on.

That's where maintenance due diligence comes in.

The goal is simple: know everything that is knowable, so that when bad news comes, and it will, you're not blindsided. You may still be wrong, but you're rarely surprised.

In the short run, stock prices are mostly story and emotion. Narratives dominate, sentiment swings, and liquidity amplifies everything.

In the long run, prices are just math: revenue, margins, reinvestment, returns on capital, dilution.

Maintenance due diligence is the practice of constantly separating those two worlds. You want to see clearly when the business is quietly improving while the stock goes nowhere, and when the stock is roaring while the business stagnates.

Microcap sentiment doesn't move in gentle waves. It swings like a wrecking ball between "this is going bankrupt" and "this is the next Tesla." It rarely hangs out in the middle.

Your job is to grab onto the business fundamentals like a safety bar on a roller coaster. You don't control the ride. But you do control how tightly you hold onto something real.

Peter Lynch said, "Stand by your stocks as long as the fundamental story of the company hasn't changed."

You must keep asking yourself: Has the story really changed, or just the price?

High expectations: The silent killer

Developing the conviction to hold and forming realistic expectations go hand and hand. Many stock pickers can't control the bullish echo chamber in their heads as they reach for reasons to justify a higher stock price and valuation.

Markets often disappoint not because companies fail, but because investors expected perfection on an impossible timeline. The business grows nicely, just not as fast as the fantasy in someone's spreadsheet.

Optimism is necessary in investing. Delusion is fatal.

One way to protect yourself is to stretch your time horizon and shrink your near-term expectations. Assume that even if you're right about the destination, the ride will be longer and messier than you think.

When you invest in a company, don't expect immediate gratification.

Joel Greenblatt said: "Unless you buy a stock at the exact bottom (which is next to impossible), you will be down at some point after you make every investment. Your success entirely depends on how dispassionate you are towards short term stock price fluctuations."

Stocks rarely perform in the time frames we predict, and it's why the market only works for investors that have more patience than they thought they would ever need.

Performance is rarely linear, up and to the right, year after year. You sometimes must hold onto a position for a year or two before it goes up 200% in three months.

How many of your successful investments have occurred on the timeline that you originally predicted? How many times do you ever remember thinking, "Well that happened a lot quicker than I thought"?

Not often enough. Most of my successful investments took longer, in some cases a lot longer, than I originally expected. History proves that even with our winners, let alone our losers, our initial expectations are too high.

Why I underwrite three years instead of three months

When I look at a microcap, I'm not trying to predict what will happen next quarter. I'm trying to get comfortable with what might reasonably happen over the next three years.

That means talking to management about where they want the business to be, not just what they hope to report next quarter. It means understanding the key metrics that really drive value and then tracking quarterly results against a long-term map instead of a short-term narrative.

Three years is long enough that one weird quarter, an order pulled forward, a customer delay, a supply hiccup, doesn't dominate your thinking. But it's not so long that you're telling fairy tales about the distant future.

Ask a CEO about the next quarter and you're asking for guidance. Ask about the next three years and you're asking about strategy. The answers tend to be more honest, more revealing, and more useful.

This shift in horizon also changes your own behavior. Most investors are fixated on the next 10% move. If you simply focus on whether a business can be worth 100% more in a few years, you're playing a completely different game.

Wrong mindset – I think the stock will be up or down 10% tomorrow, next week, next month.

Right mindset – I don't care what the stock does tomorrow, next week, next month. I think the business will be worth considerably more in one, two, or three years.

The right approach is not to choke a position at the first hint of disappointment, nor to ignore repeated signs of decay.

Hold your positions like a tube of toothpaste. Don't hold them too tight. No company is perfect. Give them a little room to disappoint you, and a lot of room to exceed your expectations. The key is having reasonable expectations.

Boredom: The hidden superpower

In the book, *The Art of Execution*, portfolio manager Lee Freeman-Shor describes how he invested $25–150 million each with 45 of the world's top investors. His instructions to them were simple, as there was just one rule. They could only invest in their 10 best ideas. Over several years he tracked their positions, trades, and performance, and was amazed at what he saw.

> The most successful investors I worked with, those who made the most money, all had one thing in common: the presence of a couple of big winners in their portfolios. Any approach that does not embrace the possibility of winning big is doomed.

Freeman-Shor also noted the best investors had a high boredom threshold. Just like a fine wine, sustainable multi-baggers often take their time to ascend and develop. Don't worry if no one likes your investment idea. Don't worry if the stock goes nowhere for months or quarters.

Let's not forget the multi-bagger first principles: If the business is growing, earning more money, and not diluting, time is your friend. The crowd will eventually find it, make it their idea, and chase it higher.

For most sustainable multi-bagger stocks, the first few chapters of the story is one of a misunderstood business that kept growing revenues and earnings and not diluting. Then all at once it seems the world wakes up to the idea and decides it's a wonderful business. The question is whether you'll still be there when it happens.

Holding ≠ Never Selling

A majority of stocks will underperform T-Bills over the long term. Only 1% of your winners deserve to be held for 10+ years. It can take a lifetime to find a handful of businesses worthy of holding long term.

"Holding" is not the same as "never selling." Very few businesses deserve to be held for decades. Most will give you a good run, then mature, stumble, or get disrupted.

Your goal is to figure out whether an investment is on a short shelf life, a medium one, or very rarely a very long one. For some, the right horizon is 18 months. For others, it's three to five years. A tiny handful might be worth 10 years or more.

The hard part is that you rarely know which is which in real time. You only realize you owned something truly special after years of drama and a giant percentage gain behind you.

So you need selling rules that are tied to fundamentals, not feelings.

Let boredom and volatility trigger questions. Let deteriorating business performance, clear strategic mistakes, broken unit economics, or permanent competitive damage trigger sales.

Most stocks will not be worth holding through multiple full cycles. Only a small minority deserve that kind of patience. It can take an entire investing lifetime to find even a few of them. That's okay. You don't need many.

Growing old together

When you do find, buy, and hold a rare 1% stock, only 10+ years into the journey do you realize how special they were.

The most cherished relationships are the ones you've held the longest. They have lasted the test of time. You've grown older together. You trust each other because you've experienced life's ups and downs. You look back at all the relationships that have come and gone, and against all odds this one has gone the distance.

You both look nothing like you did when you started the relationship. You're not even the same person. You think back at your original thesis and laugh at how wrong you've been. The stock is up 3000% since your initial purchase 12 years ago, but it didn't play out like you thought. It never does.

When I invested in Idaho Strategic (IDR) in 2013, I could never have imagined all the ups, downs, lulls, and pivots. I could have never imagined the 30 company visits over 12 years, and the thousand conversations with John Swallow. When I first met John, his sons were just children. I could never imagine I would attend their weddings. I could never have imagined the joy of looking back at their success and knowing I played a small role in making it possible.

We all picture long-term monster stocks as smooth escalator rides to heaven. They aren't.

They are elevator rides where some kid jumps in and pushes all the numbers and you sigh in disbelief. The elevator goes up and down and up and down. You almost get off but conviction and stubbornness keep you from exiting. Thankfully the last number pushed is the penthouse. When you finally make it to the top floor you feel lucky you held onto enough stock to pay for it. Now you are on top and have what everyone wants.

You look like a genius, but in reality, you were just stubborn in the right way, for long enough.

Most aspiring stock pickers want to be in the top 10%. That's a reasonable goal. But there's a big difference between good, great, and GOAT (Greatest of All Time) stock pickers.

CHAPTER 34

Good to Great to GOAT

In the book, *Golf Is Not a Game of Perfect*, Dr. Rob Rotella tells a story from the 1990s when Tom Kite was the #1 player in the world. Kite played a practice round with two collegiate Division I golfers from the University of Texas.

After the round, one of the collegiate golfers said, "Tom, we basically hit it as good as you did today. When we missed and hit a bunker, our bunker shots were as good as yours. When we missed a green, we got it up and down like you did. We scored within a shot or two of one another. So how come you're the all-time leading money winner and we're the number three and four golfers at the University of Texas?"

Tom replied, "The difference is when you guys get in tournaments, the likelihood is that you'll lose your concentration on four or five shots every round. Over a four-day tournament, even if every lapse costs you just one stroke, that's 16 to 20 shots a week, and that's the difference between being the leading money winner and losing your card. If one of these lapses costs you two or three strokes, or you get upset and lose concentration on a second shot, you can be talking about 25 to 30 strokes a week, and you won't even make the college golf team. Over a career, losing concentration can mean lots of strokes."

In 2024, Scottie Scheffler's scoring average was 68.01. This is the lowest scoring average in the modern era. The third best scoring average in 2024 was Collin Morikawa which was 69.05 and the tour average in 2024 was 70.29.

By those numbers, on average, Scheffler beat Morikawa by four strokes and the average Tour player by eight strokes in every tournament.

Being one or two strokes better per round (which equals four to eight strokes per four-round tournament) than your opponents is the difference between good, great, and GOAT.

How should stock pickers be judged?

We all have heard the expression that stock picking is both an art and a science, and it's true.

Stock picking is an art because we all express ourselves differently. We all invest differently, in small and big ways.

Where stock picking stops being an art is the end result.

Jackson Pollock was a famous artist from the 1940s and 1950s who used a drip technique to create his art. He would staple a canvas to the floor or a wall and then walk around the artwork flinging paint at the canvas.

In 2006, "No. 5, 1948," sold for $140 million. I guarantee 99% of people would find that painting ugly, which is proof that the end result of artwork is subjective.

Stock picking is the opposite. The result of stock picking is completely objective.

A 5% CAGR over 10 years is ugly.

A 20% CAGR over 10 years is beautiful.

Few would disagree.

Every stock picker is judged by performance and time. I think we would all agree it's easier to show great performance over a short period of time. Time is like gravity to an active stock picker where performance reverts to the mean.

In addition, successful active managers attract more assets under management which forces them to style drift, increase market cap, or diversify into areas before they are ready, which further increases the chances of reversion to the mean. The few stock pickers that can withstand these headwinds and gravitational forces for 10+ years become good, great, or even GOAT stock pickers.

There are two different stock picking mindsets: capital preservation and absolute returns.

Capital preservation is a *defense first, don't lose money* mindset. Absolute returns is a more *offense first* mindset. Every stock picker uses both mindsets when making decisions, but one is usually more dominant. It's like how great sports teams are known for their offense or defense.

Stock pickers who seek to manage 100% of clients' net worth are more capital preservation dominant. Capital preservation dominant stock pickers are trying not to lose money for their clients, and they are willing to give up some absolute returns for reduced volatility.

By comparison, I am absolute returns dominant and operate a niche focused fund that is meant for no more than 10% of a client's portfolio. I'm more like Stephen Curry, where I always think I can shoot myself out of a problem. If I miss five shots in a row, I don't let it destroy my self-confidence. I keep shooting.

My definitions for good, great, and GOAT are focused on absolute return stock pickers.

The Competitor – The S&P 500

Ninety percent of active managers can't beat the S&P 500 over a 10-year time frame, and for good reason. The S&P 500 is the equivalent of the 1992 "Dream Team" that won gold in the summer Olympics in basketball. The Dream Team consisted of Michael Jordan, Magic Johnson, Larry Bird, David Robinson, Charles Barkley, and others. They were unstoppable and beat their opponents by an average of 44 points per game.

Similarly, the S&P 500 is the dream team of the most popular and best-performing large caps on the planet. As of June 2025, the S&P's top players include Apple, Microsoft, Nvidia, Amazon, Alphabet,

Meta, Tesla, and Berkshire Hathaway. These are some of the best stocks of all time.

If you manage other people's money, they will compare you against the S&P 500. It doesn't matter if you tell them not to. It doesn't matter that you don't own a single company in the S&P 500. It doesn't matter that your strategy doesn't mirror anything remotely relating to the S&P 500. It doesn't matter.

Your investors will compare you against the Vanguard S&P 500 ETF and its three bps of fees. They WILL compare you against the cheapest, best-performing investment vehicle in the world. You either choose to live in this reality, or you don't.

My fund is a portfolio of sub $500 million market cap microcaps. I show my performance against the S&P 500. Why? I want to be compared against my best adversary – not a lesser adversary. I want to show that my roster of no name players can beat the dream team.

Good, great, and GOAT (Greatest Of All Time) stock pickers have this winning mindset. They want to beat the best. They are too engrossed in the betterment of their craft to worry about looking bad. They have the self-confidence and the skills to match it. They are good at all five skills of stock picking.

How do I define good, great, and GOAT?

The S&P Global SPIVA US Scorecard is a semiannual report that evaluates the performance of actively managed US mutual funds against their respective benchmarks. The scorecard assesses fund performance over multiple time horizons, offering insights into both short-term and long-term trends. I used the data from the SPIVA report and Alpha Architect to help define good, great, and GOAT when comparing all domestic US funds against their benchmarks.

Good stock picker: A 10-year track record (annualized net return) of beating the S&P 500. How many make the cut? 10% of active managers.

Great stock picker: A 20-year track record (annualized net return) of beating the S&P 500. How many make the cut? 2.7% of active managers.

GOAT stock picker: A 20-year track record of 20% net annualized returns. How many make the cut? 0.01% of active managers.

This leads to three important questions.

What are the good, great, and GOAT stock pickers doing differently to beat the S&P 500?

To beat the S&P 500 over 10 years you are in the top 10% of professional stock pickers. To accomplish this, you must be good at all the skills of stock picking and applying them in such a way that produces alpha over a relatively long period of time.

We all have skills where we are naturally gifted (strengths) and others where we are deficient (weaknesses). Good, great, and GOAT stock pickers don't waste time avoiding their weaknesses. They know where they are deficient and educate themselves, and they find tools or people to help fill the deficiencies. You can only become a good stock picker if you can become good at applying all five skills.

As an example, my deficient skill was analyzing, specifically valuation. I was a story stock investor for the first seven years of my stock picking career. I was deficient in valuation because it was the last skill I developed.

I lifted this skill from poor to good in two ways. First, I started sharing my analysis with investors who were strong in valuation. Second, I focused on simple businesses and stayed away from businesses or industries where it takes a CPA or CFA to understand the financial statements.

Good, great, and GOAT stock pickers don't take their strengths for granted. They double and triple down on their strengths to extend the duration of this advantage. Just like an athlete who is naturally gifted, those gifts will only take you so far if you don't continue to work on them.

My strong skills have always been identifying and selling. When I was a story stock investor, I became quite good at identifying great stories and later identifying great leaders. Since story stocks have shorter shelf lives, I also sharpened my skill of selling. When I launched MicroCapClub, it became a tool for idea generation, analysis, and building my investor network, further strengthening my skills.

We can all think of famous stock pickers who are better at presenting and interviewing than stock picking. Some would say my definitions aren't fair, and that these investors are still great stock pickers. No, they aren't. They are likely deficient in one or more skills, and they try to mask it with their wit and charisma. Great performance is proof you aren't deficient in any skill.

Good, great, and GOAT stock pickers are consistent. I don't mean consistency of returns, but of process. There are big advantages born out of boring, methodical consistency.

Most stock pickers say they consistently:

- Turn over the rocks and go A through Z to find ideas.
- Read all the filings, press releases, and proxies.
- Do extensive financial modeling.
- Talk to management, customers, and suppliers.
- Verify the investment thesis through ongoing maintenance due diligence.
- Create a systematic system to track current and potential positions.

Everyone says they do the work, but few actually do it.

Many stock pickers can be consistent for a few quarters or years. Few can be consistent for a decade or more. A little success happens. Priorities change. New obligations enter. Life happens. Whatever it is, these distractions form wedges in consistency, and it breaks the pattern that is necessary for good returns.

Here is an example of how consistency becomes an advantage.

One of the benefits of microcap investing is all the little niches of industries you must explore and educate yourself on and how that knowledge dovetails into something else years later in ways you never imagined.

Consistency gets amplified in returns when all the seeds you planted researching companies and industries start bearing fruit, and this is the flywheel that propels the performance of good stock pickers through the 10-year mark.

It's all the notes, analysis, financial models, relationships, management interviews you've accumulated across 100+ portfolio and watchlist companies that becomes a sustainable advantage. Those companies you intimately follow evolve and go in and out of favor. A stock picker might own the same company multiple times over a career.

Inside a watchlist of 100+ companies something new is always happening. A new management team takes over a company. A new acquisition is made. A new division gets launched. An old division gets sold. An unactionable idea can become actionable in an instant.

These old investment ideas become new ideas because the valuation or corporate actions bring them back on the radar. It's the work you did five or 10 years ago that allows you to see around corners when new events take place and act before others. This is how the skill of valuation and buying is heightened through consistency and it allows you to act quicker.

To be in the top 10% you must be good at all the skills of stock picking and apply them consistently.

What are the great and GOAT stock pickers doing differently to beat the good stock pickers?

To beat the S&P 500 over 20 years you are in the top 2.7% of professional stock pickers. Twenty years is a long time. Time acts like gravity. It is an ever-present downforce that continuously bites and claws at your returns to revert them to the mean. Great stock pickers fight off father time like King Leonidas and his 300 Spartans fought off the Persian army in 480 BC.

How do they do this?

If you've beaten the market for 20+ years you've likely had to evolve as an investor in small or large ways. Inside every stock picker is a better stock picker. It's this curiosity and ambition to expand your circle of competence and evolve that keeps you at the top of your game. The way you got in the top 10% of stock pickers is likely not how you will get into the top 2.7%.

They look like Eddie Lampert, who was a traditional stock picker the first 10 years of his career, and then successfully evolved into more of an activist the next 10 years of his career. The result was 30% gross CAGR over 18 years before Sears threw a wrench into his returns, but he still had a successful long-term track record.

There are plenty of examples of investors who put up blistering track records for one to five years who didn't evolve effectively and were slow to adapt. I can't help but think of someone like Michael Burry, or others that got locked into a bearish mindset and they couldn't break free from it. They were right once in 20 years and still believe in the same narrative and their long-term performance just keeps degrading.

There is also a graveyard of stock pickers who tried to adapt and failed. Great stock pickers adapt like chameleons to a new environment. They don't invest in a world they want. They invest in the world they have.

Great stock pickers don't become complacent. They don't slow down. They are never satisfied. They are constantly challenging their circle of competence, but they aren't doing so recklessly. They are scientists that are testing their theories in small ways. They accept small losses as they learn and then earn the right to be more aggressive.

Great stock pickers don't reminisce about the multi-baggers they had 15 years ago because they have new ones today. Great stock pickers do everything good stock pickers do, but they effectively adapt and evolve in ways that keep them outperforming for 20 years or more.

What are the GOAT stock pickers doing differently to trounce everyone?

Twenty years at 20% net CAGR is a 50x outcome.

Let's revisit the question that was asked to John Danaher, "How do you become the best in the world at what you do?"

He replied, "Any sport or profession has five or six core skills that are necessary to participate. To be the best in the world you must be good at all the skills, and best in the world in at least one, preferably two, of those skills."

He then went a couple levels deeper, "What makes people stand out is having the ability to identify the one or two skills that are currently being underutilized in the sport or profession. Then they focus massive effort on developing and innovating on that underutilized and underappreciated skill. When you innovate on an underappreciated skill and reintroduce it back to the game or industry it will surprise your opponent. It will take years for them to catch up. This is how you become the best in the world."

GOAT stock pickers innovate and redefine a skill that is underappreciated by the majority in their flavor of investing. Since their innovation normally goes counter to most long-held beliefs, it can be years before anyone takes notice outside their own investors.

Joel Tillinghast, legendary manager of Fidelity Low-Priced Stock Fund, said: "The secret of success in business and investing is to do something useful that no one else is doing."

Here are some examples:

- Perhaps it's a new way of thinking about valuation and business models like Nick Sleep and Qais Zakaria's scale economics shared. This allowed them to identify and value certain business types that others didn't. The investment world eventually saw what they saw, but this insight gave them tremendous advantage and the full benefit of multiple expansion over two decades.
- Perhaps it's developing active patience towards a very specific type of business like Reece Duca of IGSB does with vertical SaaS companies. They realized this around the same time as Mark Leonard at Constellation Software and both have made billions.
- Perhaps it's creating a more systematic approach around position sizing and valuation like Andrew Brenton and his team have done at Turtle Creek Asset Management. Turtle Creek differs from many value fund managers. They actively trade around their core positions via "continuous portfolio optimization" which adds alpha to a pure buy and hold strategy.
- Perhaps it's Ed Thorpe, or Jim Simons, who were first to apply probability and statistics to the stock market by exploiting a bunch of anomalies.
- Perhaps it's focusing on identifying special situations like Joel

Greenblatt and creating his famous Magic Formula that allowed him to deliver one of the best 10-year track records in investment history.
- Perhaps it's a deep value investor like Michael Melby at Gate City Capital that cares about assessing management quality.
- Perhaps it's Warren Buffett and the other *Superinvestors of Graham-Doddsville*, who all shared the foundational approach of Graham and Dodd by buying securities trading far below estimated intrinsic value to allow a margin of safety. Several would go on to become GOAT stock pickers.

Many of the GOATs don't just invest one way. They are more like Bo Jackson and Deion Sanders that can play at the highest levels in both professional baseball and professional football.

- George Soros – 20% net CAGR over 40 years
- Michael Steinhardt – 23.5% net CAGR over 28 years
- Stanley Druckenmiller –20%+ net over 30 years
- David Tepper – 25% net CAGR over 25 years

These investors all doubled up the S&P and they did so as versatile players. In fact, very few achieve GOAT status in modern times simply by being long-term stock pickers. Most GOATs play the investing game in multiple ways at the highest level.

Warren Buffett has produced a 20% net CAGR for 70 years. He invests in a multitude of different ways. Yes, he has a $250 billion public stock portfolio, but Berkshire Hathaway is a publicly accessible private equity vehicle that doesn't charge any fees. Buffett goes where the IRR is the highest.

Many of the GOATs went from doing it all themselves to creating winning teams. They went from playing every instrument in the orchestra to conducting the orchestra.

What about stock pickers who put up blistering track records for eight to 15 years? Aren't they GOATs?

- Peter Lynch – 29.2% gross CAGR over 13 years
- Sleep and Zakaria – 19% net CAGR over 13 years

In 2014, Sleep and Zakaria, closed the Nomad Investment Partnership. They were only 45 years old. The partnership was mostly invested in three stocks: Amazon, Costco, and Berkshire Hathaway. If they had remained in those three companies equally weighted it would have produced a 21% CAGR through 2024.

Peter Lynch could have put up mediocre returns for another seven years and likely achieved GOAT status.

So, yes, I call them GOATs too. Just because they stopped investing outside capital didn't mean they stopped investing their own capital.

In summary, GOAT investors innovate on an underutilized skill that gives them an advantage that is compounded over time into superior performance. Their original advantage might not last forever, but they have the tenacity and intelligence to find the next area. They keep adapting and successfully reinventing themselves. By the mid-point of their career, they have GOAT level competency across many areas of investing. They also evolve from playing an individual sport to a team sport.

It might seem overwhelming to think about what it takes to be a good, great, and GOAT stock picker. It isn't. Don't focus on the result. Focus on today.

In the final chapter, I'll explain the secret to compounding.

CHAPTER 35

The Secret to Compounding

Intelligent fanatics was a term Charlie Munger used to describe a great entrepreneur and business builder. An individual that founded a company and built it into one that dominated their niche, geography, or industry. The cherry on top is that intelligent fanatics don't just dominate for a year or two, but for decades.

These are the best of the best that create dominant and enduring businesses. Sean Iddings and I studied 100+ of them.

Do you know what the most common element was among all of them?

High standards. They executed on high standards every single day.

You don't start with a single store in Arkansas and in 25 years become the largest retailer in the world without high standards.

You don't launch a rocket ship into space and have it land back down to Earth again without high standards.

You don't create the most dominant quick-service restaurant chain in the United States that is also closed on Sundays without high standards.

Whether it's Jeff Bezos's customer obsession or Steve Job's relentless pursuit of design and function. High standards was the key.

High standards create dominant companies. High standards create

GOAT stock pickers. High standards create great families. High standards create great relationships. High standards change the world.

If you want to be like everyone else, lower your standards.

High standards transcend business into stock picking and even our personal lives.

I remember someone saying on a podcast, "Anyone that says time heals has never lost a child." This statement struck me since I have two young children. A few years ago, a friend of a friend lost a child in a tragic accident.

My kids were three and six at the time. I decided right then and there I needed to hug my kids more. I felt I needed to step up and raise the standard.

Every morning, I started giving them hugs. BIG HUGS. I wouldn't let go of them until they squirmed to get away. I did it consistently, every morning.

On one occasion, I hugged my daughter when she came downstairs. She giggled and squirmed to get away like she always does.

When I finally let her go she said, "Are you ever going to stop hugging me?" and I replied, "Never," and she looked at me and said, "I know Daddy."

Her response triggered something. I melted. I had to walk into the bathroom to gain my composure. I couldn't help but think to myself, "Okay she knows I love her. It doesn't matter what happens tomorrow."

I've noticed the older my children get the less they do what I say and the more they do what I do.

I've tried to become more self-aware of what I'm saying, doing, and how I'm reacting. My kids are always watching. This realization is slowly changing my behavior.

When I started viewing myself through their eyes there were things I didn't like. I needed to be a better example. To set a high standard.

The easy times are easy. The hard times are hard.

What about when they see me having an argument with their mother? Do they see me treat her with respect? Do they see me listen to her? Do they hear me say "I love you," at the end of an argument when it's the last thing I want to say?

When my kids see me step up in hard situations like this it shows them what a real relationship looks like. It teaches them it doesn't matter what we are arguing about today, we still love each other.

More importantly, it shows them how they should treat people and how they should expect to be treated. It shows my son and daughter what a man looks like.

It creates a high standard for their future relationships. I fail a lot, but I'm slowly getting better at it. I must be the example.

My seven-year-old son is going through a phase where he's thinking about what he wants to be when he grows up. I want to be a teacher. I want to be a baseball player. I want to be an astronaut. I want to work at a zoo. I want to be an uber driver. It's hilarious because every week it is something different.

Every time he asks me, "Do you think I can do it?"

I reply, "Of course buddy. You can do anything you want."

He wouldn't ask me if he could do it unless he needed that positive affirmation. All kids need it. But the older he gets, he'll stop asking me and start watching me.

He needs to see me chasing my dreams and making him a part of it. That is how he'll know he can accomplish anything he wants in life. I need to be the example for him.

I don't want you to think I'm perfect. I make tons of mistakes and say dumb things. Just ask my wife. This isn't about perfection, it's about intention.

I do have a few life hacks that I'm implementing that are very simple and extremely powerful. The key is doing them today, not tomorrow.

- When you think something good say it. Whether you are alone or around people. Say it out loud. Positivity attracts people. Negativity reverts you to the mean.
- When you think something good about someone else, tell them immediately. Most people don't know their gifts or talents. Even accomplished people don't get a lot of positive feedback. One word of encouragement can change the trajectory of someone's life.
- When you think you wronged someone, even in the slightest way, apologize to them immediately. Don't wait another day. Quick apologies make relationships three times stronger. Slow apologies

make relationships weaker. Time becomes a wedge that is hard to bring back together again.

- When you've been wronged, reach out to the person and have a hard conversation today. Try to forgive them as soon as possible. Don't let hate build up and distract you.

Stock pickers think in long-term CAGRs. We all want to compound our capital at high rates and become GOAT stock pickers.

We are always looking forward one, two, and three years, estimating what a business will look like in the future. When you know a business intimately and build conviction, those future returns feel so real. We can smell, taste, even envision spending those returns. We can feel our ego swelling from the accolades we would receive from achieving those returns.

The worst part of investing is wishing time goes faster so you can get to your returns quicker. We all make this mistake. We live in the future, instead of the present.

Focusing too much on the future, the result, distracts us from the work that is necessary today to achieve those high returns.

Here is the secret.

When you do the work today…

When you read the earnings transcripts today…

When you do those key word searches today…

When you read the press releases and filings today…

When you set up the expert calls today…

When you have that hard conversation with a CEO today…

When you do the financial modeling today…

When you set a high standard for your business today…

When you work out and eat right today…

When you hug your children today…

When you tell your spouse you love them especially when you don't want to today…

When your kids see you chasing your dream today…

When you call your parents today…

When you apologize today…

When you forgive today…

When you get on your knees and pray to your God today…

When you do these things today, you don't have to worry about tomorrow.

The secret to compounding your family, your relationships, your faith, your dreams, your business, and your portfolio – it all starts and ends with taking care of today. This is how you live an abundant life. Being present and living TODAY to a high standard.

Don't get distracted by the millions of things that are trying to make you mediocre.

I want you to do something awesome with your life and your portfolio.

Your family needs you to do something awesome with your life and your portfolio.

Your God created you to do something awesome with your life and your portfolio.

It's never too late. Today is a new day. Live it to a high standard.

When you take care of today, tomorrow takes care of itself.

I hope you enjoyed the book and it helped you gain some valuable insights you can apply to your journey. Don't invest like me. Don't try to clone me. By the time you do, I will have already evolved. You can't beat the S&P 500 by being someone else and following others. You can only crush it by being you.

Inside every stock picker is a better stock picker.

ABOUT THE AUTHOR

Ian Cassel has been a stock picker for over 20 years with a focus on microcap stocks. He started as a teenager and in college made it a goal to become financially independent. At the age of 28, he became a full-time private investor supporting himself and his family on his own capital base.

In 2011, he founded MicroCapClub, a global online community for experienced microcap investors to find new ideas, collaborate on due diligence, and network with peers. In 2018, Ian founded Intelligent Fanatics Capital Management LLC, which works with high-net-worth families to provide them with intelligent exposure to the smallest public companies in the world.

Ian has co-authored two books: *Intelligent Fanatics Project: How Great Leaders Build Sustainable Businesses* and *Intelligent Fanatics: Standing on the Shoulders of Giants*.